STRUGGLING FOR SOCIAL CITIZENSHIP

Struggling for Social Citizenship

Disabled Canadians, Income Security, and Prime Ministerial Eras

MICHAEL J. PRINCE

McGill-Queen's University Press
Montreal & Kingston • London • Chicago

© McGill-Queen's University Press 2016

ISBN 978-0-7735-4703-2 (cloth)
ISBN 978-0-7735-4704-9 (paper)
ISBN 978-0-7735-9881-2 (ePDF)
ISBN 978-0-7735-9882-9 (ePUB)

Legal deposit second quarter 2016
Bibliothèque nationale du Québec

Printed in Canada on acid-free paper that is 100% ancient forest free
(100% post-consumer recycled), processed chlorine free

This book has been published with the help of a grant from the Canadian
Federation for the Humanities and Social Sciences, through the Awards to
Scholarly Publications Program, using funds provided by the Social Sciences
and Humanities Research Council of Canada.

McGill-Queen's University Press acknowledges the support of the Canada
Council for the Arts for our publishing program. We also acknowledge the
financial support of the Government of Canada through the Canada Book
Fund for our publishing activities.

Library and Archives Canada Cataloguing in Publication

Prince, Michael John, 1952–, author
Struggling for social citizenship: disabled Canadians, income security,
and prime ministerial eras / Michael J. Prince.

Includes bibliographical references and index.
Issued in print and electronic formats.
ISBN 978-0-7735-4703-2 (hardback). –
ISBN 978-0-7735-4704-9 (paperback). –
ISBN 978-0-7735-9881-2 (ePDF). –
ISBN 978-0-7735-9882-9 (ePUB)

1. Canada Pension Plan Disability program – History – 20th century.
2. People with disabilities – Pensions – Government policy – Canada –
History – 20th century. 3. Pensions – Political aspects – Canada –
History – 20th century. 4. Social security – Canada – History –
20th century. 5. Social rights – Canada – History – 20th century.
6. Citizenship – Canada – History – 20th century. I. Title.

HV1559.C3P7575 2016   362.4'04820971   C2016-900066-4
                                             C2016-900067-2

This book was typeset by Interscript inc. in 10.5/13 Sabon.

Contents

Tables

Preface

The core of the modern welfare state – the extent and quality of the social rights that constitute social citizenship.

Walter Korpi, "Power, Politics, and State Autonomy in the Development of Social Citizenship"

The struggle for citizenship is viewed as an affirmation of the value of choice, independence and control which disabled people conceive in terms of human rights.

Len Barton, "The Struggle for Citizenship"

Struggling for Social Citizenship is for readers who are interested in examining social policies and social rights; learning more about income security, disability, and issues of administrative justice; better understanding welfare state history, and exploring the influence of government and politics on how public programs are developed and reformed. A number of audiences will find the book relevant and meaningful: workers who become disabled and their families; federal and provincial policy makers and parliamentarians; activists and administrators involved with public and private disability insurance programs; students and scholars of citizenship studies, social policy and theory, disability issues, and Canadian politics, federalism, and policy making. Readership for this volume will also include individuals from the fields of disability studies, rehabilitation and health studies, political science, Canadian history, social work, and sociology. Readers from all these groups, I believe, will find this book enlightening, challenging, and stimulating.

Struggling for Social Citizenship is the first detailed examination of the policy and political history of the disability benefit component of the Canada Pension Plan (CPP), the single largest public contributory disability plan in the country. The book focuses on broad policy trends and program developments, highlighting the role of ministers, members of Parliament, public servants, policy advisors, and other political actors. More specifically, the book examines the pension reform agendas and records of the Pearson, Trudeau, Mulroney, Chrétien, Martin, and Harper governments. The analysis covers the origins, early implementation, liberalization of benefits, and the more recent restraint and reorientation of the disability benefit program.

The book also considers how disability has been defined in programs and distinguished from ability in given periods; how these distinctions have operated, been administered, contested, and regulated; and how, through income programs, disability is kept in circulation as a social construct and administrative category. On a theoretical level, *Struggling for Social Citizenship* weaves together social policy, political science, and disability studies literatures, producing an innovative analysis of citizenship and social rights. On an analytical level, the book aims to provide a way of understanding the interplay of political and social institutions and actors in policy making in Canada at macro, meso, and micro levels of action.

Disability, income provision, citizenship, and social security are dynamic processes, rather than fixed entities. As conceptual ideas and material activities, they are subject to various interpretations and constructions, as well as changes and outcomes. I am interested in examining how income provisions for people with disabilities were established and what they mean for the social rights and citizenship experiences of Canadians. Therefore, to understand how individuals actually experience social programs and social rights, I employ a critical interpretive approach to study the immediate world of people who are applicants to and clients of the CPP disability program.

My approach to this topic is shaped by a number of experiences. Being the son of a veteran of the Second World War taught me from an early age about veterans' needs, programs, and organizational activities. As an academic trained in political science and public administration, I study the history of the welfare state and income security programs in relation to power relations, policy ideas and interests, and administrative and judicial schemes of provision. Being a consultant to governments at all levels over the past thirty years has sensitized me to the significance and complexities of bureaucratic politics, the constraints and choices of change, the often overlooked roles of members of Parliament in social issues, and the importance of appeal and redress systems to individuals seeking a social right to income support. Furthermore, serving as a community volunteer in health, law, and disability organizations connects me directly with the faces and stories of individuals and families, self-advocates, and their allies as they struggle for benefits, recognition of their identity, and ultimately their citizenship. From all these life experiences, I have learned of the essential need for critical, reflective thinking joined with social commitment.

This book greatly extends a research report, *Wrestling with the Poor Cousin: Canada Pension Plan Disability Policy and Practice, 1964–2001*, written in 2002 for the Office of the Commissioner for Review Tribunals Canada Pension Plan/Old Age Security (OCRT), of the Government of Canada. In 2013, the OCRT was absorbed into the new Social Security Tribunal. In the course of writing that report, and discovering practitioners' and policy makers' responses to it, I realized that disability income provision and the social rights of Canadians warranted a fuller, book-length examination. *Struggling for Social Citizenship* expands on that report by examining additional disability income programs over a longer period, all set within a theoretical context of social struggles and social rights and an analytical framework that addresses sociopolitical institutions, the policy community, and micro-level dynamics between clients and administrative processes.

My analysis employs several research methods: a scan of the academic literature on the CPP and related social policies in Canada; a review of government documents on the CPP, especially the disability benefit; selected interviews with both appointed and elected officials; and an analysis of administrative data regarding trends in expenditures and caseloads; and an analysis of decisions and appeals related to CPP disability benefits. The overall approach is a decision-making analysis and study of disability and social policy processes. Key concepts that inform this analysis include disability policy, policy goals, program elements, and prime ministerial eras of policy developments.

I owe a very special debt of gratitude to the late G. Peter Smith, commissioner of the OCRT from 1998 until his sudden death in early 2004. Peter sponsored *Wrestling with the Poor Cousin* (Prince 2002) and offered advice and encouragement to me in many ways. He was a fine public servant with a sincere passion for social fairness and the public good. It is most fitting that the building in which the Office for the Commissioner for Review Tribunals was located has been named in honour of Peter to mark his contributions to Canadians with disabilities. I am grateful as well to staff at the former O C R T, including Deputy Commissioner Guy Arsenault, senior counsel Tina Head, legal counsel Chantal Proulx, and executive assistant to the commissioner, Ginette Garneau, for invaluable and continued assistance. I am also thankful to Bob Baldwin, Laurie Beachell, Cam Crawford, Pierre Fortier, Lee-Anne Goodman, Rod Hagglund, Bruce Halliday, Michael Hatfield, Kathy Jordan, Steve Kerstetter, Nancy Lawand, Hon. Allan MacEachen, Hon. Alan Redway, Helen Redican, Marcia Rioux, Leonard Shifrin, Sherri Torjman, Deborah Tunis, David Walker, and William Young. I wish to thank Simone Godbout for her research assistance in scanning and summarizing the parliamentary debates on Bill C-2. A special acknowledgment must go to Tom Kent, Prime Minister Pearson's chief policy advisor, who was gracious in his advice and encouragement.

Along the way, the publisher's anonymous referees offered useful suggestions and constructive challenges that have made this a better book. Numerous federal and provincial officials, past and present, who cannot be identified, were helpful in reading drafts of the book and making time for interviews and answering specific questions and making available key documents.

I am delighted that McGill-Queen's University Press undertook to publish this book. This partnership press is a fitting publisher. Many years ago, I was a graduate student in public administration at Queen's and have remained associated with colleagues there in various disciplines, including disability studies. One of my daughters, Jessica, was an undergraduate student in political science at McGill and worked at the press through her final two years there. So I am doubly grateful to Philip Cercone, executive director of the press, for his support, and I wish to thank Joanne Muzak for her careful copy editing, which enhanced the final manuscript. Jessica also provided me with many helpful comments on drafts of the manuscript. Kathleen, my other daughter, I wish to thank for her periodic questions about policy issues and, more importantly, her comments that reminded me this study is a piece of my wider interest in matters of social justice. Above all, I wish to thank the love of my life, Karen, for her patience and encouragement as always, in letting me get this story on the page, and so it is to her that this book is dedicated.

Michael J. Prince
January 2016

STRUGGLING FOR SOCIAL CITIZENSHIP

"Citizens of that Other Place"

By the social element [of citizenship] I mean the whole range from the right to a modicum of economic welfare and security to the right to share to the full in the social heritage and to live the life of a civilised being according to the standards prevailing in the society.

T.H. Marshall, *Class, Citizenship, and Social Development*

Selfhood does not stop at the skin. But it always *begins* – literally or figuratively – from the body. There is nowhere else to begin.

Richard Jenkins, *Social Identity*

Everyone who is born holds a dual citizenship, in the kingdom of the well and in the kingdom of the sick. Although we all prefer to use only the good passport, sooner or later each of us is obliged at least for a spell, to identify ourselves as citizens of that other place.

Susan Sontag, *Illness as Metaphor*

Citizenship is an institutionalized, individual, and interactive set of group processes. Traditional analysis of social citizenship examines the nature of and extent to which welfare state provisions diminish class divisions and alleviate economic inequalities in capitalist market societies. Despite the continued importance of those questions for understanding our political economy and liberal democratic citizenship, the focus in this book is on a political sociology of disablement and the welfare state – specifically, on what social citizenship means for persons with various kinds of disabilities. How does social citizenship relate to impairment and handicap in Canadian social life? What is the relationship between political institutions, such as federalism or parliamentary government, and income security policy for disabled Canadians? What is the relationship between societal institutions such as families, health professions, or insurance companies and income security policy for disabled Canadians? And how do state and societal institutions, actors, groups, and processes interact? Along with this institutional context, the book considers the embodied individual and social citizenship, and the relationships between embodiment, well-being, and human agency. Citizenship starts and ends with embodied individuals intermingling with environments of different scales and forms through political eras.

Disablement is integral to social citizenship and attendant political conflict in four ways. First, social rights to income support are tied to the development of social welfare administrations at federal and provincial levels of government (and, historically, at the municipal level in many parts of the country) and to the politics and processes of intergovernmental relations. Second, disability as a social policy issue and state response is bound up with the growth of health professions and rehabilitation sciences and therapies. In critically important ways, modern social rights to income support are medicalized rights. Third, disablement or impairment of people poses a challenge to conventional notions of citizenship as participation in society, the economy, and the polity. Through the twentieth century, disability became viewed as not simply a personal pathology but as the product of social forces such as industrial accidents, general unemployment, wartime wounds, poverty, and family needs. In varying ways, a socio-political perspective on disability emerged, though individualistic explanations continue as a major frame of understanding disability in public discourse and public policy. The Keynesian welfare state, as a particular cultural form, assumed particular beliefs about disablement, persons with impairments and ability disability relations. Still today, it remains difficult to comprehend disablement independently of beliefs of "normal" bodies and minds. Fourth, in the Canadian context, social rights to income security for people with disabilities, chronic illness, or sickness are on the whole in congruence, not in contradiction, with market values and capitalist relations.

This Introduction argues that social rights are not political universals with a given essence; rather, any regime of social citizenship is a historically specific creation with particular institutional arrangements intertwined with power relations among numerous groups and actors. Within the field of income security in Canada, there are several different regimes of social rights in policy and practice. For each regime, we need to ask what particular income programs mean in terms of adequacy of benefits, the scope of coverage of needs, and the implications for families, work incentives, or social cohesion. A social right to a disability income benefit is not a predetermined matter or an absolute guarantee so much as a recognized claim, a series of activities that may result in an entitlement realized or in an application denied. Claiming social rights is, among other things, an ongoing undertaking by individuals with bodies navigating through, in Sontag's terms, the kingdom of the well and the kingdom of the sick. The social citizen's material body is administered through rules on labour force attachment, records of financial contributions to social insurance programs and perhaps private life insurance plans, and medical assessments of bodily conditions and functional capacities and incapacities. Bodies matter to citizenship; and matters of the body define social policy eligibility for people with disabilities.

In the rest of this Introduction, we make our way through literatures on citizenship, social citizenship, and social rights. In the first section, I set out my analytical approach to the inquiry and link it to critical social sciences, critical policy studies, and critical disability theory. The second section briefly examines the central concepts of citizenship and political communities and then social citizenship and the welfare state, including a discussion of social rights and public policies. In the third section, I present the ideas of embodied citizenship and disabled bodies.

A CRITICAL INQUIRY

A critical spirit informs this study of people with disabilities, employment, and income security. This means that attention is given to examining relations of public and private power in all spheres of life; to questioning conventional notions of disability; to revealing forms of exclusion and subordination; and to approaching policy studies with a value position based on progressive change toward a fuller measure of human dignity and social justice. As a form of explanatory critique (Neuman 2006), this book simultaneously explores how scholars, politicians, and advocates think about disability and social citizenship, and examines particular social rights and actual programs relevant to persons with disabilities. This helps to identify patterns of consensus and divergences in viewpoints within and between groups involved in disability policy systems. This approach also assists in identifying the subjective meanings of policy actors and groups that operate in and through objective structural relations of the state, civil society, and market economy.

The field of critical policy studies is coming of age in Canadian policy analysis, yet authors in this genre tend to overlook issues of impairment and disability. According to Michael Orsini and Miriam Smith, the core of critical policy studies – what makes such studies critical in effect – is the "rethinking of fundamental assumptions about political power and about the social and political structures that underpin the policy process" (2007, 15). A critical policy approach, they add, "takes seriously the perspectives of marginalized groups in Canadian society, whose interests and identities have often been absent from discussions and debates on public policy" (14). This is accomplished in part by drawing on concepts from a number of disciplines and theoretical approaches outside mainstream political science and public administration. Another aspect of critical policy studies that informs this book is the reconsideration of the relative place of the nation-state in public policy and practice. Critical policy studies aims to move beyond the nation-state as the privileged level for analysis to consider multiple levels or scales of policy action and equally to move beyond the analytical separation of the state and society as distinct institutional spheres to examine the interplay of state and societal actors and organizations. The legitimacy and capacity of civil society organizations, especially those that represent vulnerable populations and historically marginalized communities, are of interest in critical policy studies for what they can tell us about the distribution of decision makers and circulation of different knowledge forms in policy processes.

Like critical social science, critical policy studies embraces interpretive approaches of everyday life and the social construction of realities. How knowledge is situated, assembled, and contested certainly has application to understanding the struggles for social citizenship. How, for instance, is the lived experience of workers with disabilities included and interpreted by social program officials? What ways of knowing disability are valued and regarded as valid evidence in the welfare state? More recently, Orsini (2012, 808) has recognized that disability is largely neglected as a form of difference in the literature on diversity and the welfare state, and he has begun to address this oversight in his research on autism and neurodiversity.

While the critical policy studies literature may often neglect disability groups, issues of impairment, disablement, and resulting oppression are the idée fixe of critical disability theory. Richard Devlin and Dianne Pothier argue that the principal contention of critical disability theory is that disability "is a question of politics and power (lessness), power over, and power to" (2006, 2). From this perspective, fundamental issues revolve around "who and what gets valued, and who and what gets marginalized" (9). Devlin and Pothier indicate that "perhaps the most important critical claim with regard to disability is that it is a social construct" (13). Critical disability theory attends to structural inequalities and pays special attention to disadvantages and exclusions systematically produced by institutional practices, power relations, and cultural norms. Critical disability scholars do not only look at the formal promises of legislation and social policy, but they also closely inspect the substantive practices of social citizenship. In their work, Devlin and Pothier offer a critique of liberalism and the charitable and welfare responses to people with disabilities. These responses, they contend, are inadequate to be sure; but, more seriously, community charity often compounds the problems of many disabled Canadians. Critical disability theory thus aims to remove barriers and dismantle practices of exclusion, promote human rights, and advance substantive equality.[1]

Struggling for Social Citizenship is thus informed by these ideas of critical social science, policy studies, and disability theory. One of the aims of this book is to incorporate disability more fully into accounts of citizenship and social rights. As political sociologist Angharad Beckett observes, "despite the importance of 'citizenship' as a concept within wider society and the continuing interest in theorising on the topic within academia, very little consideration has been made of this issue as it relates to 'disability'" (2005, 420). The book takes a long-term and in-depth programmatic approach to studying social citizenship and disability. The approach is contextual, grounded in historical developments both material and discursive. Social rights of citizenship are examined in relation to a particular set of income programs established in Canada since the early twentieth century, which correspond to specific political jurisdictions and policy communities that are characterized by forms of conflict and cooperation, supports and struggles. All major institutions – government, health,

1 Examples of disability studies as they pertain to Canadian policy include Boyce et al. (2001); Cameron and Valentine (2001); Prince (2009); Puttee (2002); Stienstra (2012); and Withers (2012).

education, and so on – are implicated in the formation and operation of ability/disability relations. Also, this examination of state-polity-society relations considers the micro (or local), meso (or middle-range policy sectors), and macro (or overall systemic) activities and factors. State organizations and societal structures, and their myriad interactions, shape disability identities and social policies. Government influences ability/disability relations and, in turn, these relations affect politics and state activities. Likewise, structures and processes in civil society help to constitute and regulate lived experiences of disability and of claiming social rights of income support.

CITIZENSHIP AND POLITICAL COMMUNITIES

In democratic theory, disability studies, public policy, and other academic fields, citizenship is a primary investigative concept or model for examining political participation, social membership, marginalization, inequality, and the nature of the modern welfare state. Ralf Dahrendorf defines citizenship as "a set of rights and obligations associated with membership in a social unit" (1988, 31). The social unit Dahrendorf has in mind is a national political entity, one in which "all members of society are citizens ... subject to laws, and ... equal before the law" along with rights and freedoms of association, of speech and the right to vote in elections (38). These rights and obligations of citizenship, according to Dahrendorf, are public in nature, meaning they are separate from market forces, universal in principle and so equally available for all, and absolute rather than conditional.

Liberal democrats most often conceptualize citizenship as a legal status with a bundle of civil and political rights and obligations, and as membership in a constitutional community. Whether civil, political, or social, citizenship however is not an immaculate set of principles that exist independently of specific political communities, actual historical periods, or concrete public policies. Bryan Turner offers a more dynamic and sociological view of citizenship, defining it as "that set of practices ... which defines a person as a competent member of society, and which as a consequence shape the flow of resources to persons and social groups" (1993, 2). More than a bundle of formal rights and obligations, citizenship, as a set of social practices and resource flows, is shaped by political struggles over time. Through these struggles, citizenship is defined by community membership and social status "in a society which is highly differentiated both in its culture and social institutions" (1993, 5). Society is also defined in many ways by market capitalism. As Dahrendorf recognizes, any major social provision or entitlement "creates interests in change as well as interest in the status quo," thus generating tensions (1988, 28). The politics of modern citizenship, then, involve "practices through which individuals and groups formulate and claim new rights or struggle to expand or maintain existing rights" (Isin and Wood 1999, 4).

Social policy scholar David Harris also discusses community membership as foundational for citizenship. He writes, "The core of the citizenship theory of the welfare state is community membership. Community membership is the good to be promoted by welfare institutions in a market economy – from our membership of our community flow the welfare rights we can assert and the duties we owe to contribute to support of our fellows" (Harris 1987, 145). When we understand citizenship as membership in a community, Nira Yuval-Davis cautions that we do not view community "as a given natural unit. Collectivities and 'communities' are ideological and material constructions, whose boundaries, structures and norms are the result of constant processes of struggles and negotiations, or more general social developments" (1997, 8). As discussed in later chapters, membership in the struggle for social rights by disabled Canadians includes several forms of community: federal and provincial political communities, policy communities linked to certain income programs, and professional communities of law, medicine, nursing, and rehabilitation. Each community is an ideological and material construction with distinctive ideas and organizations, standards and rules, centres and frontiers. In assorted relations with other communities, each engages in regulating access to cherished resources, creating or recognizing certain identities, excluding certain people while including others on the basis of specified criteria, such as severity of impairment and labour market participation.

All aspects of citizenship, as Julia Eckert points out, are social in some manner: "Citizenship, although articulated not necessarily collectively, is nonetheless fundamentally social: the understanding of rights and perception of oneself as a rights-bearing subject emerge in social relations, collectively *with* others or by comparison *to* others, and by recognising the similarities in forms of subjection and in the needs of life" (2011, 313). Beside these aspects of general sociality, the concept of social citizenship refers to a more specific area of rights, obligations, resource flows, practices, and communities.

SOCIAL CITIZENSHIP AND WELFARE STATES

If community membership is the focal point of citizenship, social citizenship is widely regarded as the central concept of modern welfare states. Desmond King and Jeremy Waldron explain that "collective provision for welfare is associated now with an idea of social citizenship, and is taken to be comparable in status and importance to other aspects of citizenship, such as the right to own property and the right to vote" (1988, 417). Following the pioneering work of T.H. Marshall, Gösta Esping-Andersen proposes that social citizenship is the core idea of a welfare state and that the foremost principle involved in social citizenship is the granting of rights to income supports, education, health care, and other services for individuals and families (1990). Peter Dwyer describes social citizenship as "the universal right of citizens to an extensive set of state-guaranteed social and economic provisions" (2004, 6). Here Dwyer expresses the principles of general access and equal availability, a theme that runs through much of the social policy literature. Debra Cowen, for example, states, "Social policy becomes a constitutive element of social citizenship when it is structured on principles of universality and entitlement. The welfare state came into being when policies were implemented at a national scale and practised according to a logic of social citizenship" (2008, 44).

Actual practice in Canada, however, has not always mirrored a given rights logic or set of principles (Cowen 2008; Redden 2002). In a comparative study of welfare states in democratic industrial capitalist societies, Wil Arts and John Gelissen report that properties of social citizenship include "the fact that more or less extensive welfare provisions are legally provided and the fact that the state plays a principal part in the welfare mix alongside the market, civil society, and the family" (2002, 139).

The welfare state refers to the exercise of authority by state organizations and officials in relation to a specific society and political community. Julia O'Connor, Ann Shola Orloff, and Sheila Shaver define the welfare state (or what they also call state systems of social provision) as "intervention by the state in civil society to alter social and market forces" (1999, 12). The term, as they use it, includes multiple policy instruments and policy fields: income maintenance program, public services, and state regulations. In the Canadian context, the welfare state also refers to the interplay of state authority between the two orders of government; there are not one but multiple welfare states in Canada. From an institutional perspective, the welfare state also entails the interaction of power relations of societal institutions and actors.

Welfare states in Canada, through social citizenship and other practices, create categories of disablement, organize ability/disability relations, and connect the private realm of everyday life to the public arena of policy and practice. In this context, the welfare state is public intervention in regard to human bodies and selfhood. As a liberal welfare state regime, Canadian income security policy for people with disabilities involves a prominent role for social assistance, for private sector insurance plans, and work-based social insurance such as workers' compensation and the Canada and Quebec Pension Plan Disability. The Canada Pension Plan Disability (CPP/D) program, the main policy under consideration in this book, offers a modicum of economic welfare and security, but is expressly limited in its role to allow room for the market economy to provide private disability insurance plans and to emphasize values of individual responsibility. In capitalist society, CPP/D represents a form of moderate collectivism and a notable form of social citizenship.

"What the twentieth century view of social citizenship added," writes Hugh Heclo, "was a commitment to national welfare programs to deal with the shared insecurities of an industrial age" (1995, 674). In Canada, intended effects of this social citizenship regime of common benefits, federal-provincial cost-sharing, formal equality of status, and universal programs are said to include the fostering of social integration and of the national political community. Another commonly identified effect of social citizenship is said to be to lessen the dependence of people on the labour market economy, a process called de-commodification. Walter Korpi explains, "Social citizenship refers to rights that individuals have as an outflow of their status as citizens. These social rights can be claimed without citizens having to demonstrate economic need (for example via a means test). Instead, claims are accepted if the individual falls in a specific category, for example, in terms of age, health, or employment" (1989, 314). Many observers have readily interpreted this process of de-commodification as weakening economic self-reliance, as creating a passive citizenship with few if any obligations related to work. What are the connections between social security and disabled workers and disabled people? To what degree do income programs protect people with disabilities from dependence on the labour market for financial support? The interactions between market forces and the program features of CPP/D, discussed more fully in Chapters 4 and 9, are multifaceted and do not operate all in one direction.

Social Rights and Public Policy

Social rights feature prominently in political discourse and public policy. In the mid-1960s, John Porter described social rights in Canadian society as follows: "Social rights are the claims on the social system of all members of the society to a basic standard of living and to equal opportunities for education, health, and so forth" (1965, 370). While in overall terms Porter saw Canadian society as a vertical mosaic stratified by social class and ethnic groups, he did regard social rights as having egalitarian possibilities, what Ramesh Mishra calls "the ideal of equality of status" and of "equal consideration as a member of the societal community" (1981, 37, 38). For people living with disabilities in liberal welfare states, "the rights of the disabled and the rights to welfare are forms of social rights, demands from disadvantaged groups for full equality, acceptance, and belonging" (Erkulwater 2006, 218). Janine Brodie sees social rights as "the right to the collective provision of a minimum level of social security as a right of citizenship" (2009, 21), while O'Connor, Orloff, and Shaver offer a more conditional notion, describing social rights as "effective claims on the state for particular benefits or services under specified conditions" (1999, 31). In Canada, social rights to economic welfare and social security, as Alan Cairns and Cynthia Williams remark, "are not constitutionally entrenched. They are found in legislation, and are consequently subject to parliamentary supremacy conditioned by the political consequences expected to flow from their modification" (1985, 18).

With respect to income maintenance programs, Ola Sjöberg outlines the following characteristics of social rights: as positive rights, they "demand active effort on behalf of the state"; are "provided in the form of concrete measures directed to individuals"; "require an extensive administrative apparatus and some kind of distributional mechanism"; and require a fiscal basis of taxation on community resources for funding these social entitlements via public expenditures (1999, 276). The political and public nature of social rights stems from the fact that "they are directly legislated and administered by the state," with "a clear and explicit government mandate"

(Esping-Andersen 1990, 81). Social rights to income maintenance, as expected, concern the material welfare of individuals and families – usually a basic floor or modicum economic security.

The citizenship literature commonly identifies social rights as located in specific parts of the welfare state – the education system, health care services, community and personal social services, social housing, and labour market programs and employment services. This is accurate enough but it is not the whole picture of the institutional arrangements for exercising social rights to income provision. The practice of social rights take place in and though other institutional contexts too: state structures of tribunals and courts, legislatures and cabinets, societal structures of families, workplaces, and unions, health and life insurance companies, physicians and other health professions, social movements, and community organizations. The institutional locations of social citizenship rights are many, both within the state and throughout civil society and the market economy, as is discussed more fully in Chapter 2. When exercised, social rights generate, alongside public expenditures, considerable private costs for individuals, families, and community groups.

This wide-ranging landscape of institutional arrangements points to the intermeshing of social rights and other types of human rights, namely, civil rights and political rights. While some writers assert sharp differences between civil and political rights on the one hand and social rights on the other, *Struggling for Social Citizenship* explores the interconnections among these types of rights. While twentieth-century social citizenship was not especially precise as a set of guidelines, "then neither were the concepts of civil and political rights as they acquired historical force" (Heclo 1995, 673). "Political and civil rights form part of the context for claiming of social rights" (O'Connor, Orloff, and Shaver 1999, 31). Moreover, political and civil rights are integral to practices of claiming social rights. Claims by disabled workers to income provisions like CPP/D are shaped by the back-and-forth of civil rights and duties and procedural rules and legal requirements. Matters of administrative process, discretionary power, and procedural fairness are recurring issues in the determination of eligibility for disability income benefits.

Social rights link closely to political rights. As Kathryn Ellis observes, "social rights are embedded in democratic structures and processes. Consequently, the exercise of disabled people's political rights offers the potential for additional leverage when accessing directs services and direct payments" (2005, 669). That entitlements to public benefits and services are rarely boundless also connects civil and political rights to social rights. In the words of Esping-Andersen, "Social rights are hardly ever unconditional. Claimants will at least have to satisfy the condition of being ill, old or unemployed to receive the benefits. Beyond the mere presence of a problem, however, conditions are usually linked to type of social security agreement" (1990, 48). Conditions that apply in a given program can relate to one or more of the following factors: a history of work performance in the labour force; a demonstration of need through a means test or needs test of household resources; a period of residency in the jurisdiction; and a record of paying contributions for a social insurance plan. In Canada's liberal welfare state regime, contributions by the insured worker are a main funding method for social citizenship rights.

Access to social rights of income support takes two basic routes: either direct rights or derived rights. Direct social rights are individually based and targeted to a primary intended beneficiary of a public program – for example, the disabled wage earner, the injured worker from an industrial accident, or the war veteran suffering from trauma. Derived social rights are provided indirectly through a person's intimate relationship to the primary beneficiary of the program – for example, the spouse or a dependent child, often in the role of widow or orphan. Derived rights reflect an accepted level of public responsibility for the risk of a breadwinner's lost income and the legitimate financial dependence of spouses and children. This distinction between direct and derived social rights corresponds to the traditionally gendered dichotomy of the public and domestic spheres of life, to "women's social rights derived from their status as wives" (Sainsbury 1996, 49).

Where Were Disabled People in the Keynesian Welfare State?

Based on a recent survey of citizenship studies, Ruth Lister concluded, "there remains an imbalance between theoretical and empirical advances in our understanding of citizenship. The field would be enriched by more empirical studies ... of the cultural, social and political practices that constitute lived citizenship for different groups of citizens" (2007, 58). Along similar lines, Helen Meekosha and Leanne Dowse have argued that in contemporary citizenship, disabled voices are absent and that "the language and imagery of citizens is imbued with hegemonic normalcy and as such excludes disability." They contend that feminist perspectives also "largely fail to acknowledge disability experiences" (1997, 49). Though academic interest in disability is increasing, the same criticism of ignoring disability issues can be made of the public policy and social policy literatures. The risk, of course, is that the marginal status of vulnerable groups is perpetuated through scholarly oversight and through fuzzy nostalgia surrounding the post–Second World War period of Keynesian welfare state development.

Janine Brodie describes the postwar consensus on social citizenship, from approximately 1945 to the late 1970s, as conveying the ideas "that poverty was not always an individual's fault and that all citizens had the right to a basic standard of living" and "of universal publicly provided services as a right of citizenship" (1995, 56–7). Central elements of this Keynesian welfare state included broad support for public services of health, education, and, on a national basis, income supports for the unemployed, the elderly, and families with children; a federal government commitment to high and stable levels of employment; a basic safety net to relieve poverty and provide a basic level of support; a progressive income tax system and thus a degree of redistribution; a modest supplementary role by governments in the provision of child care, housing, and labour market training, supported often by intergovernmental collaboration; and labour standards and collective bargaining in key sectors of the Canadian economy. It also included a male breadwinner, female homemaker model of the family – what Cowen calls the "post-war model of 'male breadwinner' worker-citizenship" (2008, 22).

Where were people with disabilities in the postwar consensus and Keynesian welfare state? Specified groups of disabled people did figure in the Canadian political community and public policy; most notable were mentally burnt-out and physically wounded veterans from the First and Second World Wars, who had pension benefits and rehabilitation services, and injured industrial workers, with workers' compensation programs that predated the Keynesian welfare state. Of less profile and lower priority politically were social assistance programs for blind persons and for people with permanent disabilities; both are rather thin welfare-based notions of social citizenship. These too predated the postwar period of social citizenship. Over the 1945 to 1970s period, vocational and medical rehabilitation programs were introduced for the civilian population as well as for Canadian war veterans; new medical treatments and preventive measures emerged; and employment preparation and training programs for people with physical disabilities were established. At the same time, however, across the country, sheltered workshops, segregated schools, separate recreational camps, large residential institutions, and annual charity campaigns that used pity and tragedy in their images of people with disabilities materialized.

Insofar as, in the Keynesian welfare period, "social programs became an important source of Canadian national identity" (Shields and Evans 1998, 17), for most Canadians with disabilities, their relationship to the public realm was in provincial political communities. Introduction of the CPP and specifically the CPP/D, as later chapters show, shifted the balance for people with disabilities between federal and provincial governments, public and private realms, and personal obligations and public entitlements. For people living with significant disabilities, their public identity involved contradictory practices and troubling consequences. For many disabled Canadians, the Keynesian welfare state frequently meant social exclusion as well as integration; marginality and stigma as well as civic solidarity; institutional building as well as province or nation building; personal and family obligations as well as social rights of citizenship. The appropriate relation between disabled and non-disabled individuals very often was segregation. At best, there was a public culture of ambivalence toward people with disabilities, which was reflected in social policies and administrative structures of the state.

Like all state formations, the Keynesian welfare state had a particular material organization and cultural way of constructing and dealing with the disabled (Rioux and Prince 2002). For people with disabilities, the postwar consensus on social policy contained certain assumptions about the causes and nature of disability and certain beliefs about what should be done. In the evolution of thinking on disability, the postwar welfare state corresponded to a period of medicalization, among other social processes. The overall policy orientation to disabled persons was framed within the knowledge, discourse, and power of biomedical science. Persons with disabilities were viewed and treated as sick, abnormal, functionally limited, possibly rehabilitative, yet frequently identified as unemployable and therefore dependent.

From around the late 1970s onwards, the postwar consensus of the welfare state became unsettled, and, according to most social observers, the financing, effectiveness, and legitimacy of the social welfare state were in crisis (Rice and Prince 2013). This crisis, however, included a positive development – namely, the rise of advocacy groups of people with mental and physical disabilities, who questioned past practices, challenged the labels, language, and depictions of disability, and called for reforms in education, workplaces, and community environments to remove barriers, promote access, and achieve inclusion. Disablement increasingly became a more politicized identity and a new social movement for change. The disabled person strove to become the embodied citizen.

THE DISABLED BODY AND EMBODIED CITIZENSHIP

Citizenship has a bodily materiality, a fleshy embodiment in social environments. Embodied citizens are human subjects assembled materially by their bodies and minds, discursively by talk and cultural symbols, and relationally in specific interactions and circumstances. The disabled body is, at one and the same time, a biological entity, a marker of social identification that often includes stigmatization, and a site of power relations by state and societal institutions, all occurring in a local milieu of family and significant others. Along these lines, social citizenship is built upon embodied knowledge, which "emerges in situ, from sensations, emotions, thoughts, and subjectivities as well as cognition, physiology, and biology of both individual and collective bodies" (Moss and Teghtsoonian 2008, 12–13). With embodied citizenship comes politics of the individual body and collective body politics, as Susan Wendell observes: "We live with particular social and physical struggles that are partly consequences of the conditions of our bodies and/or minds and partly consequences of the structures and expectations of our societies, but they are struggles that only people with bodies and/or minds like ours experience" (1996, 79–80).

Citizenship and disablement have a troubled history. Scholars have asked if the idea of a disabled citizen is a contradiction in terms (Bacchi and Beasley 2002; Meekosha and Dowse 1997). Lennard Davis puts it starkly: "An able body is the body of a citizen; deformed, deafened, amputated, obese, female, perverse, crippled, maimed, blinded bodies do not make up the body politic" (1995, 71–2). Adults with disabilities are seen as "lesser citizens" (Bacchi and Beasley 2002) or "absent citizens" (Prince 2009). This is because the dominant paradigm of citizenship in modern societies rests on physical, cognitive, and behavioural qualities and capacities linked to cultural norms of autonomy, rationality, gainful employment, self-control, and working bodies. "In addition to their experiences of illness," Pamela Moss and Katherine Teghtsoonian add that "people must often cope with scepticism on the part of employers, health care providers, and insurance administrators that can result in being denied access to paid sick leave or other income support benefits and/or being subject to surveillance and scrutiny" (2008, 13). Trying to claim a right to a modicum of economic security, or many other social rights, can be formidable when one dwells in the kingdom of the ill and disabled. In disability studies, of course, as well as in feminist research, indigenous studies, ethnic and race studies, queer studies, and other critical perspectives, the human body and embodied experiences are central concerns of theory and analysis (Sarvasy 1997).

However, in mainstream studies in citizenship, public policy and administration, and social policy, regrettably there is comparatively little attention given to human embodiment and, particularly, disablement and impairment. What Helen Thomas has said of other social sciences applies also to these fields: they have "tended to view the body as an unquestioned 'natural' fact of existence, while offering disembodied accounts of social action" (2013, 10). Much of the writing on citizenship, certainly from liberal political thought, assumes abstract individuals, an approach roundly criticized by critical social theorists. Writing from a feminist perspective, Kathleen Jones depicted citizenship "as a practice of embodied subjects whose ... identity affects fundamentally their membership and participation in public life" (1990, 786). A generation later, Chris Beasley and Carol Bacchi wrote on the need to connect the literatures on the body and on citizenship "to bring citizenship to life by giving it material flesh" (2000, 340). And yet Lister has observed that "While a number of disability theorists have framed their analysis using the concept of citizenship, it is rare for citizenship theorists to incorporate disability in their work" (2007, 53). In public policy and administration, the emphasis on rationality, best practices, and evidence-based decision making continues to endorse notions of abstract and disembodied policy actors, program clients, utility maximizers, stakeholders, and consumers. These policy actors all have specific governance roles, vested interests, certain ideas and preferences, and resources, but rarely are they considered in terms of their bodily materiality or embodied knowledge.

In traditional social policy and welfare state studies, material realities of the human body was an important topic in regards to insecurities of life that threatened interrupting the earnings capacity of breadwinners. In the late nineteenth century and early twentieth century, governments began to recognize illness, injury, disability, and death as natural and individual risks that warranted policy responses of some kind. Vulnerable bodies of injured factory workers, sick war veterans, and blind and/or deaf persons, all were the object of state interventions, program definitions, and administrative classifications. Public financial assistance for the "able-bodied" unemployed featured powerfully, and still does, in provincial welfare policies.

In the contemporary discipline of social policy, Julia Twigg argues that the human body is almost nowhere to be seen, even though the body is evident in state interventions and public debates. In areas of social policy where the body is of clear importance, such as health care services, the body, Twigg claims, has been ignored or, more commonly, taken for granted to be a private entity, a medicalized body, or an object to be managed remotely (2000, 2004). "In social policy discourses," Amanda Coffey explains, "there is an almost unquestioning acceptance of the body as a pre-social, basic or fixed entity" (2004, 82).

Therefore, one of the aims of this book is to present citizenship and people with disabilities as embodied and contextualized subjects, and to understand citizens as having multiple differences, specificities, and commonalities in their lived experiences. The literature on bodies and citizenship speaks of "embodied subjects" (Jones 1990) and the "embodied welfare subject" (Dean 1999), "corporeal citizenship" (Gabrielson and Parady 2010), "embodied subjectivities" (McLaren 2002), and "embodied citizenship" (Lister 1997). A basic premise is that "bodies give substance to citizenship" and "citizenship matters to bodies" (Bacchi and Beasley 2002, 324), that "citizens act as embodied subjects whose interests reflect their biological and psychosocial reality" (Jones 1990, 795). The human subject must be understood as a concrete and particular citizen, embodied, socially located, and intently connected with his or her surroundings and larger institutional structures. Thinking about social citizenship in relation to bodies (and their material and discursive elements) adds new perspectives on conventional issues examined in welfare state studies, such as market (de)commodification and social solidarity. It also contributes to further consideration of other crucial issues such as the medicalization of society and the contestation of impairments.

The Embodied Social Citizen

Many people with disabled bodies, and certainly those with visibly significant impairments, are associated with beliefs about abnormality, incapacity, and therefore dependency. Yet some people with disabilities qualify for particular income support programs while other people with disabilities do not. In other words, some disabled bodies are given legitimacy in social provision while others are seemingly regarded as still capable of earning an income, of recovering from their condition, or facing less onerous costs as a result of their impairment and any attendant treatment. In any case, they are determined by the administrative state to be ineligible for public benefits. Every year, a lot of Canadians enter the kingdom of the sick and disabled, but only some gain further admittance into the realm of national social insurance; many are relegated to rely on provincial welfare systems and on their families for essential resources. Those persons who have a relatively elevated status within the income security system have qualities of severity and duration as disabled bodies, particularities of the individual grounded in biomedical practices and administrative procedures. A person's bodily presence is central to accessing social rights of the political community. In considering the embodied self, we become mindful of the material and discursive forces within given configurations of power and knowledge that give shape to the social citizen.

Social rights *in theory* assume the citizen to be an able person with an equal identity, a fixed status of formal rights and obligations. Social rights *in the flesh* viewpoint take the practice of citizenship to be a set of actions in and through bodily realties, limitations, and possibilities. Social rights of citizenship are claimed, denied, adjudicated, negotiated, recognized, or denied, and performed in personal lives. The actual exercise of social citizenship is influenced by both public judgments and self-assessments, and an array of exclusions and inclusions in everyday life. The social citizen as the holder of rights and responsibilities has "embodied potentialities" (McNay 2000, 32), relating to bodily functionalities as well as environmental supports and social possibilities. And the "embodied welfare subject" has the potential capability, Hartley Dean suggests, "of negotiating her or his dependency, of resisting exploitation, of interpreting competing moral discourses, and of generating new meanings from shared bodily experiences" (1999, xxv).

A series of implied and stated responsibilities are also associated with income support programs for people with disabilities. These responsibilities, some of which are firmer than others, deal with the verification and documentation of impairments; participation in rehabilitation and treatment programs; partaking in formal volunteering or trying a return to work; taking care of oneself; and reporting to program officials any changes in one's family composition that could affect benefits. There is also a personal rendezvous with public revenue in paying general taxes and earmarked contributions for social insurance coverage. "The acquisition of social rights is definitely among the most expensive financial investments an average citizens in the industrialized world makes during his or her lifetime" (Sjöberg 1999, 277). All these duties can be understood as embodied obligations of social citizenship for the disabled person.

CONCLUSION

This Introduction began setting out the book's approach by drawing on ideas from three strands of academic literatures: critical social sciences, critical policy studies, and critical disability theory. Other key elements of the analytical framework, dealing with disability politics and policy and state-society relations, are presented in Chapters 1 and 2. Here we have reviewed the pivotal ideas of citizenship and political communities, social citizenship and the welfare state, and the nature of social rights in relation to Canadian public policies. Over time, federal and provincial states have produced particular models of disablement and ability/disability relations through programs, services, and benefits. During the Keynesian welfare state era, disabled people were frequently segregated and marginalized; that was not a golden age or benevolent consensus for many Canadian living with significant impairments. Social rights, in both their design and exercise, are intertwined with civil and political rights as well as with conditions and rules for access. Direct social rights and derived social rights are two dimensions of social policy in welfare states with ramifications for gender relations and family supports. In general, social rights to income security benefits create political spaces in everyday life for people with disabilities. Concepts of embodied citizenship and disabled bodies point out that the human body is an intrinsic factor of political attention in disability policy and practice by means of medical diagnoses and treatment regimens and administrative decision making. The social citizen is the locus of rights and responsibilities that bear directly on bodily materiality.

Key arguments, which will be elaborated throughout the book, have briefly been indicated here. For Canadians with disabilities, the introduction of social rights to income support has meant the amplification of particularistic criteria of eligibility, not the creation of universalistic entitlements. The history of federal and provincial welfare states reveals no single model of social citizenship. Rather we see numerous formations of social rights as expressed in different programs, in different circumstances and time periods, yielding different patterns of inclusions and exclusions in coverage and adequacy of income protection. A significant development across these different programs is the central role of medical science and rehabilitation services. Another argument concerns the CPP/D program, the central policy to be studied. Coverage of most working people under this national disability social insurance program was a leading intergovernmental agreement and social policy achievement in the mid-1960s. Since then, the CPP/D has contributed to abating the economic insecurity of many disabled workers and their families. The program also contributes to a continual dynamic of political debates and personal struggles for social rights to income provision. Despite the elaborate apparatus of the CPP/D as a national disability insurance program, the position of considerable numbers of disabled workers is characterized by initial ineligibility, strenuous experiences through appeal processes, eventual rejection for benefits, and stressful changes in social status. The result most certainly compromises the ability of many disabled people to live a life in accordance with standards prevailing in Canadian society. A related argument, arising from the labour force participation test to qualify for CPP/D, is that the right to this disability income program is an earned right, which, among other things, means that the market identity of Canadians is not wholly subordinated to a notion of social justice.

The rest of the book is organized as follows. Chapter 1 sets out further elements of the analytical framework – namely, the concepts of disability politics, disability policy, and struggles for social citizenship. Chapter 2 presents the institutional context for disability policy and social rights, arguing for consideration of state and civil society structures and how they network at macro, meso, and micro levels of action. Key to understanding the origins of the CPP/D policy and its subsequent implementation is the legacy of earlier disability income programs and politics in Canada. Chapter 3 thus offers a historical policy context of Canadian disability income provision from the early 1900s to the 1960s. Chapters 4 through Chapter 8 detail the creation of the CPP/D and its developments over the past five decades, spanning the prime ministerial eras of Lester Pearson, Pierre Trudeau, Brian Mulroney, Jean Chrétien, Paul Martin, and Stephen Harper. Chapter 9 looks at how various political actors, state and societal institutions and processes have shaped income security policy and the social citizenship rights of people with disabilities. Consideration is given to the role of federalism, advocates and interest groups, elections and political parties, labour market forces, medical and other health professions, and families. The Conclusion offers reflections relating to the changes and continuities in policy and practice of the CPP/D, and the quality of social rights for working-age Canadians with disabilities as offered by the CPP/D. Suggestions are put forward for addressing the ongoing struggle for social citizenship that is the everyday reality of so many Canadians living with disabilities.

CHAPTER ONE

Disability and the Politics of Income Support

Disability today can be framed as an emancipatory movement and minority rights issue; a biomedical phenomenon; an emergent political identity; a set of social relationships and practices and as a topic of philosophical and ethical enquiry.

Jackie Leach Scully, "Disability and the Thinking Body"

Disabled people have long struggled for the right to work, but it should be remembered that citizenship also involves the right to adequate social security.

Peter Dwyer, *Understanding Social Citizenship*

In contemporary societies and welfare states, disablement is foremost a site of personal and social struggles. This chapter sets out to do three things: to discuss conceptions of disability and what makes disability a significant political issue in our times, which will include outlining several academic perspectives on disability politics; to describe the character of the overall disability policy field and more specifically the key disability income programs in Canada, with a focus on the CPP/D; and to expound on the struggles for social rights to disability income experienced and undertaken at individual, organizational, and institutional levels.

Bodily matters of disability and state responses together feature in the historical establishment and present-day composition of social citizenship rights. The political significance of disability income support is evident in how human differences and needs are authoritatively interpreted; in how groups and identities become recognized in public policies and private plans; and in how roles are distributed among professions and other societal institutions. Claims by disabled people forged some of the earliest relationships between citizens and the federal and provincial states, and produced policy legacies, such as the diverse set of categorical programs in place today and the enduring strong influence of medicalized criteria in eligibility rules. The history of income support policies reveals that social rights for men and women with disabilities has been an issue since the early twentieth century and continues to be an issue in the early decades of the twenty-first century.

Politics of disability income involve the regulation of impairments as much as the recognition of disablement. Provision of income mainten-ance to certain people with disabilities relates directly to fundamental processes of "the state categorization of individuals and populations and the twentieth century's elaboration of normalcy" (Jenkins 2004, 173). This indicates the strategic importance of definitions and eligibil-ity as well as program administration and adjudication, topics explored in later chapters. Officially established and enforced categories of nor-mal and abnormal, able and disabled, are constructed through cultural representations and public beliefs, political discourses and public poli-cies, administrative procedures, and the practices of health profession-als. The disabled social citizen is caught up with the ways in which the body is regarded vis-à-vis notions of capacity and incapacity, employ-ability and unemployable. As a general category, disability is further-more differentiated by criteria of cause, severity, and duration of the impairment. In this way, social rights to income provision create and reconstruct relations between workers and non-workers, and the eli-gible and ineligible, for support.

Canada Pension Plan Disability (CPP/D), which is a relatively large national income security program, is the political expression of a set of rights and responsibilities of social citizenship. It is also part of the historical and contemporary developments in Canadian feder-alism, a complex public service infrastructure of administration and adjudication of claims, and a disability policy subsystem linked to a variety of state and societal structures and power relations. Since its implementation in 1970, the CCP/D has been never far off the dis-ability income and pension reform policy agendas.

CONCEPTUALIZING DISABILITY

Categories of disability and ability, as well as the related distinctions between employable and unemployable and deserving and less deserving, are the outcome of exercises of public and private power. For purposes of social policy and practice, these classifications are commonly enacted as fixed and discrete reference points in programs, services, and social surveys. For people living with disabilities, however, disability can be an unstable notion, a contested symptom, an episodic condition, a phenomenon routinely visible or more often than not invisible to other people: in short, a fluid identity or series of identities. For a person who acquires a significant impairment in her adult working years – a brain injury or spinal cord accident, for example – disability becomes her new reality, an unfamiliar territory in which she is learning about the condition and effects, and adjusting her life to new circumstances in her body and mind. In this context, disability is described in the literature as a form of being and medical condition and as a marginalized and spoilt identity, the subject of social stigma (Goffman 1968).

Differences between fixed categories in public programs and fluid particularities of people living with disabilities are thus an underlying tension and source of politics in disability income support. The subject disabled, as Rosi Braidotti says of the subject woman, "is not an essence defined once and for all but rather the site of multiple, complex, and potentially contradictory sites of experience" (1994, 199). Relations of power in policy making and implementation generate specific kinds of disability identities through the processes of self-documentation and presentation to various authorities, through assessments and verification by experts, and contestation in formal appeal systems.

Traditionally, in income security policy, disability (at times called debility, handicap, invalidity, feeble-mindedness, and incapacity) was framed as a social and economic risk to individuals and their families, linked to the loss of earning ability by the breadwinner of the household. Whether from an accident, illness, or injury due to modern industrialism, military service and warfare, or the vagaries and misfortunes of everyday life, the loss of earning capacity due to disablement was and still is seen as a direct threat to family security and stability (Marsh [1943] 1975; Stienstra 2012). Here the embodied citizen appears in the conception of bodily conditions, in the policy design elements, and in concerns over the psycho-emotional effects of income provision on recipients. There is attention to the mental and physical conditions and functional limitations of the person. There emerged, as Chapter 3 will demonstrate, the creation of different programs of income assistance for different categories of needy people: the blind, the totally disabled, the distressed war veteran, the injured worker, and women with dependent children whose husbands were in asylums or otherwise incapacitated by an accident or serious illness. Income security programs for disabled people have developed in a piecemeal manner, program by program, risk by risk of disablement. Consequently, the state compartmentalizes disability. Applicants for social assistance must demonstrate their particular living requirements and needs as an individual and as a family. A version of individualization takes place in determining eligibility and benefit levels through investigation and, at times, surveillance of the intimate circumstances of the applicant. This relates to concerns, in addition to those of maintaining budgetary controls and protecting against fraud by malingerers, of the psychological effects that income provision may have on recipients' morale, work habits, and sense of "normal responsibility for self-support" (Burns 1956, 57).

Disability public policy, Deborah Stone observes, is "fundamentally the result of political conflict about distributive criteria [paid work and human need] and the appropriate recipients of social aid" (1984, 172). Stone highlights three dimensions of disability. These are disability as a deserving category, that is, a special moral worth; disability as a significant physical and/or mental incapacity; and disability as a clinical phenomenon entailing the medical verification of diseases, injuries, disorders, or conditions. Disability is a set of biomedical attributes and an elaborate business sector of insurance, research, sickness and absence management, and rehabilitation services. Moreover, in the Canadian context, disability is a legal and administrative category, a constitutionally protected ground under the Charter of Rights and Freedoms along with a term contained in provincial and federal statutes and regulations. David Cameron and Fraser Valentine, like other critical disability specialists, argue that disability is "a socially created category, a product of complex political, economic and social relationships" (2001, 7). Negative stereotypes of dependency and feelings of pity or fear toward disabled citizens, which counter the ideas of rights, self-confidence, and capacities, are significant aspects of the social constructions of disability.

The meaning of disability, then, is the stuff of considerable theorizing and inquiry, lively public debate, and varied governing practice. This book does not offer a singular or definitive definition of disability. I am, rather, interested in explicating the origins and official definitions of disability in Canadian policies, and examining the political, administrative, medical, and quasi-judicial processes through which disability is determined for the purposes of structuring eligibility for income maintenance. Generating grounded descriptions of the meaning(s) of disability in state action and inaction is itself a core task of social policy analysis.

In a review of the CPP/D in the mid-1990s, the auditor general of Canada remarked, "The status of persons with disabilities remains a complex social issue and is difficult to determine with precision. It entails especially sensitive human, moral and emotional dimensions" (1996, 17:23). For establishing eligibility to public resources, the determination of disabilities can be complicated and necessarily involves ethics and passions. Often it can involve unsympathetic techniques exercised by experts and officials over the disabled social citizen. The human dimension operates within an institutional context of competing interests and beliefs in addition to asymmetrical power relations and types of knowledge. Should consideration be given to a person's age, skill set, or the nature of the local labour market where the applicant to CPP/D resides? How should degenerative diseases, such as cystic fibrosis or multiple sclerosis, or so-called invisible disabilities such as chronic fatigue syndrome, be considered when deciding benefit eligibility?

THE DISABLED AS POLITICAL SUBJECTS

In an important paper on embodied citizenship, Carol Lee Bacchi and Chris Beasley (2002) make the point that there are two types of citizens or political subjects. First, there are those people they call full citizens. These are people deemed to be in control over their body and mind. They are active and autonomous persons, enjoying civil liberties and a degree of distance from government supervision. They are the able, functional, and socially empowered members of the political community. Bodily matters, Bacchi and Beasley contend, are largely absent from everyday discourse for the full citizen, who is taken for granted to be a healthy consumer or producer. The second type of political subject is the lesser citizen. These are people deemed to be controlled by their body. They are passive and dependent individuals who tend to be more under government surveillance than full citizens and certainly are objects of medical scrutiny. These lesser citizens are the disabled, those with dysfunctional bodies and/or minds, the biologically disempowered. For disabled members of the political community, bodily matters are ever present in their social identities and interactions. They have what Michel Foucault calls a body "that by its own causality confirms and explains the appearance of an individual who is a victim, subject, and bearer of this dysfunctional state" (2003, 313). Taken to be limited and abnormal in some manner, their prominent roles are as patients, public clients, and recipients of charity.

All citizens have a physiological existence, a material body that "is crucial to the social and political location of persons" (Turner 1986, 128). This analysis takes us far from liberal abstractions of citizenship, and echoes Susan Sontag's metaphor of the kingdom of wellness and the kingdom of illness in modern societies. Bacchi and Beasley astutely emphasize that "on both sides ... medical professionals are positioned as authorities," a theme to be examined in the next chapter (2002, 342). Of course *within* these two types of citizens delineated by Bacchi and Beasley are multiple kinds of political subjects with different bodies and minds, varied life worlds, and particular social experiences. As Lennard Davis declares, "the categories of 'disabled,' 'handicapped,' 'impaired' are products of a society invested in denying the variability of the body" (1995, xv). While multiplicities flourish among disabled citizens, there are rigidities in the programmatic definitions applied to them and a generally felt hegemony in medical categorizations and diagnostic practices. In addition to the gaze of biomedicine, people with significant disabilities have shared experiences of abnormalization, exclusion, and stigmatization.

More than victims or passive clients, however, people with disabilities, as we will see throughout this book, exercise resistance and enact creative human agency in their interactions with others. People with disabilities are active participants in both constituting and claiming social rights of citizenship as workers, contributors to social insurance programs, as applicants and recipients, and possibly as appellants of negative decisions on their entitlement claims. Disability, like other social identities, is a series of actions and performances: a doing and undoing, contemplation and preparation, a producing and reworking, accommodation and self-advocacy, achievements and setbacks, all within networks of relationships in state and societal structures. In her study on gender and agency, Lois McNay makes the case for contextualizing human agency "to explain the differing motivations and ways in which individuals and groups struggle over, appropriate and transform cultural meanings and resources" (2000, 4).

In public commentary and right-wing political ideologies, there is frequent mention that "rights talk" diminishes the idea of obligations and responsibility talk. What such remarks typically ignore is the work involved in expressing and pursuing a right, the work in presenting a claim, the work in managing a benefit, and the work in defending rights attained. Exercising social citizenship is an endless commitment, not some brief activity. Claiming a right to income support involves a series of legal and moral obligations, expectations, and requirements. For many people, exercising a right to disability insurance can involve the risk of lengthy procedures and intense investigations, which, in turn, have the risk of adverse consequences to one's health. In regard to CPP/D and other income programs in Canada, the effort of social citizenship is tied closely to labour force participation and employment status. It is linked also to the labour performed in other public and private realms of life. There is considerable emotional and material labour with bodily effects, expended by disabled citizens, associated with claiming an income benefit. Following the feminist mantra, the personal is political, *disabled bodies are politicized working bodies*.

Perspectives on Disability Politics

If politics is the authoritative allocation of values, for disability it includes beliefs of normalcy and abnormality. If politics is the exercise of power, authority and influence over others, for disability it is in relation to human bodies and to social relationships encouraged and denied. If politics is understood as being about who gets what, when, and how, for disability it involves who gets to be recognized or constituted as able and disabled, when, where, and in what ways. What should disability mean, and who, for the purposes of public provision, should be counted as disabled? The politics of disability is very much part of a person's life that is historically specific and material, both individual and collective in nature. Rod Michalko's depiction of the lived experience of disability is instructive: "It is more than merely a private happenstance that must be suffered in the realm of privacy; it is also a public matter that must be suffered in and through the polity. Disability is not an exclusively individual issue; it is a collective one" (2002, 6). As a collective issue, politics involves, in the words of Mary Dietz, the "participatory engagement of citizens in the determination of the affairs of their community" (1987, 14), be that their neighbourhood, city, province, nation-state, or beyond. For many people, the politics of disability concerns challenging traditional distinctions between the private and public realms of community life and between notions of normalcy and disablement.

Even as Canadian state institutions figure highly in the following chapters, the analysis adopts a critical and expansive conception of what is political. The politics of disability encompasses authority structures, power relations, and governance processes in and between the state, the polity, and society in Canada. Claims, struggles, and decisions occur in a number of state and societal contexts: families, workplaces, professions, interest groups, insurance companies, and community non-profit agencies as well as the public structures of government bureaucracies, tribunals and the courts, legislatures, and cabinets. Further, the politics of disability refers to the effects of allocating resources and making laws on the everyday realities of people living with disabilities. Jill Vickers characterizes a woman-centred view of politics and government as that which "comes from the bottom up and the outside in" (1997, 9). This description can aptly be applied to people who are marginalized because of disability.

ANALYTICAL FOUNDATIONS

Disability studies includes old and new styles of disability political mobilization and engagement. The old style of disability politics often involved particular groups with particular impairments – injured industry workers or damaged war veterans, for example. It centred on "battles over where to draw the boundary lines around eligibility and support needs," usually for specific impairment groups (Barnes and Mercer 2003, 35). A hierarchy of disabilities, and sometimes explicit competition among disability groups for public recognition, funding, and available services, is a legacy of this traditional politics. Another legacy is the role of charities and foundations in fundraising for essential supports for persons with disabilities and their families, and the role of some of these organizations in propagating public images of the disabled as tragic and pitiful victims. Political mobilization and state response for the so-called worthy poor led to the institutional separation of many people with disabilities from mainstream facilities of education, care, and employment (Bach and Rioux 1996; Stone 1984). In liberal democratic terms, this style of disability politics was primarily the conventional politics of elections, voting, issue campaigns, and interest groups revolving around a particular group's needs.

By comparison, a newer style of disability politics began to emerge in the 1970s, with different goals, tactics, and preferred policy instruments. Organizations controlled by people with disabilities, rather than run by parents or professionals, were established in Canada and other countries. These organizations challenged the old segregated and welfare approaches, outmoded language, and systemic barriers to access, lack of employment opportunities, and the dominance of professionals in the lives of disabled people. Equality rights and full citizenship became the ideals of the growing disability movements, and their struggles from charity to parity were joined with more critical analyses and radical tactics for social justice (Devlin and Pothier 2006; Withers 2012). The new form of disability politics is one example of contemporary identity politics and social movement mobilization on issues of recognition and cultural values, yet this disability politics is still focused on basic material matters of redistribution.

A second conceptual foundation deals with embodied politics, which has become known in feminist and disability literatures, among other social science fields. Related closely to embodied politics are the ideas of corporeal citizenship (Gabrielson and Parady 2010), embodied subjects (Wendell 1996), and bodily subjectivity (Braidotti 1994). As forms of power in action, embodied politics concern the contestation and medicalization of ill bodies, mechanisms of enforcing dominant standards of normalcy (Davis 1995; Foucault 2004), the management of stigma in interactional situations (Titchkosky 2003), and the production and circulation of embodied knowledges of disabled people (Moss and Teghtsoonian 2008). In her study on theorizing episodic disabilities, Andrea Vick uses the concept of embodied politics to refer to "the reciprocity between the lived experience of disability and its institutional interpretation" (2012, 41) and to "accentuate the experiential and discursive dimensions of disability in social policy" (42). Vick argues that how the CPP/D program defines disability, as both a severe and prolonged impairment, tends to "exclude the complex embodiment of persons with episodic disabilities" (2012, 41) – people with fluctuating materialities and thus shifting identities that ill fit the binary definitions in disability programs.

The third stream of literature relevant to understanding disability politics centres on ideas about social status and identity. Some works focus on status (Turner 1988); other works look more at citizenship (Isin and Wood 1999), while still other works examine the interconnection between disability, gender, and social citizenship (Meekosha and Dowse 1997; Morris 1993). A related theme is the political practices of citizens in pursuit of inclusion and empowerment (Andersen and Siim 2004; Bonnett 2003; Enns and Neufeldt 2003; Orsini 2012). The marginal position of most disabled people and their pursuit of inclusion and full citizenship is a clear example of status politics in contemporary life. Status politics, according to Bryan Turner, involves "the assertion of claims for social rights or entitlements against the state by aggregates who experience some form of discrimination" (1988, 13).

Status politics concerns group affiliations, the distinctive social situations of specific groups, and the differentiation of access to social rights on a group basis. It can mean a strategy of selectivity and targeting in policies as recognition of differences in the disadvantages and risks of various groups in society. In policy terms, Canadians with disabilities are highly differentiated by distinctive programs and client categories. In societal terms, clientele are stratified, that is, positioned hierarchically by the adequacy of benefits and scope of coverage for specific populations of disabled people. Alan Cairns describes the Canadian situation: "The handicapped have emerged to challenge the stigmata and socio-economic penalties attached to their physical and mental disabilities" through techniques of expanding self-awareness, expressing "political aspirations, alternative identities, competing values and new definitions of the appropriate relations between ... the able and the handicapped, and citizens and the state" (1986, 73, 74). These kinds of status politics entail a reimagining of social policy and the "model citizen." If and when such claims are accepted and addressed by governments in some fashion, the aggregate is defined in an official way and the resulting group becomes a clientele of the welfare state. This resulting client status of particular groups of people, with disabilities and other vulnerabilities, raises issues of bureaucratic encounters in claiming social benefits combined with processes of administrative gatekeeping and issues of access to social rights. Status politics for persons with disabilities is not only a project for public recognition and formal rights. It is also a project to challenge individualistic and highly medicalized notions of impairments and of people living with disabilities, and to obtain acknowledgment that barriers are socially created through cultural beliefs and physical built environments.

The fourth conceptual foundation relates to literature on human needs and how they relate to politics, discourse, and social rights. Key ideas in this context include the representation of the needs of strangers (Ignatieff 1984), the politics of need interpretation (Fraser 1987), and the contestation of illness and disability (Moss and Teghtsoonian 2008). Human needs are a key idea in the normative basis of public policy and social provision. Michael Ignatieff supports the principle that "needs do make rights" (1984, 13). The basic needs of people living in a welfare state confer on them entitlements of rights to the resources of that society. It is this occurrence, from human needs to social rights to actual provisions, that makes a moral community and establishes important relations among strangers. Ignatieff argues, however, that while some human needs "can be specified in a language of political and social rights," such as the basic goods of "food, shelter, clothing, education and employment," other needs, such as for respect, dignity, and solidarity with others, cannot be so specified (1984, 13). The expression of certain basic human needs, then, can seemingly justify a claim on community resources and assert an obligation on the part of the political community to respond in addressing and protecting these needs. This analysis begins to offer an appreciation of the place of human needs in social citizenship and how needs might correlate with rights.

Nancy Fraser enriches this line of analysis in her work on women, welfare, and the politics of need interpretation. Fraser suggests that many of the struggles over social welfare are struggles over the interpretation of social needs. The politics of need interpretation arises because human needs are not self-evident nor beyond dispute; they are interpretive and thus contestable. On whose terms should the welfare state deal with people living with disabilities? Whose interpretation of the needs of the disabled ought to be the commanding one? She maintains that "the interpretation of people's needs is itself a political stake, indeed sometimes *the* political stake" (1987, 104). In this sense, Fraser considers social programs as "institutionalized patterns of interpretation" (1987, 104) – particular ideological assumptions and cultural norms embedded in policies of the welfare state. Fraser describes the politics of need interpretation as "the processes by which welfare practices construct women and women's needs according to certain specific and in principle contestable interpretations, even as they lend those interpretations an aura of facticity which discourages contestation" (1987, 105). The processes involve the construction of identities, the interpretation of needs, and the positioning of women as subjects. Fraser proposes seeing the US social welfare system as a "juridical-administrative-therapeutic state apparatus" (1987, 113). The juridical component includes the legal system and rights and duties; the administrative includes bureaucratic agencies and managerial-defined criteria; and the therapeutic includes counselling and rehabilitation. This perspective extends the range of institutions commonly associated with social rights in the citizenship literature. Together these systems tend to implement policy, Fraser suggests, in a manner that makes it seem non-political. As well, she identifies three major kinds of needs discourse: an expert need discourse of administrators, planners, and policy makers; an oppositional movement needs discourse of feminists and other groups; and a reprivatization discourse that seeks to shift public needs into the realm of the market or the domestic sphere, which would entail economic and familial interpretations of needs.

"The disability rights movement," observes Ruth Lister "provides a good example of a political challenge to orthodox needs interpretation. It has also underlined the dangers of disconnecting a needs from a rights discourse" (1997, 86). One such danger is that social policy on the basis of need may result in "professional domination of welfare provision" by therapeutic agencies (Lister 1997, 86). Another danger is that claims rooted in a needs discourse may get caught up in administrative or reprivatization discourses that promote charitable and philanthropic responses and limit a politics of social justice in the public sphere. Fraser has written of "the tendency for the politics of need interpretation to devolve into the administration of need satisfaction" (1989, 177). On this point, Barbara Cruikshank (1999, 60) has criticized Fraser for accepting a dichotomy between politics and administration in the welfare state. For Cruikshank, politics and administration both involve relationships of power, elements of control, and possibilities for resistance. Cruikshank's argument is borne out in other studies on state restructuring of disability programs (Chouinard and Crooks 2005) and psychiatric power (Foucault 2006). In any case, a merit in Fraser's approach is its identification of multiple institutional actors and methods in how needs are interpreted and then implemented in policy. Lister is optimistic that political participation can shift power relations in specific processes of need interpretation. She writes, "Through user involvement, the politics of need interpretation can be opened up in a more democratic way to embrace the relatively powerless and to challenge the exclusive power of experts to define needs" (1997, 170). In later chapters we will see to what extent disability movement discourse plays a role in defining needs for the purposes of income security programs.

DISABILITY POLICY AND INCOME PROGRAMS

According to Lyn Jongbloed, "Disability policy is the outcome of complex social negotiations that pertain to changing definitions of *impairment, disability*, and *handicap* and notions about the rights and responsibilities of individuals and groups" (2003, 204). This description gets at the fundamental idea that disability policy, like disablement itself, is a historically contingent social construction. Disability policy is commonly identified as one segment of public policy, usually equated as a branch of social policy by public authorities. William Boyce and his colleagues offer a definition that fits well with focus in this book on different levels of action and on societal as well as state structures: "Disability policy embraces courses of action that affect the set of institutions, organizations, services, and funding arrangements of the disability systems. It goes beyond formal services and includes actions or intended actions by public, private, and voluntary organizations that have an impact on disability" (2001, 5). On disability policy and the Canadian state, Cameron and Valentine note that disability is not a coherent or comprehensive policy field but rather fragmented, with an array of distinct issues, distinct programs often introduced as add-ons to other policies, and varied definitions of disability. It is not a surprise that they conclude, "the state presents itself to the disabled citizen as a complex set of institutions" (2001, 23).

Disability policy is politically layered in relation to human bodies. This policy field involves the regulation of citizen bodies, the construction of standards of normalcy, and the formation of the disabled social citizen in the body politic. Authoritative notions of the norm – the able-bodied citizen – constitute also the other – the abnormal citizen. Disability policy is the use of state and social powers to construct identities of disablement and to modulate relations of ability/disability in the population. Disability programs are collectivist social policies of public and private interventions, yet this collectivism operates in conjunction with individualist notions of bodily functional limitations and potential workforce participation.

This book focuses on income maintenance policy – programs that offer a payment to individuals and families living with disabilities. Jane Jenson makes the important point that not only universal programs provide social rights, but that "depending on their design, targeted and insurance-based social policy can also provide for social rights of citizenship" (2003, 7). The disability income policy field incorporates programs of provincial social assistance, several federal and some provincial disability-related tax measures, federal and provincial social insurance programs for sickness and disability, and rehabilitation, medical, and employment services. Client groups include veterans, injured workers, and blind persons, working people with short-term illnesses, victims of motor vehicle accidents, working people with severe and prolonged impairments, and the surviving spouse and dependent children of insured workers. The underlying mandate of these program mechanisms is to protect individuals and households against economic and social hardship and need caused by reductions in earned income and by the additional living expenses as a result of an employment injury, sickness, invalidity, or impairment. Disability income policy therefore connects with labour market programs, old age cash benefits and survivor benefits, motor vehicle insurance, personal injury awards and settlements through civil litigation, family benefits, and health care services. All of these are significant events in the political history of disability.

Disability income programs have distinctive origins and orientations. Some programs in Canada, such as workers' compensation and veterans' allowances, were established in their own right, specifically as state responses to needs around particular kinds of disablement. Other disability income programs, such as original benefits for blind persons and the CPP/D were introduced within other public policy frameworks. This pattern of disability initiatives as a subsystem within bigger policy systems is evident also in social assistance and employment insurance. These two approaches to locating disability policy persist today, resulting in disability income support being a distinct policy domain for some groups and needs as well as a diffuse dimension in other policy areas. These diverse access points and separate program designs result in a mottled social citizenship for disabled people.

The CPP/D, as noted earlier, forms the core of the inquiry in this volume. The single largest public disability insurance program in the country, CPP/D, however, has received only marginal attention in governmental reports and academic literature on public pension policy, even in periods of great pension debates (Bryden 1974; Deaton 1989; Guest 1998). Yet, as the analysis will show, private insurers and provincial governments regard the CPP/D program as the "rich federal cousin." Most private insurance companies routinely, and some provincial governments increasingly over recent times, use the CPP as the "first payer" of benefits to many Canadians with disabilities, therefore directing claimants to this program before processing their applications for benefits from workers' compensation, social assistance, or private health insurance plans. In the early decades of the twenty-first century, the CPP/D operates within a complex and dynamic network of federal, federal-provincial, and public-private program relationships.

The Canada Pension Plan Disability Program

CPP/D policy encompasses the following authoritative actions: legislation, the most obvious example being the Canada Pension Plan Act and regulations; intergovernmental, intersector, and international agreements on social security; policy directives that interpret and direct the implementation of the legislation; guidelines, for example, for physicians and other medical practitioners inside and outside government; case decisions by Employment and Social Development Canada (ESDC) on approvals and denials; leading decisions on appeals by the Federal Court of Canada and the Supreme Court of Canada in CPP cases appealed beyond the level of review tribunals; management protocols and "best practices" such as for hearing processes; and communications initiatives that include program guides and personalized annual statements of contributions to the CPP. Along with being an authoritative mechanism for allocating benefits and rehabilitation services, CPP Disability is an expression of public purposes and certain deeply rooted social values. The original and still primary policy goal of CPP/D is to provide a degree of *income protection to insured workers* (partial financial security) that complements private insurance, personal savings and employment benefit programs by replacing a portion of the earnings of contributors who cannot work because of a severe and prolonged mental or physical disability. Other policy goals of CPP Disability include the following:

- to provide a degree of income support to families with a benefit to the children and youth of CPP/D beneficiaries, up to the age of twenty-five if they are attending full-time an educational institution;
- to ensure program integrity, fair administration, and accountability so that benefits are paid correctly, appeals heard fairly and promptly, and fraud and errors are avoided;
- to provide or, at times, restore the financial sustainability and affordability of the CPP for present and future generations;
- to promote a return to work by supporting at least some CPP/D beneficiaries to undertake gainful employment.

This last goal may now be seen as an "all-win" concept – meaning that the state and the individual benefit in the long run. At the outset, however, the rehabilitation provision was coercive in nature; the program had the power to require rehabilitation, and if the client refused, his or her benefit could be cut off. This is probably why this feature of CPP Disability was not taken up by officials for many years.

Corresponding to each of these goals is a perspective on what the role and nature of the program should, and needs to, be in practice. The income protection goal reflects entitlement; the goal of financial foregrounds sustainability and affordability, a standpoint that draws attention to actuarial concerns, economic capacity, and equity of contribution obligations across generations of Canadian workers; program integrity emphasizes compliance and enforcement; and the return to work goal stresses enabling and active programming. That CPP/D has several official policy goals raises practical and political questions about the relationship among the five goals and their ranking as priorities over time. In every period of the program's history, these goals and associated beliefs have had their champions and critics – in the federal bureaucracy, in Parliament, in intergovernmental relations, among interest groups – and all have been influential in shaping the CPP. These policy goals vary as well in the degree to which they are expressed in measurable terms that provide a standard against which to track, report on, and evaluate the results. In recent years, the goals of returning to work, assuring program integrity and financial sustainability have received greater emphasis by governmental policy makers than in earlier periods. At the same time, income security as a public commitment has been subject to some restraints.

CPP/D consists of six program elements regarding benefits, services, administrative and adjudicative processes, and intergovernmental agreements. One element is the disability pension to eligible contributors. In 2013–14, $4.3 billion was paid to nearly 330,000 contributors. A second is the flat rate monthly benefit to the children of disabled contributors. It has its own eligibility rules and benefit rate, and in 2013–14 benefits were paid to approximately 85,000 children. Third, there is a national vocational rehabilitation program and other related return-to-work support services and incentives. A fourth element is the decision-making process on applications and the three-stage appeal system for administering and adjudicating benefit claims. Fifth, there is quality assurance and related monitoring and evaluation activities related to the goal of program integrity. Sixth, there is a set of agreements between the CPP and the Quebec Pension Plan to manage the flow of work between the plans and to handle legislative changes. As well, there is a series of information-sharing agreements with provincial governments and similar agreements with provincial workers' compensation boards along with 40 reimbursement agreements with private sector insurers. Canada also has international social security agreements with about 50 other countries. Employment and Social Development Canada is the federal government department that serves as the central place for legislation development, policy direction, program design, and research on issues related to CPP/D and its clients. The relationship between the policy goals, value perspectives, and program elements is shown in Table 1.1. A more detailed discussion of the program design and political substance of CPP/D is given in Chapter 4.

Social right foundations of the CPP/D incorporate economic substance and personal status. CPP/D confers an entitlement by requiring certain market achievements in the labour force and by recognizing certain personal incapacities verified by medical personnel. With these eligibility criteria, CPP/D benefits are an individual entitlement based on market and medical references, along with other considerations. The disability benefit is a social right to partial compensation for the loss of work capacity and earned income. This is disablement interpreted as dispossession – a shortcoming of the worker-citizen in bodily functions and in personal finances, and a social risk and individual threat to income security. While the CPP/D rests, in large part, on the social insurance principle of an earned right, to a degree the disability benefit for contributors and the derived right for their

Table 1.1 Policy goals, value perspectives, and program elements of CPP Disability

Policy Goals	Value Perspectives	Program Elements
Income protection	Entitlement: individuals who pay premiums establish an entitlement to income support in the event of disability	• Disability pensions • Disability benefits for children • International social security agreements • Reimbursement agreements
Return to work	Enabling: assist and encourage those able and willing to work to return to the paid labour force	• CPP disability vocational rehabilitation program • Related assessment and support services • Work incentives, e.g., employment earnings exemption
Program integrity and accountability	Enforcement: through control and compliance mechanisms ensure that benefits are paid to the right people, at the right time, and in the right amounts	• Quality assurance program and internal audits • Information-sharing agreements with provinces and WCBs • Initial applications for CPP disability benefits and reconsiderations by Employment and Social Development Canada, and the Social Security Tribunal processes
Financial sustainability and affordability	Economy: conscious of program costs and financing in short term and across generations	• Contribution rate increases • CPP fund investment practices • Eligibility for disability benefits and their administration • Information-sharing and reimbursement agreements

children endeavours "to adjust real income to the social needs and status of the citizen and not solely to the market value of his [or her] labour" (Marshall 1964, 80).

STRUGGLES FOR SOCIAL RIGHTS

Where there is social policy there is social struggle. The awareness of struggle – specifically the citizenship struggles of persons with disabilities, and especially persons defined as having severe and prolonged impairments, who seek and claim rights of access to income benefits – is a central themes of this book. Their claims are mediated through medical, bureaucratic, and legal processes, and supported

with civil rights to administrative justice and political rights of advocacy. In the Canadian context, these struggles take place within the
institutional framework of capitalism, liberalism, and federalism, as
well as ideologies concerning abilities, families, and health sciences.
The book goes beyond the traditional focus in citizenship theory on
social class, capitalism, and legal membership by embracing and
exploring issues such as disabled persons as a distinct category in
public programming, the location of persons with disabilities vis-
à-vis mainstream society, and the role of social movements and other
groups in policy-making and program delivery processes.

Turner effectively articulates this idea of struggles for citizenship,
social rights, and inclusion in society: "To become a citizen involves
a successful definition of the self as a bona fide member of society
and thus as a legitimate recipient of social rights. Becoming a citizen
involves a process of, as it were, getting into society as an outcome of
social struggles. Entry into citizenship thus involves a process of
social conflict and negotiation since citizenship is defined by various
forms of social closure which exclude outsiders and preserve the
rights of insiders to the full enjoyment of welfare and other social
benefits" (1986, 85).

Citizenship, understood to mean social membership and participation, results from organized struggles by marginalized groups, and
successful struggles produce concrete advances in social rights (Dwyer
2004; Faulks 2000). All such claims for social rights are political,
Turner argues, because any growth of citizenship challenges "existing
patterns of power – and therefore – will be met with political struggles by dominant groups to preserve their advantages (1986, 104).
Likewise, as we will see in Chapters 7 and 8, the retrenchment and
restriction of access to income benefits and rights of appeal produce
further disadvantages, provoking additional forms of struggle. People
struggle for social citizenship to gain authoritative recognition of a
social condition or group status; to attain compensation for past
wrongs inflicted on a group; to obtain access to community resources
in the form of income benefits, employment opportunities, services
and support; and to secure restructuring of institutional arrangements to enable participation by people with disabilities.

Struggles for social rights occur at numerous personal, organizational, and systemic levels that intersect with public and private
domains of life. Political struggles for recognition are most apparent
in state arenas, as are many symbolic struggles for attitudinal and

cultural changes. Struggles for economic opportunities and financial resources focus not just on the state but also workplaces, families, and organized labour. Struggles for due process and administrative fairness are evident in interactions with medical personnel, social program administrators, employers, and private health insurance personnel. Other sites of struggles for disability income benefits, which will be discussed, include federal-provincial relations generally, Quebec–Ottawa relations specifically, political parties and federal elections as sites of policy advocacy and promise making, along with the roles of MPs and parliamentary committees as constituency advocates and policy shapers.

All struggles concern the interaction of human agency and social structures, whether at the personal level of everyday life, public or private sector programs, medical knowledge and bureaucratic administration, labour markets or insurance firms, or general cultural beliefs and attitudes on disability. In *Struggling for Social Citizenship*, the focus is not so much on the disability-related struggles associated with coping with chronic illness or managing impairments, although these are powerful experiences, and they are the interest of medical sociology and rehabilitation science plus other fields. Attention here is devoted to exploring the struggles of disabled workers who negotiate relationships and identities with social security programs, and with clients navigating systems of services and redress in an attempt to realize their social rights to income support and a modicum of economic welfare. These struggles concern both the *extent* and the *content* of social citizenship (Faulks 2000, 7). Personal and social struggles reveal the problematic nature of traditional understandings of citizenship for people with disabilities and, in turn, emphasize the importance of organized or networked action and conflict in the classification, development, and administration of social rights.

The development of social rights is a contextual process, contingent on a mixture of material and discursive factors. The social citizenship of people with disabilities is not a regime unfolding towards some ultimate policy purpose or final set of ideals, for the reason that there is no public consensus or governmental vision of such a progressive trajectory. Social change and human history do not occur in such a linear, uniform, and inevitable fashion. This tells us that struggling for social citizenship may result in various outcomes: frequent setbacks, for sure, as well as the establishment of new rights, the maintenance of existing ones, the expansion of certain rights perhaps, and the erosion of other entitlements. Across the disability income policy field, developments are always uneven and at times contradictory, and so struggles may be a proactive or defensive form of political engagement by groups in decision-making processes.

CONCLUSION

Disablement is a sociopolitical construction and a biological phenomenon. Ideas about disability are intrinsically linked to ideas about normalcy, both of which are constructed, interpreted, maintained, and transformed through social practices, subject locations, and human relationships. Definitions of disability are an intermingling of individual acceptance and self-identification, acknowledgment (or not) by family and acquaintances, politically advocated by groups for recognition of redefinition, and official assessment and assignment through legislation and professional appraisal. Notions of incapacity and severity of impairments vary across policies as well as across time and jurisdictions. The disabled as political subjects are often viewed as lesser citizens, as passive and dependent individuals, although people with disabilities exercise human agency in claiming, managing, and defending social rights of citizenship. The image of social citizen that emerges in this chapter is of disabled bodies as politicized working bodies.

The analysis here adopts an expansive conception of what is political, as illustrated by the discussion of four strands of academic literature on old and new styles of disability mobilization, embodied politics and related idea of contestation, the politics of social status and identity, and human needs and the politics of need interpretation. In turn, these four streams of thinking on politics draw attention to historical phases in the activism of disabled people themselves, to the bodily materiality and cultural dimensions of disability, and to the inevitable conflict associated with claiming citizenship rights. Relations of power operate in and circulate through state, civil, and market institutions, producing boundaries of eligibility for programs and badges of ability and disability for people's identities. Claims of identity rights for public benefits, including disability income provisions, are often claims of differentiated social citizenship – categorical programs for particular memberships. Because claims for social rights confront prevailing groupings of power, they generate conflict and struggle, even for those supposedly deserving and in need. Establishing rights to income maintenance based on disability has contributed to legitimating government interventions, outlining social citizenship, and developing federal and provincial welfare states. Income provision for people with disabilities over the last one hundred years has institutionalized rights claims that are collectively provided, medically assessed, and individually claimed, and shaped the institutional nature of state-society relations in Canada in significant ways.

CHAPTER TWO

Sociopolitical Institutions
and Prime Ministerial Eras

The meanings of public life and the collective forms through which groups become aware of political goals and work to attain them arise, not from societies alone, but at the meeting points of states and societies.

Theda Skocpol, "Bringing the State Back In"

Politics is about power; that is about the capacity of social agents, agencies and institutions to maintain or transform their environment, social or physical.

David Held, *Models of Democracy*

Disability income policy deploys state powers to mitigate the consequences of earnings loss and additional costs of care due to impairments. More than that, implementation of disability income programs involves the exercise of other kinds of power relations: the relative autonomy and expertise of medical science; the private authority of life insurance companies; and the public legitimacy of legal advice and judicial decisions. Having examined citizenship and social rights, and disability and the politics of struggles, this chapter sets out the final elements of the analytical framework. These elements are institutions of the state, polity, and civil society that bear on disability and the social rights of citizens; the three levels of micro, meso, and macro processes and key actions; and prime ministerial eras of disability policy formation. Which institutions are involved in generating, interpreting, and providing for measures that address the needs and risks of people with disabilities? How does disability income provision interrelate with state agencies, political actors, and social structures? How do individuals in their immediate milieu interact with a disability income program and the larger social context? What is the place of the CPP/D within the overall social system?

Many writers on social rights locate these entitlements squarely within the interests, resources, and actions of the welfare state. Societal institutions, however, should not be neglected in understanding social rights. That social rights are publicly defined engages political processes, to be sure, but these rights also involve the influence of values, beliefs, and attitudes within the general cultural setting in which the state governs. Life chance outcomes, and life opportunities for that matter, are conditioned by groups, choices, and activities within the market economy, families, and a host of community structures. "Citizenship in mainstream literature is adamantly public," note Chris Beasley and Carol Lee Bacchi, "in the public autonomous individual agent or in public community belonging" (2000, 340). What can get lost with this emphasis, they suggest, is "the dependence of public activities upon private ones, as well as the related difficulties attached to regarding them as entirely separate" (ibid.). The "social" then takes in the domestic realm and the official realms of everyday life, and the power dynamics of social citizenship comprise private and public material actions and discursive activities.

Providing disability income support requires other institutions besides a government department that determines and processes cash payments to clients. The effective administration of public disability programs operate through medical and rehabilitation specialists, insurance companies, labour unions, workplace human resource personnel, lawyers and legal advocates, and local service agencies. For many Canadians with disabilities, encounters with the state as citizens with rights to a benefit are indirect, convoluted, and highly ambiguous experiences. To get a disability income benefit, the social right claimant must pass through more than a few social institutions in addition to state agencies. Rights to income security for disability are a dense thicket of structures greatly consequential to shaping the identities and capacities of individuals and their prospects. Social citizenship and disability policy function at and across three levels of human action, social contexts, and institutions. In brief terms, the first is the micro level of everyday lives, practices, experiences, expectations, and the exercise of personal agency; the second is the meso or middle-range level of program sectors and policy communities; and the third is the macro level of overarching institutions such as federalism and the market economy. Social rights to disability income generate a politics that preoccupies firms and labour markets, governmental agencies, families, and medical, legal, and bodily interests.

LINKING STATE, POLITICAL, AND SOCIETAL INSTITUTIONS

On the whole, the citizenship literature has a definite state-centred orientation, shaped by T.H. Marshall's (1964) pivotal formulation on the institutions of social citizenship, in which he highlighted the educational system, national health care, and public social services. J.M. Barbalet emphasizes the centrality of the state, declaring, "it is the state which ultimately grants" rights of citizenship (1988, 110). Deborah Stone, in her analysis of disability public policy in United States, adopts a state-centred analysis that views "disability as an administrative category in the welfare state" and aims to explore "the meaning of disability for the state – the formal institutions of government, and the intellectual justifications that give coherence to their activities" (1984, 4). Bryan Turner extends the focus, adding certain political institutions, though retaining a state-centred approach: "citizenship presupposes a number of political institutions such as the centralized state, a system of political participation, institutions of political education and a variety of institutions associated with the state which protect the individual from the loss of liberties" (1986, 107). On the system of political participation, Turner is referring to political parties, interest groups, and elections, while on protection of individual liberties, he is likely thinking of the courts and tribunals (Porter 2007).

Mainstream studies of social rights typically do not examine medical practices, health insurance policies, rehabilitations services, administrative law, or the power dynamics operating within family structures. Analysis that looks more closely at social institutions will enable the study of the role of informal rules or norms and interpersonal practices that operate in these settings, for example. Broadly understood, citizenship encapsulates relations between individuals, states, and societies, and claiming and exercising social rights involves individuals, processes, and structures that span the political community and civil society. Social citizenship is not just about the state intervening in society or regulating the market economy; it is about the state interacting with societal institutions and relying on market structures. And it is about the interplay – the cooperation, contradiction, and conflict – among state and societal institutions that shape the actual practice by embodied subjects of social rights. Moreover, social citizenship involves the rights of property in the market economy, the responsibilities of individuals in households, the divided and shared jurisdictions of federal and provincial governments, and the role of physicians and nurses in the authoritative determination of disabilities.

Actors and organizations in state, political, and civil society institutions all contribute, in various configurations, to shaping disability policies and social rights. The state has degrees of autonomy; politics can and do matter; and civil society institution are more than mere context for public policy and governing. Particular processes and ideas connect state, political, and societal institutions. Citizenship, as a set of legal, political, and social rights and practices for membership in the political community, certainly links structures and actors across these institutional domains. Struggles for rights, by individuals, social groups, and program clientele similarly connect with organizations in a community, federal, or provincial polity and welfare state. Postmodernity, as a perspective on our current age, accentuates ways in which various sectors interact and collide; in how established assumptions are increasingly questioned and contested; and in which multiple identities are expressed by particularistic criterion of embodied citizens. Disability as a social construction is another example of a concept and discourse that asserts new relationships among institutional orders of society, thus challenging traditional divisions between public and private realms of life.

Disability income programs further demonstrate the intermingling of public and private and of the individual and communal: revenues from employees, employers, and the self-employed help to fund public programs through general finances and social insurance premiums; medicine and other professions are recognized as self-regulating bodies with powers granted by provincial governments; veterans' groups lobby parliamentarians and the federal government for recognition of their needs and better services as a result of their military service; public disability plans like the CPP/D and its Quebec counterpart are designed to provide room for personal savings and private industry health and life insurance plans; family members and friends offer advice and can influence decisions by potential program clients on whether to apply for a benefit or to appeal a negative decision. Through countless interdependencies like these, state, political, and societal institutions intermingle, at times as relatively autonomous actors, and at other times as subjects of actions by others. Together, though not necessarily in unison, they confer or disclaim social statuses, provide or refuse resources, and alter or maintain valued identities for citizens.

MICRO, MESO, AND MACRO LEVELS OF ANALYSIS

Deborah Cowen usefully notes that "a growing body of literature investigates how citizenship is constituted through substantive struggles ... at multiple scales" (2008, 153). These struggles for social welfare entitlements can be seen as playing out at the micro, meso, and macro scales or levels of action. There are, at the micro scale, the particular struggles of individuals in claiming an entitlement and the more general interplay of personal lives, family contexts, and social policies. A micro focus is on the individual body, the embodied claimant, coupled with activities such as specific medical assessments, employment records, and rehabilitation efforts. The meso or middle level is characterized by agenda-setting and policy-making struggles over the introduction of a new program for a specific group, struggles for the extension of a program to a new category of people, and struggles for defending a social right under direct attack or stealthy restraint by authorities. Categorizing effects are at work here with attention to issues of identified risks, the pooling of coverage, general eligibility rules, and actuarial projections of programs. At the macro level of overall social structure, struggles occur over the relative responsibilities of overarching institutions – for example, of states, labour markets, medical science, and families in addressing the needs of disabled citizens. The focus here is on fundamental systemic issues such as the scope of state intervention and the place of family responsibility.

Social rights, therefore, are practised in large part by individuals at the micro level, embedded within a policy field of social citizenship, surrounded by a citizenship regime for the provincial or national political community.

In terms of rules and norms, at the micro level are the issues of client duties and rights, questions of discretion and entitlements and of appeals; at the meso level are statutory mandates, administrative fairness, judicial review, standard operating regulations and procedures;

and at the macro level are constitutional principles concerning the rule of law, jurisdictions, and parliamentary supremacy. In terms of embodied politics and corporeal citizenship, there is the body physical of the individual self, the body policy of a program clientele, and the body politic of the state and political institutions of society. In terms of the position of medicine in disability policy (and in public policy more generally), there are practices of diagnosis and treatment of individuals as patients; the role of physicians and other health professionals as authorized gatekeepers to determining eligibility categories and those, among a clientele group, deemed qualified and not qualified for a social entitlement; and the systemic issues of medicine as a power/knowledge institution in relation to the overall population and the medicalization of modern society. We can see multiple forms and scales of power in the public administration of human bodies and social life.

Micro-level Activities and Processes

Micro-level social citizenship entails individuals interrelating in intimate and immediate contexts as well as in political and state contexts – for example, providing or receiving moral support from a relative, advocating for unmet needs, or interacting with a government program official about a benefit application. It is what Barbara Cruikshank calls a strategic field where "power is exercised both upon and through the citizen-subject at the level of small things, in the material, learned, and habitual ways we embody citizenship" (1999, 124). Informal networks of support include family, friends, and co-workers, any of which can be a source of information, contacts, funds, stories, and shared beliefs. Formal sources of contact and possible support may include a union steward, direct employer, family physician, a lawyer, local member of Parliament, or life insurance company representative.

The micro level relates to classic liberal thinking about citizenship, which upholds notions of individual capacity, autonomy, and responsibility, and meritocracy. In these locally experienced and specific realties, personal struggles readily arise from contending and shifting forms of knowledge, interactions, and authority relations. These connections shape a person's sense of self and their sentiment of belonging in wider social structures. So too does the onset of a significant impairment by a working-age adult in the labour force.

A fundamental aspect of the social nature of disability is how people interpret and take meaning from a life event, diagnosis, condition, or impairment. According to Robert Pinker, "the most important definitions of citizenship are subjective ones" (1971, 141). Acquiring a disability in the midst of one's career can give rise to changes in functional capacities that may affect work performance and probably one's self-conception, leading to personal adjustments and re-evaluations about one's future. It may result in some existing relationships falling off – as the person leaves their place of employment and applies for disability benefit – and the acquisition of new relationships with health professionals and social service workers. Routines and patterns in the personal lives of disabled citizens therefore change, as do their local social environments.

Meso-level Activities and Processes

Activities, groups, and sectors of the middle range occupy the area midway between the micro level of small things and the macro level of systemic institutions. Robert Alford and Roger Friedland call it the "organizational level," which, for them, relates to "the formation and operation of formal, bounded bureaucratic structures within a society" (1985, 17). Included here are both dominant and subordinate political, state, and civil society organizations, such as mediating associations, interest groups, political parties, corporations, government departments, labour unions, professions, and non-profit agencies. The meso level is a prime political space for the identity politics of social movements and group-based status politics.

Nikolas Rose and Peter Miller express a meso-level perspective when they write that welfare states are not so much a form of state as rather a form of governance with "alliances between private and professional agents ... formed around problems" with programs and various "centres of power or decisions" (1992, 191–2). From this vantage point, welfarism, as they call it, is a matter of "the assembling of diverse mechanisms and arguments through which political forces seek to secure social and economic objectives by linking up a plethora of networks" (1992, 192). This statement encapsulates several indispensable meso-level processes: bringing together individuals, forming and mobilizing organized groups, networking amongst interests, and marshalling arguments for policy goals. What arise from this are meso discourses (Brodie 1997). These are historical configurations of a major narrative or shared understanding of governance and a corresponding form of the state, state-society relations, and a prevailing meaning of liberal-democratic citizenship. The meso narrative of the Keynesian welfare state, as noted in the Introduction, routinely omitted or segregated many people with disabilities from the mainstream story of social citizenship.

From the field of public policy studies, a family of concepts consider the middle range: associational systems, policy communities, policy networks, and policy sectors or subsystems. These concepts share the analytical aims of disaggregating the state into subsystems, paying attention to the role of organized interests and their interrelationships. Associational systems are collections of non-governmental groups, though the groups are still political and, from civil society, active in a sector of public policy. Policy communities refer to state and non-state actors and organizations associated over time with a specific public policy area. In the words of William Coleman and Grace Skogstad, "policy communities are institutions themselves [*institutionalized* may be a more fitting term] and become integrated to a greater or lesser degree by developing a set of shared values, norms and beliefs which shape the policy networks that emerge and, ultimately, the policy outcomes in a given sector" (1990, 29). *Policy networks* is a term intended to depict the actual patterns in, and nature of, relationships in a given policy field between actors and organizations from the state, polity, and civil society. Attention to policy networks often focuses on the relative capacity and autonomy of the state in making and implementing policy vis-à-vis structures in the political system and society. From the civil society side, questions of capacity and autonomy concern the ability of, say, a social movement to develop organizationally, to conduct policy-related research and analysis, and have access to state-based policy development processes.

In practice, disability policy is "an aggregate of policies," a subsystem of several independent programs that is "diverse in the perceived needs it addresses, in the groups it seeks to benefit, in its legislative origins and purposes, and in the interest groups that battled over its enactment" (Erlanger and Roth 1985, 320). Over the last hundred years, disability income policy has expanded and differentiated in all these dimensions. This reality is reflected in the literature on disability and social security (Dixon and Hyde 2000; OECD 2003) and case studies on CPP/D (Lawand and Kloosterman 2006; Torjman 2002), provincial social assistance regimes (Boychuk

1998; Prince 2015), federal income programs (Puttee 2002), tax policy measures for disabled Canadians (Prince 2001c), veterans' benefits (Neary 2009), and workers' compensation (Jennissen, Prince, and Schwartz 2000).

Invariably, struggles over social citizenship engage struggles over the design and content of programs. This may involve debates over the basis of entitlement (need, labour force participation, residency, military service, or family status) and eligibility rules, financing methods, the scope of coverage and quality of benefits, the procedural rights and responsibilities of claimants as well as those of program administrators. These are all meso-level issues that take place through the operation of formal bureaucratic structures in categorizing disability, designing forms, requiring certain documented kinds of evidence, assessing applications, and adjudicating appeals. For those disabled making a claim for a social benefit, this is the middle world of bureaucratic encounters, program gatekeepers, and administrative practices. These rules and procedures involve a process of bureaucratic individuation (Procacci 2001). That is, through mechanisms of official identification and surveillance, individuals are positioned as unique and uniform subjects at the same time. Examples of this positioning include the use of social insurance numbers, which were introduced in Canada with the CPP; a record of financial contributions to a social insurance program; and medical assessments on an official form for program purposes. Individuation, Turner points out, "makes everybody the same while making everybody entirely different," and "makes the social control of large numbers of people bureaucratically feasible and politically effective" (1986, 119).

Macro-level Activities and Processes

Large-scale cultural values and beliefs, along with the overarching institutions of society, constitute the macro level within which citizenship, disability, and income security are developed and function. While rights to social benefits and services may be established in legislation, what matters to citizens, Marshall argued, was "the superstructure of legitimate expectations" (1965, 115), the general setting of hopes and claims, norms and attitudes. Cultural aspects of society influence perceptions, ideas, discourses, and behaviours. They also have a material expression inscribed in practices, rules, and procedures that govern the conduct of individuals and groups. Among these cultural forms are "our shared 'common sense' understandings of the appropriate boundaries between the international and the national, the state and the economy, the public and the domestic spheres, and the very definition of what it means to be a citizen" (Brodie 1995, 10). These understandings also pertain to interrelations between federal and provincial governments, ability and disability identities, and the balance between rights and responsibilities.

Dominant values and cultural practices in Canadian society portray people with disabilities as disadvantaged, charitable cases, welfare clients, or users of services. In Canada, according to William Boyce and colleagues, "the hegemonic notion of able-bodied dominance has been pervasive" (2001, 23). Iris Marion Young named this process, in more general terms, cultural imperialism. Cultural imperialism occurs through "the universalization of a dominant groups' experience and culture, and its establishment as the norm" (Young 1990, 59). Groups that differ from the dominant group are marked as "Other," and as lacking certain qualities or attributes of the dominant group in society. In the context of disability, ableism or disablism can be understood as a kind of cultural imperialism. Ableism (used interchangeably with *disablism*) refers to discrimination against people with mental or physical disabilities based on individual and institutional prejudicial beliefs and practices that assign an inferior worth to them.

Governing institutions are entrenched in power relations that are in turn rooted in fundamental social values. In the Canadian context of disability and social rights of citizenship, seven institutions of this kind must be understood: federalism; cabinet parliamentary government; the Charter of Rights and Freedoms, judiciary and rule of law; capitalism and labour markets; medicine; and the family.

Federalism enshrines a division of legislative powers between the federal and provincial orders of government. Both orders are active in disability income policy. The federal government has income programs for Canadian veterans, the Employment Insurance (EI) sickness benefit, the CPP/D, and the Working Income Tax Benefit, which has a disability supplement, and other assorted tax measures. Disability income programs provided by provincial governments include social assistance, workers' compensation, disability benefits under the Quebec Pension Plan, and select tax measures in certain provinces. Both orders of government regulate workplaces through employment standard laws and labour codes, and both orders also regulate aspects of the health and life insurance industry. Constitutionally, the CPP/D and larger CPP are shared jurisdictional responsibility of the provincial and federal governments, with attendant rules for amendments and mechanisms for regular intergovernmental reviews. In this way, CPP/D has contributed to the evolution and adaptation of Canada's welfare state, social politics, and the constitutional system.

The institution of cabinet parliamentary government at both orders of government confers most of the power to initiate policy on the executive – the prime minister and cabinet, with the senior bureaucracy as influential advisor. In theory, ministers are individually and collectively responsible and accountable to Parliament or a provincial legislature. Notably, only the federal government can initiate legislation involving money. Opposition parties and individual MPs have the right to criticize, suggest, oppose, and scrutinize policy and legislation, but only the cabinet may initiate money bills. Cabinet parliamentary government functions through the vehicle of political parties and partisan political competition. Over time, the Conservatives, Liberals, and New Democrats have tended to support enhancements to disability income benefits, as individual advocates, collectively as parties through election promises, and collaboratively in work on parliamentary committees and task forces.

The Charter of Rights and Freedoms, judiciary, and rule of law together constitute another overarching institution in Canada that affects disability policy and the social citizenship rights of people with disabilities. Entrenched in the constitution, the Charter is part of the supreme law of the country. Its basic purpose is to authorize the courts to protect a set of fundamental civil liberties from the laws and actions of public sector agencies by scrutinizing and limiting their actions. While the Charter applies to most of the Canadian public sector, it does not apply to private sector activities. The doctrine of the rule of law has deep roots in political thought and Anglo-Saxon notions of administrative law and judicial review. Precepts of the rule of law are that a separate and independent judiciary exists separately from the government executive to review the actions and inactions of public authorities; that all agencies of the state are subject to and operate under the law in compliance with the procedural requirements of natural justice; and that citizens have recourse to legal remedies through the courts and or tribunals for abuses and misuses of power by state authorities. Underpinning the doctrine is the principle of validity, that every official act must be justified by some legal authority; the principle that no law may be applied retroactively; and the principle of equal treatment under the law, implying freedom from excessive and unfair state action. These principles are subject to interpretive debates and also serve as important ideas that claimants and others can deploy in asserting a right to public income provision (Porter 2007).

Capitalism is usually thought of as an economic institution that embraces competitive market exchange, private property rights, the work ethic, and gainful employment. It is obviously crucial as a political institution as well in that the role of the state is structured on the premise that capitalism is central to personal freedom and choice, along with wealth creation and general prosperity. Capitalism supplies particular impetus to the persistent concern for efficiency as an idea or cult (Stein 2002); notions of productivity, innovation, fair return on risk; and the view that governments are inherently inefficient and should therefore be limited to performing tasks for which they are suited and not for things that the market can do better. Capitalism seeks to limit public spending on disability income maintenance programs (and other such entitlements) in order to create room for private savings and private industry to meet Canadians' disability income protection needs. Participation in the labour force, to engage in paid work, is widely held as a duty of the good citizen in modern economies. Not only is it an income source, gainful employment is a form of social participation, and a basis of self-esteem and status in market economies. Employment is also a requirement of eligibility for some public benefits, especially social insurance programs like CPP/D and EI regular and sickness benefits. For many people with disabilities, however, the labour market is a place of outright exclusion, unemployment, persistent low wages, workplace discrimination, and occupational segregation.

Medical power – that is, the influence and authority of health sciences and therapeutic professionals within society – stems from a number of sources and relationships, including a body of expertise based on systematic knowledge, skills, and training developed through various kinds of evidence; relatively high societal prestige and public legitimacy; and substantial occupational autonomy through delegated authority from the state. Medical power links with other sources of influence and key interests in the political economy, such as research funding councils and foundations, medical schools and universities, and pharmaceutical companies. The medical institution has a significant presence in Canadian disability policy, specifically CCP/D and other public income programs. Nurses, family physicians, medical specialists, psychologists, and other therapists all play important roles in the construction of disablement and the implementation of programs and services in this policy field.

David Cameron and Fraser Valentine claim that, from the early 1900s to the 1970s, "the medical profession ... controlled both the meaning of disability and the lives of persons with disabilities" (2001, 6). With the dominant medical conception of disability came certain stereotypes and stigmas, along with a series of "disability-specific, medically oriented non-governmental organizations" (2001, 5). Other writers on disability emphasize the ongoing power of medical and health science professionals, and contend that this power continues to limit the citizenship rights of people with disabilities. Helen Meekosha and Leanne Dowse, for example, argue that constraints on citizenship occur when the role of professionals "is primarily informed by the duty to care rather than an interest in promoting improved citizenship rights and democratic participation for the 'client'" (1997, 53). Susan Wendell concurs: "Scientific medicine participates in and fosters the myth of control [that we have control over the conditions of our bodies and of bodily injuries and diseases] by focussing overwhelmingly on cures and life-saving interventions, and by tending to neglect chronic illness, rehabilitation, pain management, and the quality of the patients' experiences" (1996, 94).

Medical control and medicalization are not only generated by physicians and related health professionals. Other institutions, including insurance companies and government programs, are directly and routinely engaged in these processes. Even self-advocates and clients as well as family members may adopt medical discourse and accept medical practices to advance a claim. Relations of power between doctors and patients are more complicated than the common image of doctors exercising virtually total control over their patients. Some doctors are reluctant to quickly medicalize a patient's symptoms (Moss and Teghtsoonian 2008). Some doctors easily adopt the role as advocate for the patient's claim for disability insurance benefits, while others do not. And some patients will have more embodied knowledge than their physician about their condition or impairment.

The family as a basic institution (politicians call it the bedrock of society) deserves emphasis, especially given the present diversity of family forms in Canadian life. The belief that families are the fitting venue for the care of young children, elderly relatives, and other dependent members is widespread in social policies. Underlying this ethic of family is the assumption that women will be available and responsive to others, including volunteering for work outside the home and being self-sacrificing. The welfare state, built from the mid-1940s to the 1970s, was based on a particular notion of the family. As Janine Brodie explains, "It presumed a stable working-/middle-class nuclear family supported by a male bread-winner, a dependent wife and children, and the unpaid domestic labour of women" (1995, 39). Today, ideas of marriage and family, and of what represents "normal family life," are shifting. The nuclear family, characterized by married heterosexual couples with children, which was once the predominant form of family structure in the country, now accounts for 40 percent of all families (Rice and Prince 2013). Carole Pateman (1988) was among the first feminist writers to challenge the idea that social citizenship, as a bundle of rights and duties based on membership in the community, was politically neutral and universally available to all groups. In the private or domestic sphere, most informal care for children, relatives with disabilities, and the elderly is still provided by women, regardless of the women's participation in the labour force.

SOCIAL CITIZENSHIP AND NORMALCY/DISABILITY RELATIONS

In addition to the right to economic welfare and security, Marshall (1964) defined social citizenship as the right to live the life of a civilized being according to society's prevalent standards. From a critical disability perspective, society's prevalent standards usually mean standards of normal bodies and "the normal world" (Davis 1995, 22). As Erving Goffman suggests, "Society establishes the means of categorizing persons and the complement of attributes felt to be ordinary and natural from members of each of these categories" (1968, 2). Ideas such as inclusion, positive identity, social solidarity, and social cohesion take on particular and often problematic meanings in relation to issues of disablement and to the practices of social citizenship by people with impairments. Labelling and the stigmatization of individuals and groups also occur in reference to standards and norms prevailing in society. "Historically," in social policy, notes Ola Sjöberg, "the most important norm has been the norm to perform in the labour market" (1999, 278). Longstanding concerns about potential negative effects of income programs on people's attitudes towards saving incentives and work, including a fear of welfare fraud and idleness, are linked to the labour market norm. With social norms come evaluations and thus deviations from the norms. Liberalism, according to Paul Spicker, tends to "conceptualize disability as misfortune and privilege normalcy over abnormal" (1984, 2). Norms that bear on disability and disability policy are of multiple types: ableist norms of prejudice and other societal attitudes about bodies and independence; educational norms of athletic and scholastic performance; legal norms around competence; medical norms of functioning and activity limitations; and occupational and workplace norms on accommodations (or the lack thereof due to hardship norms).

Disability is about the normal body and mind as much as the abnormal. Lennard Davis asserts, "the very concept of normalcy by which most people (by definition) shape their existence is in fact tied inexorably to the concept of disability, or rather, the concept of disability is a function of a concept of normalcy. Normalcy and disability are part of the same system" (1995, 2). Over the nineteenth century, Davis suggests, normalcy became the dominant paradigm, or the norm, and people with disabilities became irregulars in society – the suboptimal, unconventional, non-standard minority group. Goffman famously referred to "the normals" as those individuals "who do not depart negatively from the particular expectations at issue," and "the abnormal" as individuals with "an undesired differentness" from public attitudes and normative expectations regarding the attributes and conduct of human bodies (1968, 5). In examining the interactions between these groups, Goffman used the term *normalization* to refer to "how far normals ... go in treating the stigmatized person as if he [or she] didn't have a stigma." He coined the term *normafication* as "the effect on part of a stigmatized individual to present himself [or herself] as an ordinary person" (1968, 30–1). These processes are germane to practices of claiming benefits and the making of decisions on eligibility for disability income.

In mainstream twentieth-century sociology, "the test of modernity was the presence of universalistic and achievement norms over particularistic and ascriptive ones" (Turner 1986, 66). However, as income maintenance programs emerged for the disabled, particular criteria that define a person as impaired were entrenched in public policies and legislation. As a set of personal attributes and specific classification of people, disability is as noteworthy as ever in Canadian policy. Rights to social insurance income for persons with disabilities involve the ascription of bodily impairment and the achievement of gainful employment. With the deployment of these norms in income security policies also potentially comes the stigmatization of intended beneficiaries. According to Spicker, "A stigmatized person is someone whose characteristics or behaviour go far beyond the norm" (1984, 166). For Goffman, the stigmatized person is "the individual who is disqualified from full social acceptance" (1968, i). Stigma is produced through the interplay of society, the self, and service provision. Expressed another way, stigma is the interaction of political economy, the embodied person, and public programs. Disability understood as a loss or decline in functional capacity results, in liberal market societies, in diminished status and earning power, all of which raise the risk of dependency and possibly poverty. Intellectual, mental, and physical impairments also can result in stigma, social rejection, and exclusion from public services.

PRIME MINISTERIAL ERAS
AND DISABILITY POLICY MAKING

Social citizenship has a Canadian history that by nearly all academic accounts began in the post-1945 period and flourished into the 1970s. Such accounts fail to notice significant developments in social policy and state–polity–society relations with origins earlier in the twentieth century. Accordingly, Chapter 3 examines the formation of the first generation of income support programs for several categories of people with disabilities. These early developments are not marginal to the welfare state and social citizenship rights. Contemporary programs, agencies, and helping professions are influenced by these initial choices, and today's disability politics are rooted in legislation and practices established during this early period. Long before citizenship became the rallying cry of the disability movement in the 1970s and 1980s, ideas about inclusion, security, and equal opportunity figured in the policy debates of social reformers.

The story of social citizenship and disability policy has been portrayed in a number of different images. Social citizenship has been depicted as a broad sequential development, a major historical stage following progress on civil and political rights of citizenship, providing a modicum of economic welfare and security (Marshall 1964). It has also been represented as a part of a series of waves of citizenship rights, the outcome of political struggles by social movements, moving outwards covering more groups of people (children, women, and the elderly, as examples), regulating the market economy, and providing access to more services on a universalistic basis (Turner 1986). Developments in disability policy over the long-term have been characterized as a series of add-ons or layers of programming (Berkowitz 1987) and also as a hit-and-miss affair resulting in citizenship by installments for Canadians with disabilities (Prince 2004).

A core aim of this book is to examine the major policy, legislative, and administrative changes in the CPP disability pension program over its fifty-year history. The history of the CPP and the CPP/D does not merely offer general background; this history is central to documenting and understanding the phases through which the CPP has passed and the nature of the debates, decisions, and developments. The CPP/D program has been the object of reform initiatives as well as restraint measures. Looking at the past reveals what policy and program options were set aside and how and why programs were formulated the way they were. To facilitate an understanding of disability policy change, the analysis is structured around prime ministerial eras. While the organization of the book is based on prime ministerial eras and federal political parties, other actors and organizations in the state, polity, and civil society are also considered. Thomas Axworthy notes that "rarely has a Prime Minister taken up social policy as a personal cause." Then again, "Prime Ministers set a framework and juggle competing forces," and "every period of social advance has a senior Minister as a driving force," Axworthy explains (2002, 4). Chapter 3 looks at approaches to disability policy and social rights in the early 1900s to the 1960s. This period includes two world wars, the Great Depression of the 1930s, and the early years of the Keynesian welfare state. The main prime ministers were Borden, Bennett, King, St. Laurent, and Diefenbaker.

Chapters 4 through 8 then proceed chronologically through the main federal prime ministerial and governing political party eras: the policy design and formation phase of the Lester Pearson Liberals from 1963 to the introduction of CPP/D in 1970; the Pierre Trudeau Liberals from 1968 to 1984, covering the policy implementation, adaptation, and pension debate phase spanning the 1970 to 1984 period; the Brian Mulroney Progressive Conservatives from 1984 to

1993, which included major reforms to the CPP and the liberalization of disability benefits and eligibility; the Jean Chrétien and Paul Martin Liberals, from 1993 to 2006, a period characterized largely by critiques and retrenchment and the reorientation of disability benefits and goals; and the Stephen Harper Conservatives from 2006 to 2015. We will see that in each era there were specific cabinet ministers who were notably central to CPP/D and other disability policy developments: Judy LaMarsh in Pearson's era, Monique Bégin in the Trudeau years, Jake Epp and Michael Wilson in the Mulroney government, Paul Martin in the Chrétien era, and Jim Flaherty in the Harper years.

Prime ministerial eras are not watertight of course; they overlap and interact in various ways. Yet there are basic internal attributes that give each a relatively distinctive set of dynamics. These periods of policy developments are based on legislative, regulatory, and administrative reforms related to the CPP/D. For each of the eras, the following questions will be addressed. What is the scope of CPP disability policy? What authoritative actions and program elements are in place, and how are policies depicted and which goals are emphasized? What are the salient changes, if any, in legislation and program features, particularly in benefit levels and eligibility requirements for the disability programs? Who were the actors and organizations involved in making the policy and decision changes? What are the issues and trends regarding the CPP appeals system? What is the shape of disability benefit payments and caseloads? What other significant social policy and political developments were occurring that had implications for the CPP and disability policy? For example, was pension reform a high priority of government? In sum, what are the implications of the period for CPP disability applicants? Each of the five prime ministerial eras reveals partisan stances, ideological differences and similarities, as well as some surprising policy decisions set in particular political and economic climates of each regime. The Conclusion will offer some comparative assessments and conclusions on these prime ministerial and political party eras covering the past five decades in Canadian politics, disability policy, and struggles for social citizenship.

CONCLUSION

To understand social citizenship for disabled Canadians, we must look at state structures, political organizations, and societal groups simply because actors and agencies in all these domains are sources of power, knowledge, and beliefs related to income provision. This is not to suggest that a pluralistic diffusion of power is at play in disability policy. That there are inequalities in the relations of power is a common theme in the fields of citizenship, social policy, and disability studies. Relations of power can also be multidirectional and, for the embodied citizen, intensely personal or chillingly distant.

The chapter explored several key elements that inform the rest of the book: the institutional domains of the state, polity, and civil society that bear on disability and on the social rights of citizens; the three scales of micro, meso, and macro processes; and prime ministerial eras of disability policy formation. Social citizenship and disability policy function at the levels of human action, social contexts, and institutions. Rights to income security in respect to disability operate within an institutionally dense thicket of structures, so that firsthand encounters with the state by citizens can seem convoluted and highly ambiguous experiences. Struggling for social citizenship does not mean that entitlements to income readily arise or are readily achieved.

This chapter also drew attention to the cultural context of disability thinking. To a large degree, Canadian attitudes to disability and people with impairments create a culture of pity, devaluing, exclusion, and misapprehension. In short, this is a culture of limitations, and a culture that is limiting to many citizens with physical, intellectual, and mental disabilities. With respect to the institutional context of disability and social rights of citizenship in Canada, seven overarching institutions were profiled: federalism; cabinet parliamentary government; the Charter of Rights and Freedoms, judiciary and rule of law; capitalism and labour markets; medicine; and the family. Examining the roles and relationships of these institutions is one of the tasks of the following chapters.

CHAPTER THREE

Social Citizenship for Canadians with Disabilities, 1900–1960

We should study the appearance, at precise historical moments, of different institutions of rectification and the categories of individuals for whom they are intended, that is to say, the techno-institutional births of blindness and deaf-muteness, of imbeciles and the retarded, of the nervous and the unbalanced.

Michel Foucault, *Abnormal*

The genius of social insurance is that it enlists the direct support of the classes most likely to benefit, and enlists equally the participation and controlling influence of the state, at the same time as it avoids the evil of pauperization, and the undemocratic influence of excessive state philanthropy.

Leonard Marsh, *Report on Social Security for Canada*

Canada's social welfare safety net is older and more complicated than is often recognized. This chapter details the early developments of disability income and vocational rehabilitation programs as well as plans for reforming disability policy as part of a modern system of social security in Canada. Exploring the first generation of disability programs allows us to appreciate Canada's lineage of income maintenance policy and reveals the influence of early programs on subsequent policies and programs. We also see how issues of work, family, rights, and duties persist through the decades. This inquiry brings to light the authoritative meanings given to disability in social legislation and regulations. The chapter examines how disability was conceived as a public issue by leading social reformers Harry Cassidy, Leonard Marsh, and Charlotte Whitton as well as the Canadian Welfare Council.

The first generation of income support programs for specific groups of persons with disabilities in Canada spans a fifty-year period and a mix of provincial, federal, and intergovernmental measures. Over this time, the federal and provincial states introduced income programs that produced several new categories of people with disabilities as clients: the injured or diseased industrial worker; the burnt-out or physically and mentally impaired war veteran; the incapacitated husband/father and hence dependent wife/mother with children; the blind adult person; the permanently and totally disabled adult; and, in the area of medical and vocational rehabilitation, the treatable handicapped veteran or civilian. Early income programs for Canadians with disabilities were poverty-relief measures, that is, means-tested and categorical assistance targeted at a "needy" low-income group. These programs distinguish Canadian social policy efforts in this field as squarely within a liberal welfare state tradition. Contemporary notions of social rights and social citizenship as political goals and justifications for policy have roots in this period.

FIRST-GENERATION DISABILITY INCOME PROGRAMS

Establishment of workers' compensation plans by provinces marked the start of the modern era in disability policy and Canadian social security more generally. As social insurance income protection against the risk of injury, sickness, or death at workplaces, workers' compensation plans were clearly a matter of exclusive provincial jurisdiction under the constitution. Starting in 1914, provinces introduced workers' compensation plans over the next thirty years or so. Ontario developed the first workers' compensation policy when, after protracted debate in the legislature, an agreement was reached between labour interests and the Canadian Manufacturers' Association.[1] In this compromise, workers gave up their rights to sue employers for damages arising from work-related injuries in return for what amounted to "no-fault" insurance against such injuries. If injured on the job, eligible workers could be compensated without risking lengthy, expensive, and uncertain legal action. Employers for their part agreed to make regular contributions to a fund that would make payments to injured workers. The benefit of such an arrangement for employers was that firms would collectively bear the cost of compensating

1 This paragraph draws from Jennissen, Prince, and Schwartz (2000).

workers and would no longer face the potentially ruinous costs of adverse legal decisions. Other provinces followed Ontario's lead, some faster than others, in establishing workers' compensation programs: Nova Scotia in 1915, British Columbia and Manitoba in 1916, Alberta and New Brunswick in 1918, Saskatchewan in 1929, Quebec in 1931, Prince Edward Island in 1949, and Newfoundland in 1950. The territories followed much later in the 1970s.

Set up to operate at arm's length from provincial governments, the programs are governed by boards composed of equal numbers of representatives of employers and workers, reflecting the historic compromise in establishing these programs. All boards in Canada also have claims adjudication and appeals processes, including judicial review of appeal decisions. Beneficiaries under workers' compensation are categorically determined – that is, benefits are available only in circumscribed situations, namely, where injuries, disabilities, or diseases arise in the course of job-related activities. From the outset, there have been workplace injuries, diseases, and disabilities that workers' compensation in all jurisdictions did not cover. Before the establishment of CPP Disability in 1970 and the Unemployment Insurance[2] sickness benefit in 1971, injured workers who ran out of benefits or who were not eligible for workers' compensation often resorted to provincial social assistance and possibly private sickness benefit plans.

The Canadian government's earliest lasting involvement in disability-related income security policy came with the introduction of financial benefits for veterans, an area of exclusive responsibility of the federal government. In 1916, the federal government of Robert Borden established a war veterans' disability pension program. Administered by the Board of Pension Commissioners, the pensions were for soldiers and their survivors for disability or death arising from the Great War. The program's basic principle was that pensions were awarded on the basis of degree of disability without regard to other income. By 1918, fifteen thousand disability pensions and ten thousand dependents' pensions were being paid. In the immediate aftermath of that war, the federal government passed the Pension Act of 1919, giving a legislative foundation to the program. This law committed the government to providing pensions for disabled

2 Unemployment Insurance (UI) is now known as Employment Insurance (EI).

members of the Armed Forces and their dependents, on a scale based on the degree of disability and the military rank of the veteran.

For the first time, federal public policy instituted the principle of income support as partial compensation for disability or death. Disability pensions awarded under the Pension Act were the first universal income benefits in Canadian social policy, as the entitlement to a pension or the amount of a pension was not determined by the financial circumstances of the veteran. Pensions were granted to members of the Armed Forces who suffered disability when the injury, disease, or aggravation was attributable to or incurred during military service. Medical examinations by physicians and surgeons determined the nature and extent of disability.

Over the following decades, the Pension Act was amended several times, expanding eligibility of benefits to widows and orphans, increasing benefit amounts, and establishing and reorganizing the structures to hear and give decisions on appeals concerning refusals of pensions. This last point indicates another important principle of the veterans' disability income program: if applicants were dissatisfied with a decision made by the minister under the legislation, they could apply to a review and appeals board for a reassessment of the decision; and at all such proceedings, an applicant could be represented by a veterans' organization. This is an early example of the interweaving of civil, political, and social rights of citizenship in policy.

In 1930, Parliament enacted the War Veterans Allowance Act (WVA) in response to "considerable pressure from veterans' organizations" who argued that existing programs dealt inadequately with the problem of "burnt out" veterans (Bryden 1974, 79). Initially, the WVA program provided means-tested allowances for veterans aged sixty or over, or who were permanently unemployable because of a physical or mental disability, and for allowances on behalf of their wives and dependents. The WVA was an example of classical federalism, with the federal government introducing its own program within its own sphere of jurisdiction. The policy design of this initiative, nonetheless, was shaped in some important ways by an earlier policy developed through collaborative federalism, the Old Age Pension Act of 1927. The WVA's basic benefit and means-testing features were the same as under the Old Age Pension Act, although eligibility was set at a younger age. Under the old age pension law, benefits were payable to certain individuals seventy years of age or older, while the WVA was available to certain veterans at age sixty. An amendment to the WVA in 1936 provided for special consideration to veterans aged fifty-five and over who, because of "pre-aging" combined with disabilities, were deemed incapable of maintaining themselves. Also in 1936, a War Veterans Allowances Board was formed, replacing the committee first established to administer the WVA program. A further amendment in 1938 made it possible for veterans with disabilities younger than fifty-five to be considered for benefits.

With the introduction of the Old Age Pensions Act in 1927, the federal government formally entered the social security field in a major way for the second time. This legislation represented "an ingenious compromise between provincial responsibility and federal initiative" (Bryden 1974, 77). To deal with provincial resistance to Ottawa entering into their jurisdiction of social welfare, and the related constitutional problem, the Mackenzie King government offered to finance the old age pension in the form of a conditional grant. The legislation authorized federal reimbursement of 50 percent to any participating province for pensions to British subjects (Canada did not pass a citizenship law until 1947) aged seventy or over who had resided in Canada for at least twenty years and in the province for at least five years. Indians were excluded from the program. The maximum pension was means-tested and initially $240 per year, an amount unchanged until the 1940s. While the federal government established some broad conditions for the program, the provinces operated and co-financed the programs. In 1931, as an extra inducement to attract provinces to enter the plan, the Old Age Pensions Act was amended to increase the federal share of pensions from 50 percent to 75 percent. By 1936, all provinces had developed public pension programs for low-income seniors.

The early story of the Old Age Pensions Act is relevant to Canadian disability policy making in two respects. First, the initiative served as a precedent of federal action and intergovernmental cooperation in the social welfare field, prompting other groups, even during the Great Depression of the 1930s, to press Ottawa for similar support for veterans and for persons with certain disabilities. Second, old age pensions became the model, in terms of program design, for cost-sharing arrangements for benefits for blind persons. In 1937, the Old Age Pensions Act was amended again to include a provision for means-tested plans for the blind and other people with disabilities who were not covered by provincial workers' compensation plans or the veterans' allowance and pension programs. The qualifying age for the blind was forty or older, and the limit of allowable annual income ($440 if unmarried and $640 if married) was set at a level higher than for the aged. With the federal government's contribution at 75 percent, all the provinces rapidly reached agreements with Ottawa. The agreements allowed provision for the payment of a pension to blind persons, defined in the legislation as persons who are, and continue to be, "so blind as to be unable to perform any work for which eyesight is essential."

During the 1940s, the blind pension benefit was raised four times by the federal government and the age of eligibility was lowered from forty to twenty-one. Both the initial provision for this benefit and the subsequent amendments were, in large part, in response to persistent lobbying by the Canadian National Institute for the Blind (CNIB) and the Canadian Council of the Blind.

PROPOSING DISABILITY POLICY REFORM

Envisaging a comprehensive and modern social security system for Canada began in the 1930s and intensified in the 1940s. Social researchers and government bodies gathered information, nationally and internationally, drawing lessons from the harsh experiences of the Great Depression, and looking at the social risks, human needs, and general hopes of Canadians during the Second World War.

Choices of policy instruments are integral to debates over the development of social rights and welfare states. Various policy instruments have long been held to have different implications for expressing certain values and for defining specific relationships between state and society, the state and market, and the state and citizens. This is demonstrated by the range of ideas expressed by Harry Cassidy, Leonard Marsh, and Charlotte Whitton, three pioneers of Canadian social welfare reform. Each articulated a position on the desired balance between social assistance and social insurance as policy instruments for providing income support. This section surveys leading documents by these pioneers – the Cassidy Plan, the Marsh Report, and the Whitton Critique – as well as the Green Book proposals of the federal government, and a report by the Canadian Council of Welfare. All deal with particular ideas about what Canadian social policy and society ought to look like. How did issues of disability figure in policy reform proposals for social security reform? As a personal and social phenomenon, how did these social

Table 3.1 Disability income policy reform ideas of the 1940s

Cassidy (1943)	• National disability insurance plan, earnings-related benefits financed by employers, employees, and the federal government • A disability allowance for blindness and permanent disabilities, cost-shared between the federal and provincial governments
Marsh (1943)	• Sickness benefit for temporary illnesses and disabilities, linked to the Unemployment Insurance program • National disability insurance plan for total and permanent disabilities, financed by employers and administered by the federal government • National flat-rate benefit for incapacitated, with provision for child dependents, financed by employees and the federal government
Whitton (1943)	• Social assistance delivered by provinces perhaps with municipal involvement, funded from general revenues of provincial and federal governments • Social utilities of custodial units, hostels, and vocational guidance • No role for social insurance
Canadian Welfare Council (1946)	• Unemployment Insurance sickness benefit • Disability and survivors' benefits on a national and social insurance basis that would require a constitutional amendment

policy advisors depict disability? Table 3.1 provides an overview of the key ideas on disability income policy reform from the 1940s.

In his 1943 book *Social Security and Reconstruction in Canada*, Harry Cassidy set out a plan for a modern system of social service in the postwar period. A Canadian social welfare researcher, Cassidy had taught social work at the University of Toronto and later was the director of social welfare for the province of British Columbia. At the time of the book, Cassidy was professor of social welfare at the University of California. His analysis and thinking ahead to the postwar reconstruction period was informed by a blend of empirical research, practical experience in public administration, and a strong commitment to extensive economic and social changes.

The central question Cassidy addressed was this: "Assuming that the Canadian people want a national system of social security, what are the essential measures to be adopted?" (1943, 18). Openly critical of the system of social services and programs then operating in Canada, especially when compared to Great Britain, the United States, and

New Zealand, Cassidy argued, "Canada's services are backward and weak in many respects. Essential services such as old age insurance and health insurance are totally lacking. In general, but with honourable exceptions, the existing services are poorly organized, their administration is mediocre, their personnel is weak, and they lack life and vitality" (1943, 11–12). Major elements of a national system of social security were absent in Canada due to federal-provincial controversy over the distribution of responsibilities for social policy.

Disability income maintenance policy had several defects. Social insurance schemes to protect against the economic risks of sickness and disability, considered internationally to be essential elements in a total program of social security, were not to be found in Canada. Instead, public assistance and public institutions were the policy instruments mainly relied upon for addressing sickness and disabilities. Of persons dependent on public aid in 1940, a group Cassidy estimated at 881,400 people or about 7 percent of the total population, 44,200 were patients in mental hospitals, 38,000 were in receipt of veterans' allowances, and 5,800 were in receipt of blind pensions (Cassidy 1943, 40–1). Provincial mental hospitals were "grossly overcrowded," and disabilities arising from industrial diseases were only partially covered in worker compensation schemes across the country. The scheme of blind pensions was "in line with modern trends to remove certain classes of needy persons from the hold-all of local poor relief," although the maximum grant was inadequate and excluded those under forty years of age (Cassidy 1943, 66, 74). Veterans' income programs, and related health and social services, on the whole provided generous and good care to veterans of the First World War, Cassidy concluded. Along with the old age pensions, blind pensions and the veterans' allowances were the only public assistance programs in effect throughout the country. Certain provinces offered other selective programs for some persons with disabilities, producing an uneven and inadequate patchwork of benefits and services.[3]

The existing system, therefore, fell well short of two core goals of social security: income maintenance for all at a minimum level, and

3 For example, Cassidy (1943, 24) noted that in 1942, Ontario, which had established a system of medical care for relief recipients in the mid-1930s, extended coverage to recipients of old age and blind pensions, and mothers' allowances.

reasonable opportunity for personal development. To adequately meet these goals, Cassidy suggested Canadian income security should be provided through a different channel, a system other than poor relief granted through a means test. He wrote, "For centuries, the poor law has offered, in theory at least, public aid to those stripped of all resources, under conditions that have been universally recognized as humiliating and degrading. Progressive thinking in recent years has supported devices of income maintenance that grant benefits as a matter of right to those whose income from wages or other sources is curtailed, before they are forced to the level of complete destitution" (1943, 63–4).

Cassidy's proposed disability income system contained· a social insurance program and a public assistance component. A new extensive program of social insurance would provide income protection against disability from industrial accidents or other causes. To ensure a unified national system of administration, the federal government would handle this program. Cassidy was explicit that the underlying principle for coverage and provision was social insurance, not universality. The program would be financed by contributions from employees, employers, and the federal state, and benefits would be graded in accordance with earnings. He expressed the need "to preserve the traditional insurance principle of granting benefits only to contributors and their dependents, if only for the psychological advantage of showing that the scheme is not 'something for nothing' and of distinguishing it sharply from public assistance" (Cassidy 1943, 140).

A disability income safety net would be needed to provide aid for people who were inadequately protected or even excluded from the social insurance scheme, so Cassidy proposed disability assistance covering blindness as well as other forms of permanent disability. Provisions for this public assistance counterpart of the social insurance disability benefits could be the same as for the existing old age pensions program.

The *Report on Social Security for Canada*, authored by McGill University economist and social analyst Leonard Marsh, was commissioned by the Advisory Committee on Reconstruction and presented to the House of Commons Special Committee on Social Security in 1943. The Marsh Report has been called "The most important single document in the history of the development of the welfare state in Canada ... a pivotal document in the development of war and postwar social security programs" (Bliss 1975, ix). Marsh recognized disability as one of the significant risks or contingencies of modern society that can interrupt the earning capacity of a worker, impose additional costs of care, and threaten the financial security of families. On the coverage of disability by Canadian social legislation, Marsh noted the fullest coverage was in industrial-related disabilities provided for by worker compensation schemes, and he was complementary about "the substantial and well-coordinated provisions for disabled ex-service men" (Marsh [1943] 1975, 139). Pensions for blind persons were deemed adequate, and two provinces, British Columbia and Quebec, had small monthly allowances under their mothers' assistance programs for totally incapacitated fathers or husbands. Regarding "this large field of non-industrial disability," Marsh concluded "there is only a fragmentary recognition in a few pieces of legislation" (139).

Along with proposals on children's allowances and national public investment, strong advocacy for social insurances was the other big idea in the Marsh Report. He argued for greater use of social insurance as a policy instrument in place of the traditional public assistance, and set out the rationale for and the elements of an extensive system of social security. Marsh acknowledged that a residual application of the assistance approach might be justified in certain circumstances, but his clear and strong preference was for social insurance. Social insurance had many advantages over the public assistance method of relief and means testing: it held the recipient partly responsible for meeting the costs of the program through mandatory contributions or general taxation; encouraged a feeling of self-dependence; readily identified who in the population was eligible to receive benefits; ensured a broad financial base through the shared pooling of risks and funds; and was a policy mechanism that did not have the flavour of charity.

Marsh approached the matter of disability in a relatively broad fashion, stressing the importance of public health, medical care, and related services (such as early diagnosis and contagious disease prevention) as well as rehabilitation and employment services as central elements of postwar public policy. Specific to social security, Marsh examined disability, especially permanent disablement, as an employment risk. Recognizing that permanent incapacity "might strike any member of the family," Marsh believed "it would naturally be more serious if it occurred for the principal earner, usually the husband" ([1943] 1975, 245). Guided by practices in various disability programs, Marsh drew distinctions between industrial and non-industrial disablement, partial and total disability, and short-term and permanent disability. In framing policy recommendations, he assumed that workers' compensation schemes across the provinces would substantially stay the same, although he believed that both these schemes and Unemployment Insurance (UI) would be extended in coverage over time.

For temporary illnesses or disabilities, Marsh recommended a sickness cash benefit, seeing it as a logical supplement to the recently established Canadian UI program, and as a complement to, rather than a substitute for, sickness benefits provided by various business firms across the country. This benefit would include all employees covered by the UI program, be federally administered, and financed by employee and employers' contributions. Intended for temporary situations, the sickness benefit would tide over an individual and family for a short period of interrupted employment income. As with UI, there would be a series of sickness benefit rates proportionate to wages.

In the event of total and permanent disablement, Marsh proposed a nationally based contributory disability insurance plan. With Marsh's analysis of disability as an employment risk, coverage would be of "all gainfully occupied persons and not wage earners alone." The program's administration would be a federal responsibility, with funding through social insurance premiums from employers, as the case with workers' compensation. Benefits would be wage-related, graduated in accordance to a series of employment income levels. Marsh set out a template, now familiar to Canadians, for linking broad income levels with premium contribution levels to finance health insurance, disability insurance, and other social security programs.

Where the incapacitated individual was fully withdrawn from employment, Marsh proposed a flat-rate benefit for wage earners and employees to be financed by employees and the federal government. The value of the benefit would be around the mid-point of UI benefit scales. In conformity with the UI program too, there would be no provision of benefits for child dependents. For that, Marsh saw his proposed children' allowances program playing a central role. Thus, for permanent disability, "a feasible rate would be $30 monthly for the breadwinner, $15 for his wife, in the case of permanent disability, securing a minimum income of $45" ([1943] 1975, 235). To put these rates in context, when Marsh made this recommendation, the maximum monthly amount of the blind pension was twenty dollars, which was raised, later the same year, to twenty-five dollars a month.

The disability income benefits Marsh foresaw were *social rights*, obtainable as a result of making contributions and meeting other criterion, but they would also be *social minimums* – what T.H. Marshall later, when defining social citizenship, would call the right to a modicum to economic welfare and security. Marsh reasoned that since disability payments would be essentially continuous over a long term, they would be relatively costly and, therefore, "from the national point of view it is not possible to set an objective higher than the maintenance of the minimum" (Marsh [1943] 1975, 241). Nonetheless, he contended that "a minimum, obtainable as of right and in the company of all other citizens, is immeasurably better than uncertain aid from relatives, charitable institutions or the state" (241–2). A modest minimum in this program, and others he was outlining, would be an improvement for many people in the "poorer rural classes" who at the time had no provision at all for the risk of disability. Beyond the minimum income benefit, in all of the branches of social security he examined, Marsh expected that "there would remain scope for additional services and considerable leeway for individual insurance provision" (247).

Lastly, Marsh suggested that advantage could be achieved by applying the performance of workers' compensation boards to the broader field of disability insurance. He argued that "procedures adopted by the Boards in the realm of disability treatment, relations with doctors, specialists and hospitals, the sympathetic handling of claims, and progressive work in physical and vocational rehabilitation, are widely regarded as having measured up to good standards" ([1943] 1975, 193). These ideas about the best way to organize service delivery were not taken up in the immediate postwar period, but, as we will see in later chapters, became recurring issues in relation to the CCP/D in the 1990s and early 2000s.

Like Cassidy and Marsh, Charlotte Whitton was a leading researcher and commentator on matters of social service administration and policy in Canada. Until 1942, Whitton was the executive director of the Canadian Welfare Council and had considerable experience in the early decades of professional social work in the country. Aptly described as "a feminist on the political right" (Rooke and Schnell 1987), Whitton was "the most prominent spokesperson of the conservative position in social work" (Struthers 1994, 321) in this period, emphasizing individual adjustment through casework. Quickly following the appearance of Cassidy's book and the Marsh Report, Whitton published a short pamphlet called "Social Security for Canadians" (Whitton 1943b) and a book titled *The Dawn of Ampler Life* (Whitton 1943a). The pamphlet previewed much of the arguments outlined in more detail in the book, the later having been commissioned by John Bracken, recently elected the national leader of the Progressive Conservative Party. Whitton was a fervent skeptic of the wide applicability of social insurance as a policy instrument to Canada.

Preferring a limited and selective welfare state, Whitton was highly critical of much of the Marsh Report and the Beveridge plan, a British report on social insurances published the year earlier. She offered her suggestions on "what might be the characteristic features of a distinctive and suitable programme of greater economic security for the Canadian people" (Whitton 1943b, v). Her critique was twofold: first, that the social insurance philosophy of Marsh and Beveridge was "premature and inapplicable" to Canada's circumstances of a relatively small, scattered, and still sizable rural population, and federal system of government. Second, concentrating on social security as income maintenance could exclude other elements of "spiritual and economic security" (Whitton 1943a, 1). Whitton argued that providing wage-related cash benefits to replace loss of income offered little difficulties for the insured population of wage earners in cities, but it faced serious challenges in providing support for the self-employed, low-wage earners, and agriculture workers in rural areas.

While holding a fundamentally different approach to social security than Marsh and Cassidy, Whitton shared with them a medical and labour market conception of disability. Disability was a functional limitation and an economic hazard to families. Sickness and disability were "maladjustments" that "strike with individual features but occur with common manifestations, over a broad cross-section of the population." Furthermore, "with their resultant inroads on income, [sickness and disability] are potent forces threatening income security, creating fear, need and dependency" (Whitton 1943b, 3, 25).

For Whitton, the favoured approaches to income maintenance were, in order of priority, (1) gainful employment; (2) a series of strong "social utilities" such as educational programs, public health, child and family protection, and vocational guidance; (3) general and specialized forms of social assistance for the relief of distress;

and (4) social insurance "for those needs arising from risks that are susceptible to actuarial anticipation and underwriting" (Whitton 1943a, 13). It would be harder to find a clearer expression of liberal welfarism. Within this framework, the provision of disability allowances themselves would not meet the problem of the care of infirm, chronically ill, or mentally impaired persons dependent on others for treatment. Rather, the greater need, Whitton claimed, was for social utilities, the community provision of services under public or private management, such as custodial units, rest homes, or hostels for special needs. With this, she proposed "an improved, humane and adequately integrated system of Social Assistance at need, adjusted with understanding help and service to meet each individual case" (Whitton 1943b, 45).

Whitton saw no potential application of social insurances in Canadian income maintenance policy, except for unemployment insurance. She declared, "The blunt, inescapable fact to be faced is that Canadian citizens, must look, today, through the immediate post-war period, and for some years to come to the provision of Social Assistance ... for maintaining minimum income standards" (Whitton 1943b, 46). There were constitutional questions regarding the scope of application of social insurance by the federal government, an issue that both Cassidy and Marsh had acknowledged. Whitton estimated that social insurance would not cover one-third of the gainfully occupied population, working on their own or, as farm labourers, not for wages. Social assistance measures would therefore always be needed.

Whitton accordingly recommended a system of social assistance to meet the needs of all the population in loss or impairment of income due to sickness, disability, and "physical, mental or character handicap" (Whitton 1943b, 46). Administrative responsibility for the program would be with the provinces, possibly with a continued role by municipal governments. Funding would come from the general tax revenues of the provinces and, with virtually no conditions, from the federal government. In short, Whitton was calling for an expanded reliance on existing means-tested social assistance programs to address the income security needs of people with disabilities.

In August 1945, following the end of the Second World War and a national election in which the King Liberals were again returned to power, the federal government called a Dominion-Provincial Conference on Reconstruction. Federal officials presented what became called the Green Book proposals, a confident and expansive design on economic and social security. The proposals sought to ensure for all Canadians high and stable employment and income, and individual economic security and welfare. Policy means to attain these objectives were fourfold: assistance to private enterprise, state action in public enterprise, public investment to provide productive work when unemployment threatens, and social welfare measures to protect the individual against the exigencies of unemployment, sickness, and old age.

Although the federal government had been providing disability pensions to veterans for close to thirty years and to blind persons for almost a decade, disability insurance was not included as a cornerstone for a comprehensive system of social security. This was puzzling since Cassidy, Marsh, and Whitton had all written on disability reform. The absence of disability income proposals by the Liberal government did not go unnoticed by social reform organizations. Within months, a report by the Canadian Welfare Council (cwc) declared that a total national plan of social security must contain a ui sickness benefit, disability, and survivors' benefits. Gaps in the Green Book proposals included an income maintenance program with "benefits as a matter of right for wage-earners absent from work on account of illness" and "similar benefits for the chronically handicapped or disabled and the widows and surviving minor children of bread-winners who die" (Canadian Welfare Council 1946, 12–13). Echoing proposals they had advanced several year earlier to the Rowell-Sirois Royal Commission on Dominion-Provincial Relations, the cwc urged that serious consideration "be given to the establishment of benefits as a matter of right to persons who are chronically unable to take employment, such as certain categories of the blind [and] persons suffering from chronic heart conditions" (Canadian Welfare Council 1946, 13).

The cwc made the case for a national disability insurance benefit in the following terms:

If a national system of old age insurance were established the insurance benefits for the disabled group and the survivor group might be associated with it, as has been done in the United States and Great Britain. A national programme is necessary if insurance benefits are to be provided for these groups. For reasons of inter-provincial migration and because of other factors, it is unlikely that any province would find it possible to work out satisfactory plans for them. As in the case of old age insurance, a constitutional amendment would be necessary to authorize disability and survivor benefits on an insurance basis. But this is surely not an amendment, which would seriously affront the provinces. (1946, 16)

In this statement, we have reference to constitutional amendments that, in fact, would take place in Canada in 1951 and again in 1964 to enable the federal government to legislate, respectively, on old age insurance and on supplementary benefits for disability and survivor groups. The cwc's statement also contains the prophecy that a national disability benefit would be, in all likelihood, associated with a national system of old age or retirement insurance. Here, then, are traces of policy thinking on what, in just a generation, would become the Canada Pension Plan and the Disability program within it.

Despite the omission of disability insurance in the federal government's 1945 Green Book, disability issues appeared on the postwar social policy reform agenda. In the first place, an expanding community of organized interests consisting of veterans groups, disability organizations, labour councils, and social welfare councils applied pressure on the federal government to enhance existing programs for veterans and blind persons, and to introduce new sickness and disability measures. Joining older interest groups, such as the CNIB, were new ones: the Canadian Paraplegic Association, formed in 1945, and the Canadian Arthritis and Rheumatism Society, formed in 1948, which contributed to a growing societal constituency for reform. In second place, the array of benefits and programs for veterans with disabilities had an impact on civilian social policy in Canada after the Second World War. As Mary Tremblay documents, "success of the programs for World War II veterans provided an impetus for a re-examination of Canadian policy for civilians with disabilities, which began in the late 1940s" (Tremblay 1998, 161). In the third place, rehabilitation emerged during this period as a field of medicine bringing "new respectability to the idea of rehabilitating the handicapped within policy-making circles" (Berkowitz 1987, 47). Medical rehabilitation and vocational training for persons with disabilities, veterans and civilians alike, was seen as a way of restoring people to active and productive lives.

DISABILITY INCOME POLICY REFORMS

Since the 1920s, organizations representing the blind had advocated for a specific piece of social legislation, at the national level, to provide income support for this group of Canadians. Blind organizations partly succeeded in 1937 when the Old Age Pensions program was amended to provide pensions for blind persons aged forty and over. With this breakthrough, during the 1940s, organizations representing the blind effectively secured a series of enhancements to the blind pension through regulatory and legislative changes. An amendment in 1942 allowed payment of provincial supplementary allowances without reduction of the pension for blind persons. A 1943 amendment increased the maximum pension to $300 a year from $240 a year. Additional significant changes took place in 1947: an increase in the maximum pension to $360 a year; an increase in the maximum amounts of income allowed; deletion of the nationality requirement and the provincial residence requirement; and the lowering of the qualifying age of a blind applicant from forty to twenty-one. In 1949, the maximum pension was raised again, this time quite substantially, from $360 to $480 a year. With this series of enhancements, the *Report on the Administration of Allowances for Blind Persons in Canada* showed, the number of blind pensioners grew from 1,946 in 1937–38 to over 6,000 through most of the 1940s, rising to over 11,000 following the amendments made in 1947 and 1949 (National Health and Welfare, *Blind Persons*, 1953, 5).

Reforms by Ottawa to the old age security system in 1950–51 prompted changes in the income maintenance policy for blind persons. A joint parliamentary committee on old age security recommended a universal old age pension of forty dollars a month at age seventy and a federal-provincial old age assistance program of the same amount at age sixty-five with a means test for determining eligibility. When the federal government adopted these recommendations, which largely reflected the Green Book proposals, it necessitated termination of the 1927 law for old age pensions.[4] Disappearance of

4 Passage of the Old Age Security Act and the Old Age Assistance Act in 1951 followed a constitutional amendment approved earlier that year by all ten provinces and the federal government giving the Canadian Parliament authority to make laws in relation to old age pensions. The Old Age Security

this legislation meant a new statutory platform for the payment of benefits for blind persons was required. In theory, the blind pension program could have been incorporated in the new legislation for old age pensions but the lobbyists won the day, following a long campaign for a specific law for blind benefits (Haddow 1993).

The Blind Persons Act of 1951 replicated many design features of the 1927 Old Age Pensions Act. The federal program offered allowances to blind persons' aged twenty-one to sixty-nine, cost-shared with the provinces on a 75 percent federal/25 percent provincial foundation. When recipients reached age seventy, they were to be transferred to the Old Age Security (OAS) program and granted federal pensions. In fact, in 1952, when the OAS program started, 3,212 blind pensioners over the age of seventy were transferred to the new program, shifting 28 percent of the caseload to the OAS from the blind allowances program (National Health and Welfare, *Blind Persons*, 1953, 5). By early 1952, all ten provinces and two territories passed legislation or ordinances to provide for the payment of allowances for blind persons.

Under the new legislation, payments were "allowances" rather than "pensions," as they were called under the old age legislation, a change to emphasize that this was a social assistance program, not a contribution-based social insurance. The previous residency requirement of twenty years was shortened to ten years and the provision excluding Indians was dropped. In regulations for the legislation, a person was deemed to be blind "only when their visual acuity or field of vision, after correction through the use of proper refraction

---

Act introduced Canada's third universal income benefit (after the WVA and the Family Allowance), with a flat-rate pension of forty dollars a month offered to persons aged seventy and over, regardless of their financial or family circumstances. For this program the twenty-year residence rule remained. Along with this universal program for those aged seventy and over, the Old Age Assistance Act introduced a revamped means-tested selective program for persons aged sixty-five to sixty-nine, cost-shared on a fifty-fifty basis with the provinces. Recipients of the blind person's allowance and war veterans' allowances were excluded. Here too there was a twenty-year residence requirement. Again, we see the situation of a program influencing the design of subsequent federal initiative on disability income policy.

lens, was not more than 10 per cent." Such a test of visual acuity, of course, required a medical examination.[5]

The maximum blind allowance was the same as under the repealed Old Age Pensions Act, although the total allowable income for a blind recipient was higher than for old age assistance and was raised several times during the 1950s. As was the case with other social programs, the maximum yearly income allowed varied with the status of the recipient as unmarried, dependent child, married, or blind spouse. In 1955, the eligibility age was lowered from twenty-one to eighteen. The blind allowance yearly maximum was raised twice in 1957, first by the St Laurent Liberal government before the federal election, from $480 to $552 a year, and then by the victorious Diefenbaker Conservatives after the 1957 election to $660 a year. The maximum allowance payable was next raised around the 1962 federal election, to $780 a year, and then after the 1963 federal election, to $900 a year. In 1966, the Blind Persons Act was amended to allow provinces to switch the financing and administration of the program to the newly established Canada Assistance Plan (CAP). That reform, coupled with the transfer of tax points to the provinces under fiscal arrangements for financing this and other social welfare programs, effectively took the blind persons allowance off the federal policy agenda. The Blind Persons Act was finally repealed in 1983, having long ceased to be necessary with the Canada Assistance Plan in place.

While the Blind Persons Act was the consolidation and expansion of an existing practice of federally cost-shared benefits for blind persons, the Disabled Persons Act, enacted in 1954, was "a new departure for the federal government and established an important precedent of federal involvement in income protection for the disabled" (Brown 1977, 301). Though a new undertaking for the federal government, at least three provinces – Alberta, Ontario, and Newfoundland – had disability allowances in place before the Ottawa entered the field in the mid-1950s (Willard 1964a, 59).

Under the Disabled Persons Act, the federal government offered to share, on a fifty-fifty basis with the provinces and territories, the cost of allowances to "permanently and totally disabled" persons aged eighteen to sixty-nine. There was a ten-year residence requirement

5 Blind Persons Regulation, P.C. 1955–49, for the *Blind Persons Act*, RSC, 1952, c. 17.

and the allowance, also means-tested, was not payable to a recipient of other federal and provincial income benefits. By October 1956, bilateral agreements were reached between the federal government and all provincial and territorial governments. Permanent and total disability was defined under the program's regulations as "(a) the person is suffering from a major physiological, anatomical or psychological impairment, verified by objective medical findings; (b) the impairment is likely to continue without substantial improvement during the lifetime of the person and is one to which the concept of cure cannot be applied; and (c) as a result of such impairment, the person is severely limited in activities pertaining to self-care and normal living." Conversely, a person was deemed to be not totally and permanently disabled where "a favourable rehabilitation prognosis is obtained, or approved therapeutic measures are recommended, by the provincial authority, and the requisite rehabilitation services or therapeutic measures are available."[6]

Comparing the legislation for blind persons and for disabled persons reveals differences that suggest a form of "special treatment of the blind," a feature noted in the social policy of Canada and other countries (Berkowitz 1987; Struthers 1994). Under the Blind Persons Act, Ottawa assumed a larger funding share (75 percent) than under the Disabled Persons Act (50 percent – the same share as under the Old Age Assistance Act). The maximum income allowed for various categories of people was more generous for recipients of blind allowances than for the disabled allowances. In addition, there were no restrictions on receiving the blind allowance if a person resided in an institution, whereas disabled persons dwelling in mental institutions or health facilities (tuberculosis sanitaria, homes for the aged, nursing homes, or institutions for the care of incurables) were excluded from receiving the disabled allowance. Still another difference was that provinces and territories had more authority to vary the requirements

6 Disabled Persons Regulations, P.C. 1954–1831, November 23, 1953, p. 3. The regulation went on to explain that severe limitation in activities included being bedridden; unable to leave home without being accompanied by another person; normally in need of care and supervision for one or more of such self-care activities as dressing, body hygiene, or eating; unable to perform such routine activities as climbing a short stairway or walking a limited distance on a level surface; or certified by a qualified physician to be under medical instructions to forbear from walking and climbing activities.

and add conditions of eligibility for disabled allowances than for blind allowances (National Health and Welfare, *Blind Persons*, 1968, 14).

Edward Berkowitz, a historian who specializes in the welfare state, offers the following reasons for the special treatment of the blind in disability programs: "Possibly it is because the unimpaired can easily imagine and sympathize with their plight; unlike mental illness, for example, the state of blindness involves little stigma. Possibly it is because blindness has existed since the beginning of history, so that the blind have had more time to secure a place for themselves as legitimate objects of aid from the state. The very fact that their impairment is less disabling than others gives the blind advantages in political organization" (Berkowitz 1987, 168).

A contributing factor in the Canadian context was that a key organization to assist visually impaired and blind persons was linked to veterans and their political activism. Soldiers returning to Canada from the First World War founded the CNIB. War-blinded and blind veterans comprised a significant component of the CNIB's constituency, which no doubt added to the political legitimacy and policy influence of the organization. Another contributing factor for the special treatment of the blind, compared to the poor and other welfare clients, was that the target population was a relatively stable group and, thanks to the CNIB, was largely documented. This meant government officials could readily estimate program costs, which facilitated budget planning and eased their concerns about spending pressures (Struthers 1994, 204).

Despite these differences in program design and political influence, the ensuing story of the disabled persons program was similar in many ways to that of the blind person's allowance. Increases in benefit levels were introduced around federal elections in the later 1950s and early 1960s, keeping the value of the maximum annual disability allowance in-line with that for the blind allowances. As well, the program was incorporated by the Canada Assistance Plan in 1966, and the Disabled Persons Act, like the Blind Persons Act, was eventually was repealed.

VOCATIONAL REHABILITATION PROGRAMS

The 1950s and early 1960s also witnessed collaborative federal-provincial initiatives for the vocational rehabilitation of disabled persons. Impetus for these initiatives came primarily from the activities and experience of the Department of Veterans Affairs (DVA), through medical treatment and rehabilitation programs for disabled veterans. Building on this success, DVA officials, in conjunction with other federal officials in Labour and National Health and Welfare, and others outside government, began "to address the needs of civilians with disabilities" (Tremblay 1998, 173).

In 1951, the National Conference on Rehabilitation of the Physically Handicapped was held, co-sponsored by the federal and provincial governments. From a suggestion by that conference, Ottawa responded quickly by forming a National Advisory Committee on the Rehabilitation of Disabled Persons. The committee had thirty-seven members with representatives from federal and provincial governments, health and welfare voluntary agencies, the medical profession, organized employers, organized labour, universities, and other interested groups. Notably, representatives from disability groups themselves were not specified as interests warranting designated membership on the committee. Also that year, the federal department of labour established a Civilian Rehabilitation Branch. In 1953, the federal cabinet extended the National Health Grants Program, first created in 1948 to assist provinces with health care research and hospital construction, to include payments to health and social service agencies for occupational therapy and medical rehabilitation services.

Ottawa's entrance into cost-sharing rehabilitation services for persons with disabilities began extremely cautiously. In 1953, the federal cabinet authorized the minister of Labour to enter into agreements with the provinces for developing rehabilitation activities for disabled persons, to assist them in re-entering the labour force. Provinces would be reimbursed, under certain conditions, for one-half of the expenditures incurred in the administration and rehabilitation of disabled persons. The cabinet order-in-council authorizing this federal move specified that the federal allotment to each province should not exceed $15,000 for 1953–54, and thereafter an amount approved by the minister of Labour from monies appropriated by Parliament to the labour department for this purpose.[7] In the first year, just $11,930 was transferred to one province, Saskatchewan. And even by the final year of this arrangement, in

7 Order-in-Council, P.C. 1953–1087, July 6, 1953. Under the *Vocational Training Co-ordination Act*, 1942, R.S. c. 286, the federal government entered into agreements with provinces to provide 50 percent of costs incurred on approved training projects. For the training of persons for defence

1961–62, just $195,752 was paid by Ottawa to nine provinces to coordinate and develop activities for the rehabilitation of persons with disabilities. In no year was the full federal allotment actually spent, likely because of the narrow scope of the program and the conditions.

This administrative practice in intergovernmental relations was adapted, expanded, and codified with the passage in 1961 of the Vocational Rehabilitation of Disabled Persons Act (VRDP). The VRDP offered agreements to the provinces and the territories with the federal government sharing 50 percent of the costs for providing a comprehensive a range of services designed to help people with physical or mental disabilities become capable of pursuing a gainful occupation. With the exception of maintenance and training allowances, personal financial need was not a consideration for eligibility and provision. Effective April 1962, federal payments through the VRDP program were $333,015 in its first year, a 70 percent increase over the previous year of the administrative arrangement, and payments grew rapidly and steadily over the years.[8] The VRDP legislation further designated the labour minister as the lead federal minister, authorized to undertake research on persons with disabilities and to coordinate federal activities in the field of vocational rehabilitation of disabled persons, in cooperation with the minister of National Health and Welfare and other ministers engaged in this field. The legislation also established a twenty-five-member National Advisory Council on the Rehabilitation of Disabled Persons, replacing the earlier and larger advisory committee, appointed by cabinet, for advising the minister in the administration of the VRDP.[9]

CONCLUSION

Canada by the early 1960s had several distinct programs for different categories of persons with disabilities. These included (1) workers' compensation schemes in all ten provinces, (2) veterans' pensions, war veterans', and civilian allowances, (3) allowances for blind

---

industries, including vocational training for the physically disabled, Ottawa's contribution to provinces was 75 percent.

8 Canada, *Public Accounts of Canada*, vol. 2, selected years.

9 *Vocational Rehabilitation of Disabled Persons Act*, S.C. 1960–61, c. 26.

persons, (4) allowances for permanently and totally disabled persons, and (5) vocational rehabilitation services for military personnel and civilian Canadians with disabilities. In the tax system, the earliest disability-related tax measure was the non-taxation of workers' compensation benefits, followed by a customs tariff measure in 1930 allowing for the duty-free entry of certain devices for disabilities. The non-taxation of veterans' benefits, the disability tax deduction, and medical expense deduction were all introduced in the 1940s.

Collectively, these expenditure programs and tax measures constituted Canadian disability income policy at the time. Introduced in a piecemeal fashion, benefits were limited and the administration stern. The incremental and inadequate nature of these programs did not mean, however, that they were uncoordinated. Disability income programs at the federal level were considered in relation to one another and synchronized in policy design to avoid the stacking of benefits. For example, the Blind Persons Act set out that persons qualified to receive that allowance could not receive assistance under the old age assistance program, an allowance under the wva program, or a pension under the Pension Act or the Old Age Security Act.

From the mid-1940s onward, there was a broadly shared body of ideas held by many social reformers and government welfare officials of a modern and comprehensive system of social security. Cassidy, Marsh, and Whitton, while they had differences, all accepted the primacy of the market economy as the provider of employment and income for most people. They all accepted a mix of social provisions with shared responsibilities among markets, governments, and families, with Cassidy and Marsh more inclined to a social insurance rights-based role by the state than Whitton. Disability was a physical or mental impairment that posed an economic risk to individuals and families because of the loss of earning power by the breadwinner and the associated costs of care. For Marsh and Cassidy, the policy response to this "hazard of life" and "economic risk" was to establish a major social insurance program, backed by a social assistance program.

Disability income policy in the 1950s illustrated the exercise of administrative federalism with cooperative action between governments, guided by program specialists in the federal public service and their provincial counterparts. Programs for blind persons, disabled persons, and vocational rehabilitation all were joint programs between Ottawa and the provinces, based on conditional and shared cost grants. Unlike conditional grants in other policy areas, these disability programs involved consultation with provincial governments and were generally welcomed by provinces. Furthermore, provinces had explicit authority to set additional eligibility rules and take measures to ensure compliance. That authority included suspending payments to recipients who, in the opinion of provincial authorities, unreasonably neglected or refused to avail themselves of training, rehabilitation, or treatment measures provided or made available by the province.[10]

Federal legislation on disabled persons, blind persons, and vocational rehabilitation shared common features of governance with little recognition of civil rights or political rights. In contrast to workers' compensation and veterans' programs, there was no provision for an appeals process in these programs' legislation, nor was the matter of appeals identified as an item on which regulations could be made. Perhaps the only reference to due process dealt with the formation of administrative tribunals to make decisions on whether an applicant had reached the age of twenty-one to qualify for the allowance for a blind person or disabled person.[11] Legislation on disabled persons and blind persons did provide, though, for the creation of advisory boards consisting of representatives of the federal government, appointed by cabinet, and representatives of the provinces with which agreements were made, also appointed by the federal cabinet on the recommendation of the participating provinces. However, the purpose of the advisory boards was not oriented to policy making or citizen engagement but was limited to administrative matters that could be addressed through changes to the regulations. As of the early

10 See, for example, the *Disabled Persons Act*, 1954, s. 7 (vi) and (xi).

11 An administrative tribunal was to be formed when satisfactory documentary evidence on the age of an applicant could not be found. Then a tribunal would be created, comprising three people. The provincial government designated one person, and the federal government selected another person. Together, they selected a third member who was to be "a disinterested person" to serve as chair. The legislation for both the blind and the disabled programs specified that such a tribunal should in all cases interview the applicant. On the issue of whether an applicant was yet twenty-one years of age, the decision of such tribunals was deemed to be final and conclusive.

1960s, then, the history of disability policy suggested that, for the most part, Canadians with disabilities were commonly pitied, some were officially recognized in policy and provided compensation or assistance, but comparatively few were entitled to adequate income security based on social insurance.

CHAPTER FOUR

Canada Pension Plan Disability Policy Making: The Pearson Years and Legacy, 1963–1970

In rising today to introduce this resolution dealing with the Canada pension plan, I have the honour to speak to the implementation of one of the most important and far reaching plans of action put forward by this or any other government. It is the natural next step in providing rounded welfare legislation for Canada.

Hon. Judy V. LaMarsh, Minister of National Health and Welfare, *House of Commons Debates*, 18 July 1963

The pension plan fitted into the fabric of Canadian society.

Tom Kent, *A Public Purpose*

By 1960, the Canadian field of income support for people with disabilities comprised three major models of public provision: a social insurance model in workers' compensation for industrial-related injuries and diseases; a social assistance model of means tested support for blind persons and permanently disabled persons; and, for war veterans, a universal model in pension allowances. Alongside these public approaches were the private models of personal provision in the form of household savings and, for a limited number of Canadians, life and health insurance plans through their workplace. For many citizens then, disability represented a serious risk to their economic and social security for which there was not a public policy – a missing piece to their social citizenship. Against this backdrop, political and public interest in a national disability insurance program steadily grew.

The story of CPP Disability can be traced to more than one date, and further back than many Canadians perhaps realize. In 1919, for example, the Liberal Party of Canada passed a statement at their convention that said, "So far as may be practicable having regard for Canada's financial position, an adequate system of social insurance against ... disability ... should be instituted by the Federal Government in conjunction with the Governments of the several provinces" (quoted in Guest 1998, 66). Closer to the genesis of the program, the story can be said to have started in 1957, when interest about a contributory public pension plan among Canada's main federal political parties noticeably emerged in convention resolutions and election campaign statements.[1] Pension reform priorities of the 1950s in Canada focused on eliminating the means-tested Old Age Assistance, enhancing the value of the universal Old Age Security, and improving the coverage and features of occupational pensions in workplaces (Bryden 1974, 137–46). The United States had introduced an earnings-related public pension plan, called Social Security, in 1935, extending it in 1939 to include survivors, and then in 1956 adding disability insurance for contributors. Over the years, the American plan was discussed within Canadian political and bureaucratic circles, and this latest extension drew additional attention.

Establishment of the CPP/D was part of the grand social policy innovations in the country between 1963 and 1968, during the minority federal Liberal governments of Lester Pearson. Indeed, Pearson called the CPP "a great and progressive reform" (LaMarsh 1969, 314). To say that governments in the 1960s thought they could do anything when building new social programs (Little 2008, 22) is overly simplistic and historically inaccurate. Such a view of carefree interventionism certainly does not apply to the Canada Pension Plan and the CPP/D. As will be shown in this chapter, politicians and governments faced strong pressures from chambers of commerce

---

1 Other dates in the story behind the creation of the CPP Disability include 1937 and 1954. In 1937, an amendment to the Old Age Pensions Act, passed a decade earlier, made provision for a means-tested, cost-shared plan for the blind and other people with disabilities who were not covered by provincial workers' compensation plans or veterans' allowance and pension programs. In 1954, with the passage of the Disabled Persons Act, the federal government offered to cost-share with provinces the cost of allowances for persons totally and permanently disabled, between the ages of eighteen and sixty-nine. Within two years, bilateral agreements were reached between the federal government and all ten provinces.

and the life insurance industry (Kent 1988; LaMarsh 1969). In response to this pressure, the CPP retirement pension was limited to replace just 25 percent of average earnings, thus leaving substantial room for private sector savings and insurance vehicles. Compromises and trade-offs also characterized intergovernmental relations over the policy in this time of growing Quebec nationalism and more assertive province-building.

Formulation of the CPP and CPP/D were exercises in statecraft of federal and provincial bargaining, a mix of pragmatics and principles, ideological orientations, and political and bureaucratic relationships. Social technology also played an important role in terms of researching the means to achieve policy objectives, generating actuarial projections, and undertaking economic analyses on the costs and effects of the program on public and private budgets. Supplementary programs in the CPP – namely, the disability and survivor benefits – required a constitutional amendment for their inclusion in any federal plan, and the implementation of the CPP/D was delayed until 1970 to allow the Department of National Health and Welfare, the federal bureaucracy responsible for putting the disability program into practice, to build the necessary capacity.

Tom Kent, an instrumental participant in the development and adoption of the CPP and CPP/D, years later wrote that "the pension plan fitted into the fabric of Canadian society" (1988, 255). Kent was referring to Canadians' widespread acceptance of the CPP and the financial contributions that working people paid into the plan. The CPP and CPP/D fit into a social fabric defined by a capitalist market economy, the federalized political system, the parliamentary and political party dynamics of the day, and prevailing beliefs about disability.

POLITICAL AND ELECTORAL ORIGINS

Following the 1957 federal election, in which old age pensions were a major issue, Prime Minister John Diefenbaker declared "that a Conservative government would look into the possibility of restructuring the old age pension along contributory lines" (Bryden 1997, 23). In 1958, Diefenbaker commissioned a university economics professor to undertake a comparative study of the Canadian and American pension systems, but he took little further action until early 1962, when he wrote the premiers seeking an amendment to section 94A of the British North America Act to allow federal legislation on a social-insurance-based pension plan that could include disability and survivor benefits along with retirement pensions.

By the 1962 and 1963 federal elections, thinking within the political parties, especially the Liberal Party had yielded more detailed ideas and a stronger public commitment by the leader to an earnings-related public pension plan for Canadians. The initial design of the CPP was done between 1957 and 1963, when the Liberals were in opposition. An ad hoc advisory committee devised the preliminary Liberal plan on a pension scheme in 1961 and early 1962.[2] A 1962 Liberal Party paper outlined a compulsory, contributory scheme with payments from employers and employees, portable benefits, and coverage on a national basis. The paper specified that the scheme would take ten years to be fully operational (Bryden 1997, 69–71). Around this time, Prime Minister Diefenbaker contacted the premiers, requesting their support for a constitutional agreement to pave the way for federal legislation on a pension plan. In the June 1962 federal election, health insurance and pensions were the prominent social policy issues. Diefenbaker's massive majority was reduced to a minority government, and in January 1963 the Quebec government declined to support an amendment without first seeing the details of Diefenbaker's legislation, a stipulation that Diefenbaker rejected.

2 Bryden (1997) offers an excellent historical summary of the events and players and issues involved in this period. To summarize, a Liberal Party committee on social security, chaired by Senator David Croll, was established in 1957 to provide input to the 1958 party convention. Among the policy ideas outlined was a universal, contributory, and portable pension plan. At the 1958 convention, the approved resolutions recommended the extension of disability pensions and the introduction of a new, universal, contributory, and portable pension plan. These ideas were part of the 1958 election platform. Renewed thinking by the Liberals on what to do about pensions occurred at the Kingston Conference in September 1960, in an ad hoc policy committee chaired by Walter Gordon and assisted by Tom Kent among others, and the Liberal Rally of January 1961. That rally passed a resolution on pension policy, echoing the 1919 statement that "a new contributory scheme, if this can be worked out with the provinces on a sound actuarial basis" (Kent 1988, 92). Later that year, in a national radio address, Liberal leader Lester Pearson pledged a national contributory pension plan as Liberal policy.

In the April 1963 federal election, Pearson promised "60 days of decisions" by a Liberal government, of which a national pension plan would be among the most important. Indeed, a contributory pension related to earnings was the key part of the Liberals' three-point pension program. The other parts were to raise the Old Age Security (OAS) benefit for those aged seventy and over, and to make the OAS available on a graduated basis for those between ages sixty-five and sixty-nine. Upon winning the 1963 election, the Liberals set up an interdepartmental task force on pensions involving all the relevant federal agencies, chaired by the deputy minister of Welfare, which reported to a cabinet committee on social security. Officials were extremely well-informed of pension systems in other industrial countries, and a detailed, workable outline of the contributory pension plan was drafted and approved by the federal cabinet within three months. The task of securing provincial approval was not so quick or easy.

Negotiations and Decisions

Appreciating the necessity for a constitutional amendment, Tom Kent, Pearson's policy advisor, recommended that insurance benefits for people with disabilities could be discussed with premiers and that the prime minister inform them that the federal government was willing to add such a benefit to the CPP. In June 1963, in a letter to the premiers, Pearson outlined federal plans on pension reform, noting that a full discussion of disability insurance would be deferred to allow a focus on improving old age benefits (Bryden 1997, 84–91). As far the Pearson Liberal government was concerned, the emphasis was on survivors' benefits because they were typically part of a pension plan, whereas disability was not. Indeed, federal welfare department officials would have favoured a separate disability program, comprehensive and universal, rather than tying it to the CPP, but that was not in the political cards. The policy question was framed as whether disability would go through social assistance, through what became the Canada Assistance Plan (CAP) or through the CPP. Agreement on a universal contributory pension plan was reached by the federal cabinet in July 1963, to be presented to a federal-provincial conference of welfare ministers that September. In her memoirs, Judy LaMarsh, then the minister of National Health and Welfare, singled out Tom Kent's role as crucial to the CPP coming into being at all (1969, 80).

In the Pearson Liberals' first pension policy formulation in July 1963 and their first draft legislation, Bill C-75, placed before Parliament in January 1964, disability benefits were not included. Welfare ministers, in their September 1963 meeting, agreed that a constitutional amendment should be made to allow the inclusion of benefits for people with disabilities and survivors. In the wake of a federal-provincial First Ministers' conference in November 1963, in which various premiers had raised some concerns about the federal plan, a federal cabinet committee on social security was formed to revise the federal CPP proposal. According to a main federal participant, around this time, "provinces hedged on co-operation with the pension proposals. Some of them were cool for partisan, political reasons only, but others on more substantial financial or philosophical grounds" (LaMarsh 1969, 121). At a First Ministers' conference in late March and early April 1964, the revised federal plan was presented and a Quebec plan was unveiled. Constant communications, consultations, and negotiations played a central part in shaping the CPP and QPP, and with them the disability pensions associated with the plans.[3] Over the policy development stage in 1963 and 1964, there were confidential meetings between Quebec Liberal ministers in the Pearson cabinet and the Quebec premier, and private meetings and communications between the Quebec premier and the prime minister and his senior policy advisor and the secretary to the cabinet. There also was a conference of federal and provincial welfare ministers that discussed pensions as well as three federal-provincial conferences of first ministers. Federal officials had numerous meetings with their Quebec and Ontario counterparts, and Pearson had extensive correspondence with the provincial premiers (Simeon 1972).

3 The story of the political struggles over the CPP and the QPP and their actual implementation is well told by academics and participants (LaMarsh 1969; Simeon 1972; Bryden 1974; Kent 1988; Bryden 1997). One participant in the policy process, Tom Kent, has described the creation of the CPP and the QPP as "the constructive expression of the idea of co-operative federalism ... a balanced combination of the best of federal and provincial ideas" (1988, 284). For Kent and the Pearson Liberals of the 1960s, cooperative federalism implied a mutual respect for federal and provincial jurisdictions, two-way consultation, and the coordination of parallel actions on common interests.

The Quebec government was determined to develop its own public pension plan, and Quebec's legislative assembly passed a resolution to that effect in 1963. At a federal-provincial conference in April 1964, the Quebec premier, Jean Lesage, outlined what the QPP would be. Kent, who was part of the federal delegation at the conference, recalls that "it was an excellent plan for its purpose. It would provide appreciably larger pensions than we proposed, and with the supplementary survivor and disability benefits that we did not have the constitutional power to include. It would generate, for many years, large investment funds. One could almost see the other provincial premiers licking their lips" (1988, 274).

As the social reformers of the 1940s well recognized, a constitutional amendment was needed to enable Parliament to make laws in relation to supplementary benefits of old age pensions, including survivors' benefits and disability benefits. In 1964, all ten provinces agreed to section 94A of the British North America Act. In return for provincial assent to this constitutional extension of jurisdiction to the federal sphere, the Pearson government had to grant provincial control over the scope, amendments, and financing of the CPP. The federal concessions to the provinces included the following specifications:

- Any province can opt out and establish its own plan, in which case the CPP ceases to operate generally in that province.
- Major amendments and "amendments of substance"[4] to the CPP must be approved by Parliament and at least two-thirds of the

---

4 Major amendments and amendments of substance as listed in the legislation contain the following areas: the general level of benefits provided under CPP; the classes of benefits; the rates of contributions; the formulae for calculating the contributions and benefits payable; the management or operation of the CPP Account and CPP Investment Fund; and the constitution of, or duties of the CPP Advisory Committee. Such amendments require a two-year notice before coming into force unless all provinces agree to waive this requirement for notice. The appeal system, therefore, is not designated, in the CPP legislation, as an area of policy substance that requires this formal process of notice and intergovernmental consensus. Whereas substantive amendments are seen as changes that "go to the very root of what a beneficiary is entitled to receive and what a contributor must pay," the appeal procedure, and many other aspects of the plan, is viewed as an "administrative feature" (Thorson 1964, 449).

provincial governments representing no less than two-thirds of the population (a provision including Quebec).
• Surpluses from the CPP Fund are loaned to the provincial governments on special terms of borrowing.

In the estimation of the federal welfare minister, "The plan was really a monument to Dominion-Provincial relations although not to the best of its relations. Out of near disaster came real progress. Agreement was reached, and a request was sent forward to the Government of Great Britain to amend the BNA Act" (LaMarsh 1969, 132). The CPP is not only an example of collaborative federalism, therefore, but it also contains within its own legislation elements of classical federalism with opting-out and entangled federalism with an amending formula of multiple vetoes. The amending formula gave recognition, and perhaps some reinforcement to the power shift taking place within the Canadian federation toward the provinces. Pearson and his senior advisors were firmly of the view that a shift in public activity to the provinces after the postwar centralization was bound to happen. The CPP thus gave concrete meaning to the philosophy of cooperative federalism espoused by the Liberal government. And, while it reflected the asymmetrical arrangements between the CPP and the QPP, a natural thing to do from Pearson's viewpoint, the constitutional amendment also gave the other provinces a genuine formal voice in the governance of the CPP. The veto power on changes to the CPP was resisted within the federal bureaucracy as a move away from the ideas and practices of the 1940s and 1950s; yet, in the words of LaMarsh, "participation of the provinces in the Canada Pension Plan was very important to us. It would have been impossible to bring in a universal, portable plan without provincial participation" (1969, 119).

When, in July 1963, the Liberals first unveiled the CPP proposal, some MPs and public groups criticized it as inadequate given the absence of supplementary benefits for people with disabilities, widows, and orphans. With the constitutional amendment secured the next year, survivor, death, and disability benefits were included in the federal design of the CPP. Provincial governments were very much interested in the inclusion of disability benefits under the CPP, as it would offer relief to the provinces on social assistance and workers' compensation outlays. Indexation of the disability benefits made them more attractive than provincial social assistance programs, which had never been automatically indexed to changes in cost of living.[5]

Negotiations between Ottawa and Quebec directly influenced the nature of the disability benefit in the plans. Quebec, in their pension plan proposal, included a disability benefit but restricted eligibility to those aged sixty and over, apparently due to financial concerns (Bryden 1974, 247).[6] When Ottawa added a disability benefit to its legislative proposal of November 1964, in Bill C-136, no age limit was attached. In the end, both the CPP and QPP incorporated a disability benefit without an age restriction. Ottawa adopted two other features from Quebec's proposal that were important to low-income persons with disabilities: (1) contributions were not be collected on the first six hundred dollars of annual income; and (2) benefits were to be adjusted to cost-of-living increases up to 2 percent a year. In the end, both governments influenced the other's position on disability benefits, resulting in less restrictive eligibility requirements and more generous benefit amounts.

PROGRAM GOALS AND DESIGN

The use of a social insurance model, with compulsory contributions, broad coverage of the working population for a range of risks, and benefits bearing some relation to contribution, was familiar to Canadians because the model resembled workers' compensation schemes and unemployment insurance, programs that had been operating for two or three generations. Adoption of the social insurance technique here, however, was a departure from prevailing federal and provincial income policies for people with disabilities. Before the CPP, social assistance was a dominant means of providing basic income to persons with disabilities (Prince 2015). The social assistance model involved welfare programs commonly cost-shared between the federal and provincial governments, delivered by the provinces, and with eligibility determined by a needs or means test.

5 See Prince 2001b, 797.
6 When the United States added disability insurance to Social Security in 1956, it was for people with permanent physical or mental disabilities aged fifty years or older. Not long after, in 1960, Congress repealed this age limit (Dixon 1973, 13).

At the time of its enactment in the mid-1960s, the CPP had a number of innovative features. As a contributory, public pension plan, the CPP would now deliver disability benefits and retirement pensions as a right and on a national basis. While workers' compensation and veterans' disability pensions were categorical programs offering compensation for specific conditions under particular circumstances, the CPP disability would be a general program that provided benefits regardless of the cause of the disability. The intent, as the original legislation stated, was "to establish a comprehensive program of old age pensions and supplementary benefits in Canada payable to and in respect of contributors" (CCH 1968).

Positioned firmly upon the policy instrument of social insurance, the CPP and CPP/D exemplify a liberal welfare state approach, one clearly articulated by Marsh and other reformers in the 1940s. As Norman Barry explains, "social insurance is basically a liberal notion, although the fact that it is compulsory does mark a departure from strict individualistic principles, since it links, in theory at least, benefits to contributions and therefore eliminates means-testing" (1999, 73–4). Its intentions are to emphasize individual responsibility through working and making financial contributions, to remove any trace of charity and stigma associated with benefits, and, through the use of compulsory contributions, to provide "an economic check on a potentially limitless expansionary process of state expenditures" (Barry 1999, 115).

The CPP was the first public pension law in Canada to impose an earnings or retirement test for eligibility to old age pensions (Bryden 1974, 4). Similar provisions were in place under the National Insurance program in the United Kingdom and the Social Security scheme in the United States, but Canadian social policy had no counterpart until the CPP. For CPP applicants, the retirement test meant that a person under age seventy had to be retired from regular employment in the paid labour force in order to qualify for and receive a retirement pension. A related distinctive feature of the CPP was that it contained a slightly broader definition of disability for the purposes of conferring benefits. The Disabled Persons Act, the existing federal disability law at the time, had a definition of disability that stressed a permanent and total condition. CPP introduced the concepts of severe and prolonged disability, as related to a person being capable or not of pursuing substantially gainful occupational work. The CPP thus added the concept of "employability" to disability income policy in Canada (Willard 1964b, 247).

The primary goal of the CPP/D was, and still is, to provide, as a right, a reasonable minimum level of income replacement to workers who experience a *prolonged* and *severe* disability. Throughout legislative debates, ministerial speeches, and government statements, the entitlement perspective of this earnings-related program was stressed. The policy aim was that the benefit would be non-stigmatizing and provide a degree of protection against the loss of wages due to disability, thus contributing to family income security. Making contributions to the CPP was not necessarily seen as a tax, as is more the case today. In the context of the early 1960s, when most Canadians lacked pension plans and retirement savings plans, paying CPP contributions was widely regarded as an opportunity to secure an entitlement to benefits that would otherwise not be available to most working people and their families (Kent 1988).

Three other goals were reflected in the original CPP legislation and thinking behind the disability program's design. The legislation allowed for vocational rehabilitation measures to be funded as part of the CPP and for a three-level appeals system to be established, officially acknowledging the desirability of return-to-work as well as program fairness and integrity as program goals. In addition, perhaps equally or more important than the income protection goal, government and business interests especially gave consideration to the financial affordability and economic effects of the overall CPP. At the time, concerns were raised over the effects of the CPP on investment markets, private savings, occupational pension plans, and the inflation and growth rates of the Canadian economy. Reflecting these concerns and pressures, governments therefore limited the maximum CPP and QPP retirement benefits to 25 percent of earnings up to the average wage, leaving considerable room for private sector pension plans, tax-assisted retirement plans, and personal savings to meet the retirement income needs of Canadians. Concerns over costs also shaped the eligibility rules, indexation formula, and implementation schedule for the new disability benefit. About the initial eligibility rules, many years later a government member remarked with justification, "A look back at the discussions surrounding the development of the CPP makes it clear that no other benefit posed as many problems or raised as many questions as did the disability provisions" (Tremblay 1991, 5389).

Table 4.1 Original program design of the Canada Pension Plan and the disability component

CPP GENERAL DESIGN FEATURES

• Federal and provincial government program with federal administration
• Compulsory contributions from employees, employers, and self-employed: 1.8% of salary or wages between $600 and $5,100 a year with employers matching, and self-employed contributing 3.6%
• Broad national coverage of working-age population
• A range of risks addressed: retirement, death, and disability
• Benefits include: retirement pensions, death benefits, disability pensions, disabled contributors' children benefits, disabled widowers' pensions, orphans' benefits, survivors' pensions, and widows' pensions
• Risk pooling with no differentiation of individual rates in relation to types of risk
• Benefits related to contributions and average industrial earnings
• Main goal: reasonable minimum level of income support and wage replacement
• Provided as of right to eligible applicants
• Vocational rehabilitation measures permitted
• Three-level appeals system
• Automatic indexation of benefits of not less than 1% and not more than 2% a year
• Benefits paid monthly
• Benefits taxable income by federal and provincial governments
• Contributions tax deductible for income tax purposes
• Phased implementation with collection of contributions as of 1966, and the payment of retirement pensions in 1967, survivors' benefits 1968, and disability benefits 1970
• Retirement test: applicants must be retired from regular employment
• Eligibility for retirement benefits lowered from age 69 in 1966 to 65 by 1970
• Actuarial report on the CPP account at least once every five years
• Major changes require approval of Parliament plus at least two-thirds of the provinces with not less than two-thirds of the population

DISABILITY PROGRAM DESIGN FEATURES

• Benefits are a combination of earnings-related (75% of the amount of the contributor's retirement pension, which is an amount equal to 25% of the average monthly pensionable earnings) and flat-rate ($25 multiplied by the ration between the Pension Index for the year against the Pension Index for 1967)
• Eligibility rules for disabled contributors: between the ages of 18 and 65, made contributions for five years, and experiencing a severe and prolonged mental or physical disability
• Must apply in writing and provide a medical report
• Three-month waiting period before benefit payments
• At age 65 disability benefits stop and the recipient starts receiving a retirement pension
• For dependent children of disabled contributors: a child 18 or under or between 18 and 25 if attending school or university full-time
• An equal amount for each of the first four children and one-half that amount for each additional child in the family

Defining Disability for a Public Policy

The original eligibility rules for CPP disability benefits included criteria of age, a certain degree of disability, and contributions from past employment. To qualify, a person had to be between the ages of eighteen and sixty-five, had to have made earnings-related contributions to the CPP for a minimum of five years, and was now experiencing a severe and prolonged mental or physical disability that prevented him or her from working regularly at a paid job. The rationale behind these rules was that an applicant for the disability benefit must have had a recent and a substantial attachment to the paid labour force.

The CPP definition of disability is noteworthy in several respects. First, it is enshrined in the legislation rather than left to be defined through regulations and administrative procedures; this gives the definition a statutory and thus parliamentary status. Second, the definition refers to *prolonged* disability – that is, likely to be long continued and of indefinite duration or likely to result in death – rather than the term *permanent*, which was used in the earlier Disabled Persons Act. This left open the possibility of a return to employment for at least some program clients. Third, the notion of disability covered by the plan includes both mental and physical disabilities. Fourth, the definition includes a functional model of disability, meaning the incapacity of regularly pursuing any substantial gainful employment is taken into account. The embodied citizen makes an appearance here as the disabled worker. Fifth, like the US Social Security Disability Insurance program, the CPP/D program does not provide benefits for partial or temporary disabilities. Only persons with full and permanent disabilities may be eligible. We have here "the logic of binary opposites and its connection to the belief in fixed subject identities" (Leonard 1997, 40). This meant effectively that CPP/D would not be a time-limited benefit for an eligible person up to the age of sixty-five. At the time of its introduction, provincial programs of social assistance and workers' compensation did offer benefits for people with partial and or temporary disabilities.

Compared to the other supplementary benefits under the CPP, the survivor and death benefits, the disability pension had a more stringent test for eligibility. The reason, as the deputy minister of welfare, Dr Joseph Willard, explained, "arises from the problems that have surrounded the provision and administration of disability benefits.

We have tried to develop the disability benefit along the lines of the one in the United States, but in some instances it is actually more generous" (Willard 1964b, 250). Canadian officials were aware that since 1956, when the Americans introduced disability insurance as part of social security, the disability component had been amended in 1958, 1960, and again in 1965, and so was regarded as "an administrative can of worms" (Stone 1984, 71). One difference in program design, for example, was that the waiting period for disability benefits was six months under US Social Security, compared to the three months under the CPP. To launch the disability program, federal officials believed "that the qualification period should be fairly rigorous, until we have gained some experience under the program" (Willard 1964b, 250).

In addition, the disability benefit was set at an amount higher than the other CPP supplementary benefits. The notion of an entitlement or right was tied to the mandatory contribution from the potential beneficiary. Funded through required contributions, the disability payment was thus regarded as a pension benefit rather than a public handout. The principle of an earned right to income without the stigma of welfare was a clear motivation behind the CPP and the CPP/D. As a basis for the CPP/D in particular, the idea of earned right did mean, however, a loss of status as a gainfully employed person and the assumption of another status as a severely disabled person who was unable to work as before and most likely not suitable for vocational rehabilitation. The general presumption was that if a person met the medical definition to receive a CPP disability pension – that is, severe and prolonged disability – the chances of rehabilitation were minimal at best. As will be shown in subsequent chapters, political and public expectations about return to work and the potential of vocational rehabilitation services shifted in later decades in the CPP/D's history.

Recognizing Family Needs and Other Innovations in the CPP

For the disability benefit to dependent children of a disabled contributor, the original eligibility criteria involved age, an education test, and the number of children in the family. To qualify for a dependent's benefit, a child had to be eighteen or younger or between eighteen and to twenty-five if he or she continued to attend school or university full time. An equal amount was payable for each of the first four children and one-half that amount for each additional child in the family. Coming at the recent end of the baby boom, this provision reflected the size of Canadian families at the time, and the reduced benefit amount was a cost-control measure. It also illustrated status politics inscribed in policy as the federal government recognized certain identities within families and provided specific benefits for those identified groups in need.

Interestingly, the category of dependent children of disabled contributors was absent from the original CPP draft bill. It was the Special Joint Committee of the Senate and House of Commons, which was created to examine the bill, that recommended there be such a benefit for each child of a disabled contributor. Comprised of twelve senators and twenty-four MPs, the Joint Committee held fifty-one sittings from late 1964 to early 1965, hearing from over one hundred witnesses as well as officials in eight federal government departments and agencies. In the end, in addition to endorsing the principles of the CPP, the Joint Committee recommended changes in a handful of areas. One of their proposals was that a further benefit, a dependent child benefit, be included in the CPP, and that the amount of the benefit be the same as for the orphan's benefit. The additional costs for this measure were projected by the chief actuary to be modest. The Pearson government agreed with the proposal and amended the bill. This constructive and substantive amendment is an instance of input from civil society organizations and parliamentary influence on social legislation; in this specific case, this input resulted in the addition of a derived social right to the policy, a claim to income support based a familial relationship to an adult client. The Joint Committee made other recommendations about the disability program that dealt with the use of rehabilitative measures, the costs of medical examinations, and the need for flexibility in the determination of disability. The Pearson government regarded these suggestions as worthwhile and the minister indicated they would be addressing them in regulations to the CPP (LaMarsh 1965, 11844).

Automatic indexation of benefits against inflation, by means of a pension index, was another innovative feature of the CPP legislation that enhanced the quality of this new social right. As Dennis Guest writes, "For the first time in Canada's history of social security, the decision was taken, while drafting the provisions of the Canada and Quebec Pension Plans, to provide for an automatic increase in line with increases in the cost of living" (1998, 154). A study at the time showed that of nearly fifty-five countries with public pension systems, only nine had legislative provisions for the automatic adjustment of pension benefits.[7] Having benefits pegged to the cost of living index was a provision that took effect in 1968, a year after the first retirement benefits began to be paid. Canadians were now assured that their pensions would keep up to date in purchasing value, an issue that had troubled recipients of old age pensions, old age assistance, and disabled allowances for the previous forty years.

For government, indexation appeared to promise a reduction in partisan and pressure group demands for increasing pension benefits. Indexation therefore made both political sense and social policy sense. For the person receiving CPP disability, indexation of benefits was particularly important because provincial social assistance benefits were anything but indexed. At first (from 1968 to 1973), the indexation formula was limited to a year-to-year increase of not less than 1 percent and not more than 2 percent. No question that Finance officials were determined to place some limitations on this alarming new idea of indexation, as they regarded it. The compromise was the 2-percent ceiling. If the average of the consumer price index, as the official inflation rate, was less than 1 percent for the previous twelve months, then the pension index remain unchanged so as to avoid making small increases or even decreases. If the average was more than 2 percent, the increase to the pension index was limited to 2 percent. There was also a banking provision that worked this way: if inflation was 2.5 percent one year, then the benefit increased the maximum 2 percent, and if the next year inflation was only 1.5 percent, the difference could be added and benefits would rise again by another 2 percent. This ceiling on indexing benefits reinforced the aims, held especially by Finance officials, of limiting the cost of the CPP and of not wishing to fuel inflation in the Canadian economy.[8]

Still another design feature of the CPP was the phase-in of its various dimensions. CPP came into effect in 1966 with the collection of

7 See Joint Committee 1964, 133–45. The nine countries with automatic adjustment of pension benefits included Chile, Israel, and several European countries, mainly the Scandinavian states. Thus, with the pension index in the CPP and QPP, Canada introduced an automatic cost-of-living adjustment to public pensions before the United States, United Kingdom, New Zealand, Australia, and many other liberal welfare regimes.

8 For further details on the pension index, see the Joint Committee 1964 and Bryden 1974, chapters 7 and 8.

contributions from employees, employers, and the self-employed. Benefits were introduced over the next four years: retirement pensions became payable in 1967; survivors' benefits, including benefits for children of deceased and disabled contributors, and combined survivor/disability pensions began in 1968; and disability benefits started in 1970. Full retirement benefits were not to be payable until 1976. Concurrently, the eligibility age for CPP retirement benefits was lowered to age sixty-five one year at a time, beginning with age sixty-nine in 1966. Similar staged approaches to implementing major social insurance programs took place with Canada's Unemployment Insurance scheme in the 1940s, America's old age retirement insurance in the 1930s and 1940s, and Canada's national medical care program over the late 1960s to early 1970s (Berkowitz 1987; Rice and Prince 2013). This tells us that state administrative capacity is a key factor in the timing of implementing a new social right. Noting that the disability benefit was not to be paid before 1970, the minister of National Health and Welfare told the Joint Committee of the Senate and House of Commons that was examining the legislation, "If this seems unduly harsh, remember that it is a very generous and long term benefit. A man or woman who has paid a contribution for only five years may, on disability, be drawing from the pension plan for the rest of his or her life" (LaMarsh 1964, 20–1). Moreover, a phased approach was a prudent strategy given the cost projections as well as the enormous administrative tasks and complexities to be tackled in setting up any single large-scale social program, not to mention the crowded social policy agenda of the mid- to late 1960s in Canada.

SOCIAL POLICY CONTEXT AND ADMINISTRATIVE FORMATION

Establishment of CPP Disability took place within a political setting of active and substantial reform in social policy in Canada and within an administrative setting of putting into place the required structures, staff, and delivery supports.

The CPP was introduced in a context of the OAS and the means-tested Old Age Assistance (OAA), which both began in the early 1950s. The OAA was phased out by 1969, with some provinces bringing the program under the recently (1966) introduced Canada Assistance Plan (CAP). To complement the OAS and CPP, a new income-tested benefit, the Guaranteed Income Supplement (GIS), for low-income seniors, was introduced in 1967. By the late 1960s, therefore, the public pension system had three-levels of programming: the universal OAS, the selective GIS, and the earnings-related CPP. Unlike CPP retirement policy, the CPP/D entered a less developed disability income policy field. There was a system of private and public pensions and Registered Retirement Savings Plans in place when CPP arrived, and the GIS made the system more complete. CPP/D links with group insurance and aspects of workers' compensation and welfare, but the disability income system itself was not often understood in such terms as a system and was spottier in coverage. At the time, some Canadian policy makers suggested that the CPP/D should serve an analogous role to CPP and OAS in the retirement income system, which becomes evident in the presence and later build-up of the flat-rate component of CPP/D that occurred in the 1980s. However, the arrival of the GIS (and, in the mid-1970s, the spousal allowance as another part of federal elderly benefits) had no parallel in federal disability income policy, and in the absence of a group plan there was no practical way to build on CPP/D protection as with retirement savings.

Within disability policy, the CPP was introduced in a context of the Vocational Rehabilitation of Disabled Persons (VRDP) program and the CAP. Introduced in 1961, the VRDP offered agreements to the provinces and the territories of federal sharing of 50 percent of the costs for a range of services designed to help people with physical or mental disabilities become capable of pursuing a gainful occupation. Ottawa's financial offer was open-ended, a function of how much provinces/territories wished to spend on these rehabilitation services. Provinces entered into two- or three-year agreements with Ottawa, which were regularly renewed from the 1960s to the late 1990s when the VRDP was replaced. (The current successor program is the Labour Market Agreements for Persons with Disabilities). Under the VRDP, the federal government specified the terms for obtaining cost-sharing, and the provinces were solely responsible for the administration of their programs, including the design, eligibility requirements, and mode of delivery. VRDP benefits and supports were provided directly by provincial government departments and agencies or through provincially supported voluntary agencies. With the exception of maintenance and training allowances, personal financial need was not a consideration for eligibility and provision. The federal government also added benefits to the Youth Allowances "to disabled or retarded young people" (LaMarsh 1969, 124).

CAP was the invention of federal and provincial social service ministers and senior program officials with a broadly shared vision of building a more comprehensive and progressive social security system for the country. Notably, much of CAP's origins lie in disability policy. CAP consolidated a number of welfare programs, including the cost-shared programs under the Old Age Assistance Act of 1951, the Blind Persons Act of 1951, the Disabled Persons Act of 1954, and the Unemployment Assistance Act of 1956. Around the time that the CAP legislation was introduced, the Established Programs (Interim Arrangements) Act passed, providing for the Blind Persons Act and the Disabled Persons Act "to be wholly financed and administered by a province with the federal contribution being replaced by a tax abatement and adjustment payments" (National Health and Welfare, *Blind Persons*, 1966, 15). At their peak, in the mid-1960s, the Disabled Persons benefit program had approximately 54,000 recipients with annual federal payments of $23.4 million, and the Blind Persons program had about 8,600 recipients and an annual federal payment of $5.6 million. In 1966, an amendment to the Blind Persons Act allowed provinces that had signed agreements under the new Canada Assistance Plan Act to discontinue accepting applications for blind person allowances and assist this group under CAP. Existing recipients who transferred to CAP would qualify for comparable or greater benefits. The same offer was made with regard to the Disabled Persons Act. By the mid-1970s, most provinces had transferred their clients for the blind persons and disabled persons allowances to CAP, and federal payments under these older programs dwindled over the years.

In relation to these earlier programs, CAP's conditions marked a significant change in social policy. These conditions were that assistance be assessed on only a needs test; that there is no residency requirement for income assistance applicants; that provinces establish formal system of appeal for their welfare administrations; and that annual audits and records are provided to the federal government. Federal welfare officials hoped that, in the long term, the CPP disability program, in conjunction with the retirement and survivor benefits, would reduce the social assistance caseload of provincial authorities (Willard 1964b, 82). As will be discussed in later chapters, this hoped-for effect has not happened.

To oversee formulating the plan's administrative infrastructure, the first director of the CPP was appointed to the Department of National Health and Welfare in 1965. In those early years, more than two hundred staff were recruited and trained; and close to forty full-time district offices and over one hundred part-time local offices were set up across the country. Within the federal bureaucracy, an interdepartmental coordinating committee was formed, and a CPP advisory committee of external members, mandated by the legislation, also was created. Numerous regulations, policies, procedures, forms, and systems were developed, including orders-in-council regarding the new system of social insurance numbers (SIN) for over 9.6 million Canadians. These administrative measures represented a process essential to the effective development of social citizenship – administering a large population through techniques of bureaucratic individuation such as SIN that situate people individually and homogeneously at the same time. A public information program was launched. Liaison with the new Quebec Pension Board was developed and a series of agreements signed with foreign governments to bring their locally employed staff under the coverage of the CPP.

A much-needed three-stage appeals process for benefits was set out in the legislation. In designing the appeal process, Canadian officials had examined comparable social legislation at the federal level, including the appeal procedures for personal income tax, old age security, and unemployment insurance. The first level of appeal was to the minister, delegated under regulations, to an assistant deputy minister or director general of CPP for reconsideration. The second level of appeal would be to a review committee composed of three people, one appointed by the appellant, one by the minister, and a third agreed to jointly. According to the legal advisor to the Department of National Health and Welfare, the idea of review committees was that, as locally constituted ad hoc bodies, they would be close to where the applicant or beneficiary lived, so as to minimize the costs of travel and the expense of a formal application to a court (Curran 1964, 338). The third level would be to the Pension Appeals Board (PAB).

According to the minister of National Health and Welfare, who oversaw the passage of the law, the three-level process was "modelled somewhat along the lines of the appeal procedure in the United States old age security legislation," in particular the idea of a judicial body at a third level. Overall, the appeal system was designed to offer "a simple, expeditious and inexpensive disposition of decisions relating to matters under the act which affect individuals" (LaMarsh 1965, 11846). Work on establishing the appeals system began in 1965–66, including the development and approval of rules and procedures, and the establishment of the Pension Appeals Board. With a view to ensuring consistency in judicial decisions, negotiations with Quebec resulted in the PAB being designated as the review commission for the purposes of the QPP (National Health and Welfare, *Annual Report 1966, 1967*, 25–6).[9]

NEW POLICY PROCESS DYNAMICS

As a new social program of major proportions, the CPP was not only a pension policy with various kinds of benefits. It was also a set of values, practices, and rules that together created some new dynamics for policy making. These dynamics, as will become apparent throughout the book, have had important consequences for the development of the CPP in general and the disability program. The origins of the CPP disability program closely entwined with a broader approach to progressive social policy and cooperative federalism, and to the electoral strategy of the Liberal Party of Canada.

A national disability income program would not have happened in Canada in the 1960s without the larger reform project of establishing a contributory retirement pension plan. This larger scheme supplied the program vehicle and the financing on which to add the disability pension program, which provided income support for the non-elderly. Some federal government officials had favoured a separate national disability insurance program, but the idea was not really on the political agenda of the country during this period. Nor, as we will discuss later, did a comprehensive disability program become a reality in the 1980s, even though it was suggested by experts and studied by an intergovernmental working group of officials. A major argument against a separate national disability program in the 1960s, and later, was that financing it would require raising federal taxes. Another option was to include disability benefits under the new Canada

9 The initial three members of the Pension Appeals Board were a judge of the Superior Court of Quebec as chair, and, as members, a justice of the Court of Appeal in Manitoba, and a judge of the County Court in British Columbia (National Health and Welfare, *Annual Report 1966, 1967*).

Assistance Plan proposed by the Liberals, but this had the disadvantages of narrow coverage of the public and the stigma of welfare administration. There was strong support for including disability benefits within the CPP because of the broadness of coverage of the population, the numerous international examples of public contributory pension plans with disability benefits, including the United Kingdom and the United States, and because the contributions to the CPP were not seen in negative terms as a tax.[10]

Actual authority to establish the disability program came from provincial agreement to a constitutional amendment, while the particular program design features came from policy work done by the Liberal Party and, more intensely, within the federal bureaucracy, as well as in negotiations between the federal and provincial governments, most significantly between Ottawa and Quebec.[11] As part of a federal-provincial program, CPP/D became subject to an amending formula, which was included in the legislation, that required agreement of Parliament and at least two-thirds of the provinces, having not less than two-thirds of the population, to any future changes to the level of benefits, the rate of contributions, or the investment policy. This necessity of a substantial intergovernmental consensus meant that executive federalism became a critical arena for reforming the CPP, thereby limiting the role of Parliament as a change agent by itself.

The fact that Quebec established its own pension plan similar to the CPP produced what may be called a systemic goal of parallelism; that is, it maintained a close degree of consistency between program provisions in the CPP and QPP. The wish to ensure uniformity in public pension standards has meant that changes in one plan, often the Quebec plan, generated pressure to amend the other plan in order

10   Indeed, the idea of a comprehensive national disability income plan was raised again in the mid-1990s, this time by provincial governments. Yet another federal-provincial working group examined the concept without major results (Torjman 2001).

11   Key actors included David Croll, Tom Kent, and Keith Davey of the Liberal Party; Joe Willard, Richard Splane, Robert Bryce, and Gordon Robertson of the federal civil service; Judy LaMarsh, Walter Gordon, Maurice Lamontagne, and Maurice Sauvé of the federal cabinet; Prime Minister Lester Pearson and Premiers Jean Lesage of Quebec and John Robarts of Ontario, and certain of their ministers and officials. For further details see Simeon 1972, Kent 1988, and Bryden 1997.

to restore comparability. This was apparent in the 1987 reform to the flat-rate portion of the CPP disability benefit and, later, for other reforms to the CPP in the 1990s and early 2000s (Béland 2013).

The original legislation also contained several accountability and public reporting requirements. At least once in every five years, the federal government's chief actuary was to prepare a report based on an actuarial examination of the legislation and the state of the CPP account, including projections for a period of at least thirty years. A CPP advisory committee was established to produce an annual report that would provide policy and program advice to the minister of National Health and Welfare, who, in turn, was to include the advisory committee's report in his or her own annual report to Parliament on the administration, programming, and financing of the CPP. The legislation further stipulated that any federal action to amend the CPP must have a study done by the chief actuary, with that information placed before Parliament to inform consideration of any proposed amendments. These provisions illustrate how the perspective on financial sustainability and affordability was firmly rooted in the CPP from its beginnings. They also helped to ensure that financial concerns were systematically placed on political and policy agendas, conveying a message every few years about the immediate and longer-term sustainability of the CPP and so also the CPP/D.

CONCLUSION

Through the exercise of the constitutional powers of the provincial and federal governments and intergovernmental relations, the CPP/D was born – the child of electoral, political party, and bureaucratic politics. In the policy design and administrative formation of the CPP/D, legislative, medical, quasi-judicial/judicial, and bureaucratic forms of power and knowledge were deployed. The conceptual framework of disability in the legislation for CPP/D eligibility rested on conventional understandings of bodily impairments as identifiable entities manifested by specific symptoms, privileged the role of medical professionals to diagnosis and gauge the severity and duration of disability and, for some time, downplayed the potential role of vocational rehabilitation services. Provision of disability income benefits to contributors and other family members was shaped largely by executive decisions and federal-provincial negotiations, especially between Ottawa and Quebec, civil society groups, through a parliamentary committee, had a specific influence on the issue of benefits to children of disabled contributors. The three-level appeal system for CPP/D illustrates the exercise of quasi-judicial logic and judicial authority patterns, and draws form American experience with social security.

The CPP/D exemplifies a trend in public policy toward disability issues in that it is a subsystem within the larger retirement income policy system of the Canada Pension Plan. National public disability insurance would not have happened otherwise in the 1960s. As an expression of social rights, the CPP/D established a legislated direct right to cash benefits for those with severe and prolonged mental or physical disabilities and with labour force participation, as well as derived rights for certain immediate family members. The whole idea, as the minister at the time, Judy LaMarsh, said, was to provide benefits not burdens. As a new social right for a group of people previously uncovered, the CPP disability benefit was not in opposition to the market economy. Eligibility tests concentrated on the severely disabled and required a recent and significant degree of work life coupled with financial contributions. Of course, eligibility rules invariably produce legally defined entrances and exclusions, the advantaged and disadvantaged, thus generating personal struggles and political conflicts over the boundaries of coverage. These struggles took place in the 1970s onwards, when the CPP/D was implemented.

Effective provision of social rights always necessitates an institutional framework centred largely in the state. For the CPP/D, the federal government, in cooperation with the provinces, established an infrastructure of program financing and administration, public information, medical evaluation, and review and appeal mechanisms. The CPP/D occurred well into the so-called postwar consensus on the Keynesian welfare state. The story of how the CPP and the CPP/D emerged and were formulated, and the linkages with other old and new programs, indicates that the consensus on the welfare state in Canada was not settled in the late 1940s or during the 1950s, although certain ideas expressed in earlier decades continued to resonate. Understandings on the role of social policy and the meaning of social citizenship were continually being expressed, debated, and negotiated; and the meaning of social citizenship changed and adapted as new policies, like the CPP/D were introduced. The Keynesian welfare state was always a complex set of ideas and practices in process, and, as the following chapters show, so too has CPP Disability.

CHAPTER FIVE

Policy Implementation and Reform Ideas in the Trudeau Era, 1970–1984

Some rights, such as welfare rights, which entitle persons to a minimum level of material well-being, provide access not simply to opportunities but also conditions.

J.M. Barbalet, *Citizenship*

An incremental policy process rather than a transformational policy process may result, with gains being made slowly rather than with vigour, as disability advocates prefer.

William Boyce et al., *A Seat at the Table*

The years 1970 to 1984 cover nearly all of the Trudeau prime ministerial era and mark the second phase in the development of CPP disability policy. During this period, the emphasis by federal and provincial governments was on implementing the CPP, making a series of modest adaptations to eligibility and benefits, and, from the late 1970s to the mid-1980s, engaging in a significant process of pension reform analysis, debate, and recommendations. Due in large part to the expertise of the intergovernmental group of federal officials chaired by the deputy minister of Welfare, Dr Joe Willard, formed to design and oversee the introduction of the CPP, the implementation went reasonably smoothly for such a major new national social policy. Disability benefits first became payable in 1970 and, with that, a large increase in appeals of decisions on disability pension applications also occurred. As soon as the CPP disability came in, insurance companies altered the way that their disability insurance policies were formulated to take into account that there was now a national disability insurance program, and they integrated their coverage around the CPP/D. The federal public service pension was also integrated with the CPP/D. Also as of 1970, retirement pensions became payable to contributors who were age sixty-five and older. Throughout the Trudeau era, the retirement test of age sixty-five and the combined contribution rate of 3.6 percent remained unchanged, with the CPP in a "surplus" into the 1980s. During this period, then, extensions to benefits and liberalization of eligibility rules were not accompanied by increases in contribution rates, as the case in more recent phases of CPP policy development.

GROWTH OF DISABILITY CASELOADS AND APPEALS

Implementation of income benefits for working adults with disabilities and their children had an immediate and significant impact on the organization structure, caseload, and appeals system of the CPP program. In the Department of National Health and Welfare, the Disability Determination Division, which had been part of the Health Services Branch, was transferred in 1972 to the CPP Branch, making it easier to integrate the work with disability benefits (National Health and Welfare, *Annual Report*, 1972, 3).

Within five years of being introduced, the average number of monthly disability benefits for eligible contributors and children numbered about fifty thousand, climbing to one hundred thousand by 1980 and reaching two hundred thousand recipients by the mid-1980s. As a percentage of total CPP benefits, the disability benefits rose to about a 10 percent share by 1975 and stayed at the level for the rest of this period. Disability expenditures quickly came to constitute between 13 percent and 14 percent of total CPP expenditures for the period, paying out over $1.1 billion in disability benefits by 1985–86. Reasons for this continual growth in the disability caseload related to growing public awareness of the program; the ever-increasing and aging Canadian population and workforce; and modest legislative changes in easing contributory eligibility requirements and enhancing benefits. In addition, there were "changing labour market conditions resulting in the unemployment of older workers, referrals to the CPP by provincial social assistance programs and referrals to CPP disability from insurance companies which also were experiencing an increase in applications" (Torjman 2001, 20).

The 1971–72 annual report for the CPP captures the impact of disability benefit applications on appeals this way: "As anticipated with the advent of disability benefits in 1970, which are difficult to decide, the number of appeals increased greatly with approximately 95 per cent of them stemming from disability cases. This growth has taken place despite the fact that about 80 per cent of disability applications [at the initial stage] are approved for payment" (National Health and Welfare 1972, 4). Statements similar to this one reappear in CPP annual reports throughout the Trudeau period. Of the disability applications that went to appeal in this period, approximately 88 percent, as an annual average, were handled at the first level to the minister; 9 percent were dealt with at the second level of Review Committees; and fewer than 3 percent went to a Pension Appeals Board for resolution. Table 5.1 presents information on the number of appeals on CPP disability benefits by level for the years, 1969–70 to 1984–85.

Some of these factors behind the growth in disability caseloads raise issues about the program's integrity and its connections with related income support programs of provincial governments and private sector insurers. It was not until the 1990s, however, that a strong effort was taken by federal officials to build information-sharing agreements with provinces and private insurers. Moreover, it was not until the late 1980s and 1990s, following major expansion of benefits in 1987 and 1991, that the financial sustainability of CPP disability expenditures became a hot political issue.

During the 1970–84 period, concerns centred more on the administration of the disability appeals system, with complaints from applicants, questions by members of Parliament, and performance audits from the auditor general of Canada. Concerns involved the adequacy of information and communication between applicants and the department; the time taken to process applications, hold hearings, and render decisions, which resulted in frustrations and backlogs; and the absence of rules, procedures, and control systems for effectively and efficiently managing the disability program. "As a result of a review of the appeals process," the 1984 annual report for the CPP noted that "the Administration has established time standards for the first two levels of appeals and an automated monitoring system … [in order to] help reduce the processing time and provide pertinent data for management's review" (National Health and Welfare 1984, 13).

LEGISLATIVE AND OTHER POLICY DEVELOPMENTS

No sooner were disability benefits paid out in 1970 than proposals for amending the CPP, including the disability component, emerged from federal sources. As we will see in this chapter and the next, a

Table 5.1 Appeals on CPP disability benefits by level, 1969–70 to 1984–85

Fiscal year	To Minister	To Review Committee	To Pension Appeals Board	Total
1969–70	98	0	3	101
1970–71	232	20	3	255
1971–72	700	45	4	749
1972–73	1,750	250	45	2,045
1973–74	2,025	369	114	2,508
1974–75	1,800	274	55	2,129
1975–76	1,500	257	48	1,805
1976–77	2,300	300	35	2,635
1977–78	2,900	330	50	3,280
1978–79	3,197	282	77	3,556
1979–80	5,623	648	85	6,356
1980–81	4,385	480	125	4,990
1981–82	5,760	560	175	6,495
1982–83	5,025	425	205	5,655
1983–84	4,633	367	195	5,195
1984–85	7,299	719	66	8,084

Source: *Annual Reports for the Canada Pension Plan*. The figures of appeals to the minister of National Health and Welfare for 1971–72 and 1972–73 are approximate figures, as given in the reports.

number of these proposals resulted in changes to the CPP and the disability program over the next dozen years or so. One such source of reform ideas was the 1970 *Report of the Royal Commission on the Status of Women*, which "threw attention onto the state as the principal site for addressing many of the concerns and claims of women for equality and equity" (Rice and Prince 2013, 100). Some measures to advance women's equality entailed making changes to the CPP and the QPP, and the Royal Commission report was certainly an input to that debate, as was the Advisory Council for the Status of Women, a federal agency established to advance the position of Canadian women in all areas life. It was Judy LaMarsh, the minister of National Health and Welfare in the first Pearson government, who sold the idea of the royal commission to Pearson, and on which Monique Bégin, a future minister of National Health and Welfare, became co-chair.

In November 1970, the federal government released a white paper called "Income Security for Canadians" by the minister of National

Health and Welfare, John Munro. In it, the government argued that priority be placed on anti-poverty measures to better concentrate available resources on those individuals and families with the lowest incomes in Canada. The main focus was on converting the universal family allowance to a selective family income security plan. This new emphasis, away from universal programs and toward more selective programs, also envisaged an important role for social insurance programs, such as the CPP, in alleviating poverty. The white paper noted, "there is a very uneven distribution of income protection for retirement, disability and survivors available through private industry" (Munro 1970, 47). In retirement income policy, the proposed strategy had three aspects: freeze the universal Old Age Security (OAS) at current benefit levels; target future increases to the selective Guaranteed Income Supplement (GIS) (which was to be made permanent; to this point it had been a temporary feature for persons too old and poor to qualify for CPP benefits); and make several changes to the CPP in consultation with the provinces. Proposals for reforming the CPP included an increase in the maximum retirement benefits as well as in the flat-rate portion of disability benefits; and a new benefit of eighty dollars per month for wives of disabled contributors under age sixty-five with dependent children to support (Guest 1998, 267).

As part of a major overhaul of the Unemployment Insurance program in 1971, a sickness benefit was added. This was, in a sense, the federal temporary disability program that Leonard Marsh had recommended in his 1943 report on social security for Canadians. In fact, Canada was a relative latecomer among industrial countries in legislating in the area of income protection against the risk of income loss due to the illness of a wage earner. This new special benefit was a statutory provision at the national level, through social insurance, for short-term health conditions. The maximum duration was (and still is) fifteen weeks of earnings-related benefits. Hence, the coverage was limited to people with insurable earnings in the paid labour force.

In the October 1972 federal general election, the Trudeau Liberals lost their majority status and formed a minority government with support from the third party, the New Democrats. The effect of this balance of power in Parliament for social policy and pension reform was quick and direct. In April 1973, the new federal minister of National Health and Welfare, Marc Lalonde, released a "Working Paper on Social Security in Canada" (Lalonde 1973), which rejected the selective philosophy espoused in the 1970 white paper, and in fact recommended enriching the universal family allowances and OAS programs. The working paper did, nonetheless, reaffirm the white paper theme that social insurance programs ought to be the first line of income protection against retirement and disability or death, supplemented by private pension arrangements. Reform ideas on the CPP included a full cost-of-living adjustment of benefits. At an intergovernmental conference in October 1973, federal and provincial representatives agreed to the full indexation of all CPP benefits along with some other changes, but not disability reform measures. It was decided that the question of the value of disability benefits would be given attention at future federal-provincial meetings (Bryden 1974, 181–2). Quebec, however, legislated the flat-rate increase of eighty dollars, an amount that would have matched the OAS basic amount had the federal government not in turn increased to one hundred dollars the OAS.

Over the next ten years, several amendments and other policy changes were made to the CPP, most of which had direct or indirect significance for disability benefits and programming. These developments are summarized in Table 5.2. A noteworthy set of legislative changes took effect in 1975, designed to make the CPP appeal system more accessible, flexible, and fair for applicants. Legal expenses incurred by an applicant or beneficiary when the appeal against a review committee was launched by the minister would now be paid from the CPP rather than the individual. Third parties were given the authority to appeal a decision on behalf of an incapacitated person. The size of the Pension Appeals Board was expanded from a maximum of six to a maximum of ten members to permit regional panels. A provision was also added to give a vice-chair all the powers and duties of a chair, if the chair were absent. These reforms were in response to the growing caseloads and appeals under the CPP and the advocacy of various MPs to enhance the efficiency and effectiveness of the appeals system.

This was an active period of policy development in the CPP in response to a number of factors, as Table 5.2 shows. One was the rising rate of inflation in the late 1960s and 1970s, which provoked concerns about the declining value of pension benefits. A second factor was the growing influence of the women's movement in Canada, catalyzed in many respects by the work of the Royal Commission on the Status of Women. Throughout this period, women's groups voiced concerns about pensions and gender equity and equality, reinforced

Table 5.2 Key amendments and policy changes to the CPP, 1974–1983

Year	Development	Policy perspective
1974	Raising of the year's maximum pensionable earnings (YMPE)	Income protection: Ensuring pension benefits equal the average of industrial wages over time
1974	Setting the year's basic exemption (YBE) at 10 percent of the YMPE	Income protection: Exempting very low-income earners from making contributions
1974	Removal of the ceiling on the Pension Index, to allow full annual cost-of-living indexation of benefits	Income protection: Offsetting the risk from inflation to income adequacy of benefits
1974	Elimination of the retirement and employment earnings test for retirement pensions for people age 65 to 70	Income protection: Allowing retirement recipients to continue working beyond age 65
1975	Guarantee that benefits are available to both male and female contributors to the CPP, as well as to their surviving spouses or common-law partners and dependent children	Gender equality and societal trends in income protection: Recognizing trends in public opinion, labour force participation, and changing family forms
1975	Several amendments made to the appeals system to broaden access, affordability, and flexibility	Program integrity and fairness
1976	To be eligible for disability benefits, a contributor must have contributed for any five whole or part calendar years in the last ten-year period	Income protection: Introducing flexibility in the period required to accumulate the necessary length of contributions.
1978	Permit the splitting or division of CPP credits earned by one or both spouses upon dissolution of the marriage	Gender equality and societal trends in income protection: Recognizing the work of a spouse in the home
1978	Elimination of reductions in children's benefits so that each child receives an equal amount even if there are four or more children in the family eligible for the disabled contributor's benefits	Income protection: Equalization of children's benefit contributes to financial security of family
1978	Enhanced ability, under Bill C-49, to negotiate and sign international social security agreements	Income protection
1979	First International Social Security Agreement signed between Canada and Italy	Income protection: Allows for the portability of benefits, including CPP disability pensions
1983 (retroactive to 1978)	Exclusion of periods of zero or low earnings while caring for a child under the age of seven	Gender equity in income protection: Improves the value of average lifetime pensionable earnings, typically for women, for determining benefits

Source: National Health and Welfare, *Annual Reports for the CPP*, selected years.

by the growing participation of women in the Canadian labour force and the continuing poverty among many elderly women. A third factor was the major increase in marriage dissolutions and remarriages, in the aftermath of changes to the Divorce Act in 1969, which, at that time, expanded considerably the grounds for divorce. A fourth factor was that some of these changes were first adopted by the Quebec Plan, providing a stimulus for comparable reforms to the CPP to maintain a degree of parallelism between the plans. The reverse has also occurred.[1]

The drop-out provision for child care, for example, which was introduced to the QPP in the mid-1970s, did not become part of the CPP until the early 1980s, but it was retroactive to 1978, when the Ontario government abandoned its rejection of the provision. The drop-out provision was one of two main amendments contained in Bill C-49, introduced in 1977; the other was the splitting CPP pension credits, earned by both spouses during their marriage, upon divorce or annulment. Both changes were discussed during the federal-provincial social security review process of 1973–76. The credit-splitting amendment was endorsed by all ten provinces, while the drop-out provision, which was initiated by Quebec, was endorsed by all other provinces except Ontario. The amendment did pass, with the approval of all parties in the House of Commons. This example showed that a change to the CPP could be considered and passed by the federal parliament even with the knowledge that it would not take immediate effect because of insufficient support under the amending formula of two-thirds of the provinces and two-thirds of the population of the country. In more recent times, during the prime ministerial era of Stephen Harper, this kind of federal leadership has been denied.

These changes to CPP were motivated by a need to improve the level of income protection. Some changes redefined entitlement in relation to the equality of status between men and women. The splitting of pension benefits upon marriage breakdown not only gave women fairer treatment, but also shifted the view of spouses from

1 In the early 1970s, the Quebec government decided to eliminate gradually the children's benefits under the QPP by de-indexing them. This policy change was not followed by the CPP. Later, in the 1980s, the QPP partly restored the benefits and re-indexed them, but at a lower level than the CPP benefit.

dependants of contributors to partners in marriages. Many other pension issues were discussed in the 1970s but were not taken up, most notably perhaps the complex and controversial idea of a home-maker's pension to be delivered through the CPP and QPP (Guest 1998, 188, 220–2).

The end result of the changes outlined in Table 5.2 was that disability benefits, like all other CPP benefits, were now adjusted each year to reflect the full increase in the cost of living as measured by the Consumer Price Index, a modest improvement to the quality of this social right. In addition, the contribution requirement for quali-fying for disability benefits was eased somewhat;[2] children's disabil-ity benefits were improved for a small portion of eligible families; gender equality was provided for in a range of benefits; and, with the introduction of international social security agreements, disability benefits were now portable across signatory nations.

THE GREAT CANADIAN PENSION DEBATE

In 1977, NDP Member of Parliament Stanley Knowles suggested to the federal government that the minimum contributory requirement for CPP disability benefits be reduced to a one-year attachment to the labour force. The minister of National Health and Welfare responded by referring the suggestion to the CPP Advisory Committee. In a June 1980 report, the Advisory Committee rejected Knowles's proposal of a single year's contributory requirement, although they had alterna-tive ideas, which became part of federal-provincial discussions on comprehensive pension reform in the early to mid-1980s. This is but one small example of what came to be called the "Great Canadian Pension Debate."

From 1978 to 1984, there was an extensive and intensive set of consultations, discussions, and recommendations on reforming the overall retirement income system, certain pillars of it, or specific pro-grams. Drivers behind the debate included the inadequate coverage of workers by occupational pension plans, the insufficient protection of private plans and personal savings against inflation, and deficiencies

---

2 Prior to 1976, a contributor was eligible for disability benefits after mak-ing contributions in five calendar years. As of 1976, a contributor must have contributed for any five whole or in part calendar years in the last ten-year period (National Health and Welfare 1975, 10).

in the vesting and portability of most workplace pension plans. There also was the continued precarious status and inequitable treatment of women, elderly and non-elderly alike, under the pension system. That 1981 was the United Nation's International Year of Disabled Persons was a related consideration. Federal and provincial governments as well as economic, financial, and social organizations joined the pension debate and produced "a prolonged, animated and polarized public policy review" (Deaton 1989, 107). To discern the place of CPP disability benefits within all this sound and fury, Table 5.3 offers a summary of CPP disability reform recommendations by various governmental and parliamentary bodies and business and labour organizations from 1978 to 1985.

This overview points out the subsystem character of CPP/D benefits as a policy issue in the overall pension and retirement security reform debate. Several key pension reform documents were silent on the question of CPP disability. This may not be all that surprising. Indeed, the prime focus of the retirement income policy debate was on the private pension system – with its issues of coverage, inflation protection, and vesting, portability, and survivors' benefits. Within the public system, most political attention focused on improving tax assistance for retirement savings, addressing poverty among current elderly women, and the great unresolved issue of whether to significantly expand the earnings replacement role of the CPP.

In addition, Table 5.3 reveals a correspondence between certain interests and positions on pension reform (Prince 1985). Business groups and financial industry studies mainly expressed opposition to expanding the CPP disability program, while provincial government studies paid little if any attention to this branch of the CPP. Provincial governments engaged with these reform ideas through intergovernmental arenas in response to federal proposals advanced in the early 1980s. Organized labour, along with disability organizations and political bodies at the federal level, addressed CPP disability and put forward definite proposals for liberalizing eligibility and benefits and for improving related program elements. CPP disability reform proposals addressed the policy purpose of income protection and entitlement. Issues the recommendations dealt with included whether a disability insurance program actually belonged in the CPP or was better placed in a comprehensive disability insurance program; improving awareness of, and access to the disability program; lowering the minimum contributory requirement to ease access; and that benefit levels were inadequate.

Table 5.3 Canadian thinking on CPP disability reforms, 1978–1985

Source	C/QPP Disability Reform Recommendations
Quebec Government, *Financial Security of Aged Persons in Quebec* (1978)	• Maintain current benefits • Improve benefits for those under 35 with dependent children
Economic Council of Canada, *One in Three: Pensions for Canadians to 2030* (1979)	• The federal and provincial governments should consider easing the CPP and QPP disability provisions and expanding the disability program
Federal Task Force on Retirement Income Policy, *The Retirement Income System in Canada: Problems and Alternatives* (1979)	• No specific recommendations or options
Parliament, Special Senate Committee on Retirement Age Policies, *Retirement without Tears* (1979)	• No specific recommendations • Noted that mental and physical disabilities are social problems not dealt with adequately in the private sector • Favoured increasing CPP benefits over a five-year period from increased contributions
Ontario Government, *Report of the Royal Commission on the Status of Pensions in Ontario* (1980)	• No specific recommendations • Generally opposed to raising CPP benefits
Parliament, Standing Committee on the Disabled and the Handicapped, *Obstacles* (1981)	• Expand the disability benefit by raising the flat-rate portion to that of the QPP (which had increased a few years earlier) • Ease the definition of disability in the program • Allow recipients to retain earnings and more assets without reducing benefits • In long term, implement a comprehensive disability insurance program
Government of Canada, National Pensions Conference (1981)	• No consensus or specific recommendations • Primary focus on private pensions for retirement
Canadian Labour Congress, *The CLC Proposal for Pension Reform* (1982)	• Raise the flat rate of the disability benefit to the level of the OAS • Raise the earnings-related component to 100% of the retirement benefit to which the contributor would have been entitled had they been 65 at the time of the disability

Table 5.3 Canadian thinking on CPP disability reforms, 1978–1985 (*Continued*)

Source	C/QPP Disability Reform Recommendations
Business Committee on Pension Policy (a coalition of nine business organizations), *Consensus Statement* (1982)	• No specific recommendations • Generally opposed to raising CPP benefits
British Columbia Government, *Developing a Pension Policy for the Future* (1982)	• No specific recommendations
Government of Canada, *Better Pensions for Canadians* (1982)	• Federal green paper, which noted that discussions were underway with provinces in regards to increasing the flat-rate benefit to the level of the OAS; increasing the maximum earnings-related benefit to the maximum retirement benefits; and reducing the minimum contributory requirements to contributions in one of the last two years
Joint Federal-Provincial Task Force, *Study of a Comprehensive Disability Protection Program* (1983)	• Did not make recommendations but did note that the CPP uses a strict definition of disability and that the benefits provided by the C/QPP are extremely low and payable only in the event of total disability
Parliament, House of Commons *Report of the Parliamentary Task Force on Pension Reform* (1983)	• Discussed sympathetically the need for a significant and early increase in benefits yet made no specific recommendations
Government of Canada, *Action Plan for Pension Reform: Building Better Pensions for Canadians* (1984)	• Noted discussions with provinces on federal proposals still in process
Government of Canada, *Changes Proposed to Canada Pension Plan* (1985)	• Tentative agreement between Ottawa and provinces to increase the flat-rate portion of disability benefit from $88 per month to $224 per month, as under the QPP

Source: Prince 1985; Burbidge 1987.

During the last Liberal government of Pierre Trudeau, from 1980 to 1984, pension reform was a high social policy priority, but it was competing for attention and resources against a new national energy policy, intense constitutional reform efforts, and the mounting fiscal challenges associated with a serious economic recession. The minister of National Health and Welfare, Monique Bégin, was an active champion of pension reform, favouring a significant expansion of CPP disability benefits and the liberalization of eligibility rules. The February 1981 *Obstacles* report by the House of Commons Standing Committee on the Disabled and the Handicapped called for the gradual establishment of a comprehensive disability insurance program, integrated with the CPP and QPP benefits on an actuarially sound basis. In the short term, the committee called for expanding the CPP disability benefit flat-rate component to an amount at least equal to that of the QPP; enlarging the definition of disability to include more people; allowing earnings on a sliding scale while in receipt of benefits; and providing for special needs of pensioners with disabilities.

The Standing Committee knew that the federal government would be hosting the National Pensions Conference in the spring of 1981 and suggested therefore that the conference examine all aspects of disability with respect to public and private pensions. Disability pensions were not, however, on the agenda, as the primary focus of the conference was private pensions for retirement. The conference, which was opened by Prime Minister Trudeau, examined the issues of inadequate coverage, portability, vesting, and inflation protection of occupational pension plans. A federal government position on pensions was planned for July 1981, as a follow-up to the conference, but it was delayed until December 1982, emerging as a green paper – a document in which a government sets out its thinking and invites reactions to those ideas. No doubt, the delay was due to the conference failing to achieve broad consensus on pension reform directions. High expectations for the conference were dashed by deep differences between business organizations and other groups over what the problems were and what then should be the solutions. These divisions were reflected within the Liberal government and cabinet itself between pro- and anti-CPP expansionists, anchored structurally in the National Health and Welfare and Finance portfolios, respectively.[3]

Before the federal government produced its green paper, Bégin took action in the intergovernmental arena using the recommendations and momentum generated by the *Obstacles* report. In December 1981, Bégin proposed four improvements to CPP disability for discussion at

---

3 The corporate sector in Canada was also quite angry about the 1981 federal budget, which planned the closure or tightening of numerous tax breaks for business firms. As the recession deepened through 1981 and into 1982, Ottawa's focus shifted to matters of inflation and soaring mortgage rates, deficit management, and economic recovery.

a federal-provincial conference in January 1982.[4] The proposals were, first, to raise the earnings-related part of the disability benefit from 75 percent to 100 percent of a contributor's imputed retirement pension (that is, from $230 per month to $307 per month); second, to raise the flat-rate portion so that it equalled the OAS pension (that is, from $71 per month to $228 per month); third, to lower the minimum requirements for eligibility for a CPP disability pension from five years over the past ten years to contributions in one of the last two years; and, fourth, that the CPP contributory period over which earnings-related benefits are calculated end in the month in which the contributor is deemed to have become disabled rather than three months later (National Health and Welfare, *Annual Report*, 1984; Canada, Secretary of State 1985). Presented to provincial ministers of Social Services early in 1982, the proposals were linked to a federal-provincial task force set up to examine the issue of comprehensive disability income protection in Canada.

When the federal government's green paper on the retirement income system finally came out in December 1982, it cautioned that "pension reform will of necessity be a lengthy process because of the time required for consultation, negotiation, legislation and implementation" (Canada 1982, iii). Reform proposals put forward in the green paper were referred to a parliamentary task force to allow for further public debate and consultations. With respect to CPP disability benefits, the paper noted that the federal government was already discussing improvements with the provinces. Because of the intergovernmental process, when the Parliamentary Task Force on Pension Reform reported in December 1983, it made no recommendations on disability

---

4 Health and Welfare Minister Monique Bégin accepted many though not all of the recommendations from the *Obstacles* report dealing with disability income support. On the proposal that special needs for disabled pensioners be provided under the CPP, Bégin did not agree, apparently feeling "that such a provision would involve a drastic change and expansion of the administrative structure of the CPP disability program." Such special needs, Bégin felt, were "more appropriately addressed through provincial programs" (Canada, Secretary of State 1985, 87). Likewise, the Trudeau Liberal government did not take up the recommendations that an income-tested flat-rate disability supplement be added under the Canada Assistance Plan or that an extended benefit for unemployed disabled workers be provided under the Unemployment Insurance plan.

benefits, focusing on improving assistance through RRSPs and on making it easier for people to get into occupational pension plans.[5]

The federal-provincial task force, formed in February 1982 to study the federal proposals and the wider question of a comprehensive disability insurance plan, completed its work in September 1983. Federal and provincial ministers of Social Services agreed that further policy work was warranted. "In this phase, the task force was asked to develop detailed design options for comprehensive disability protection, and to report back by December 1985" (National Health and Welfare, *Estimates*, 1986, 19). According to federal politicians and officials involved at the time, provinces were not interested in opening up the CPP to add other programs or benefits. This intergovernmental task force of officials produced further reports that, although not publicly released, did accept an increase in the CPP disability flat rate, paving the way for the 1986 legislation.

The Trudeau government's concluding statement on pension reform accompanied their final budget of February 1984. In their *Action Plan for Pension Reform* (Lalonde 1984), the Liberals concentrated on raising the minimum standards of private pensions, enhancing tax assistance for retirement savings, and improving public pensions in a few select ways. With respect to improving public pensions, the main action was a fifty-dollar increase in the monthly GIS for the single elderly, introduced in two stages in June and December 1984. On the CPP, proposed Liberal reforms included splitting of pension benefits upon marriage breakdown or when the younger spouse reached sixty-five; continuation of survivor benefits on remarriage; and the raising of pensionable earnings to the average industrial wage by 1987. The action plan noted that there was widespread public support for these changes. Other changes to the CPP were under discussion with provinces.

---

5 Interestingly, the Parliamentary Task Force on Pension Reform did devote a half page to disability benefits even though no disability organizations appeared as witnesses or made submissions. Furthermore, the CPP disability program was not an explicit part of the task force's mandate and order of reference from the House of Commons. Most political and policy attention was on tackling poverty among current seniors, especially single elderly women, and on the issue of a homemakers' pension. On disability benefits, MPs on the task force felt strongly about stressing the importance of the CPP meeting the more generous standards of the QPP at the time.

Also on the agenda were the federal proposals for improving the CPP disability benefits, and the raising of contributions to pay for the current benefits levels and future improvements. These issues, the action plan stated, "are complex and require further discussions with the provinces and other interest groups before action can be taken" (Lalonde 1984, 14). The implications of Ottawa's proposals were an almost doubling of the maximum benefits paid to contributors, which would provide income support comparable to that under the OAS, and a significant lowering of the eligibility requirements.

CHANGING GOVERNMENTS, CONTINUING PROCESSES

Although governing parties changed in Ottawa in September 1984, with the election of a massive Progressive Conservative government under Brian Mulroney, the federal and federal-provincial processes set in motion around pension reforms continued. In the Conservatives' November 1984 speech from the throne, pension reform was a prominent theme with several promises very similar to those expressed in the Liberal's final budget eight months before. These promises became concrete in the Conservatives' May 1985 budget, which announced proposed reforms to tax incentives for retirement savings and amendments to the Pension Benefits Standards Act, which governs plans established by companies in federally regulated industries. As previously planned, over 1984–85 the Department of National Health and Welfare began sending CPP contributors periodic statements on benefits earned and accumulated contributions, along with a description of the plan.

Part of the public education campaign on CPP was a booklet released jointly by the ministers of Finance and National Health and Welfare, Michael Wilson and Jake Epp. *The Canada Pension Plan: Keeping It Financially Healthy* (Canada 1985a) reassured Canadians that the CPP was on sound financial footing, but it also argued the need for an increase in contributions at an early date to keep the plan in a healthy financial state. Echoing a point made in the Liberal's *Action Plan*, the Conservative ministers' pamphlet said, "Since 1966, CPP benefits have been improved a number of times, but premiums have not gone up to pay for them. New financing arrangements will have to take this into account" (Canada 1985a, i). What this document, and many others since, failed to mention was that revisions to the contributory structure at approximately this point was anticipated at the creation of the CPP. As projected, until 1983, contributions to the plan exceeded benefits, and surpluses built up annually, augmented by the interest on past investments. In 1983 onward, contributions would not cover all benefit payments, and by the early 1990s the principal in the CPP fund would begin to decline.

Finance Minister Wilson agreed to a provincial consensus proposal that employee and employer CPP contributions be increased. In December 1985, Wilson released a document called *Changes Proposed to Canada Pension Plan* (Canada 1985b), which summarized the tentative agreement reached between the federal and provincial Finance ministers on changes in financing the CPP and on certain reforms to benefits. The flat-rate portion of the disability benefit would increase from $88 per month to $224 per month, bringing it in-line with the prevailing QPP disability benefits.

Attempting major pension reform in Canada can be a lengthy exercise. It occurs within a series of processes involving an assortment of policy actors and arenas, with varied decision-making rules, constraints, and opportunities for making or stalling change. In the areas of elderly income benefits (the OAS, GIS, and Spouse's Allowance), pension standards legislation for certain industries, and tax assistance for retirement savings (such as RRSPs and RPPs), the federal government has the authority to make changes without the approval of provinces. By contrast, the CPP as a policy area of shared jurisdiction requires proposals, consultations, negotiations, amended proposals, further negotiations, and so on.[6] When Monique Bégin left office as minister of National Health and Welfare in 1984, she had achieved notable successes, including raising the benefit levels of the GIS for the single, low-income elderly and seeing the landmark legislation,

6 In the event that both parents died or became disabled, the CPP orphan benefit of $88 per month was to be doubled in value. There was insufficient support among provinces and the federal government to expand the survivors' benefit to keep it in-line with QPP rates. Consequently, ministers agreed to leave the flat-rate portion of CPP survivor benefits at about $84 per month compared to the $275 under the Quebec Plan (Burbidge 1987, 84). Proposed changes to the CPP survivor and children's benefits were set out in a federal consultation paper in September 1987 and referred to a parliamentary committee for hearings and feedback. Negotiations occurred with the provinces on possible legislative amendments through 1988 and 1989, and, in response to provincial responses, the federal government was refining policy options into 1990. This example illustrates how pension reforms can be a lengthy process.

the Canada Health Act, enacted. Bégin skilfully used the political party dynamics at play between the Liberals and the Progressive Conservatives to get these reforms through. Viewing the GIS increases and the Canada Health Act as moves by the Liberals to embarrass them, the Conservatives supported both measures; those who remembered the Diefenbaker era saw the Canada Health Act as compatible with their past record on health policy. Bégin also spent considerable time defending existing social programs from cutbacks. This was no small achievement in the face of a serious economic recession and escalating budgetary deficits over the 1980–84 period. Reform of the CPP, however, was unfinished business.

As the lead social policy minister, Bégin had done what she could within federal jurisdiction by convening the National Pensions Conference in 1981, co-sponsoring the 1982 green paper, using a parliamentary task force on pensions to hold cross-country hearings and report back by December 1983, and getting pension reform profiled in the February 1984 budget. Bégin's department also conducted surveys of CPP disability applicants (National Health and Welfare, *Applicants Study*, 1983) and CPP disability benefit recipients (National Health and Welfare, *Benefit Recipients*, 1982) to generate up-to-date information on the characteristics and unmet needs of this clientele for use in the policy debate and cabinet decision making.[7] But time ran out for Bégin and the Trudeau Liberals. Public pension reform remained a work-in-progress within the ministerial and administrative committees of executive federalism.[8] Without doubt, though, the seeds for much of the next period of growth in the CPP disability program had been planted in the early to mid-1980s.

7 The Old Age Security program was subjected to a "6 and 5" indexation limit by the federal government over the 1982–84 period (that is, a 6% and then 5% annual limit in the increase in the consumer price index) as part of the Liberal anti-inflation strategy. The CPP was exempted, presumably because it was self-financing and its amendment would have required broad provincial support.

8 Internal program evaluations and surveys done by the Income Security Branch of National Health and Welfare found that CPP disability benefits were the single most important source for many recipients, accounting for nearly one-third of all the income reported, and that benefit levels were too low and ought to be increased.

On the larger policy record of the Trudeau era, mention should be made of two legal developments. One is that, in 1978, the mandate for the Canadian Human Rights Commission was expanded to include disabilities as prohibited ground of discrimination, and all of the provinces followed suit. This meant that disability was being viewed as more than a medical condition; it was being presented and defended as a human right issue. The second development was patriating the Canadian constitution and the entrenchment of a new Charter of Rights and Freedoms, a fundamental reform with implications for the Canadian state and politics and for disabled people. Entrenching the Canadian Charter of Rights and Freedoms in 1982 offered a challenging yet also strategic process for organizations that represented people with disabilities to obtain explicit inclusion and recognition in the Canadian constitution. Explicit constitutional reference to people with mental and physical disabilities is a tribute to the tenacious and artful efforts of disability activists in the early 1980s, finally moving the Trudeau government to add disability to the list of protected groups. Specifically, adding the phrase "physical and mental disability" to section 15 of the Charter "ensured that disablement and persons with disabilities [were] recognized politically" in equality rights and affirmative action provisions in Canadian public policy (Cameron and Valentine 2001, 35). Under section 15 of the Canadian Charter of Rights and Freedoms, which took effect in 1985 to allow the federal and provincial governments time to review and adjust their laws, people with disabilities are specifically included and guaranteed a set of equality rights. Section 15(1) states that "Every individual is equal before and under the law and has the right to the equal protection and equal benefit of the law without discrimination and, in particular, without discrimination based on race, national or ethnic origin, religion, sex, age or mental and physical disability." This equality section applies to the administration and enforcement of law, the substance of legislation, together with the procedurally fair provision (and non-provision) of benefits, be they regulations, transfer payments, or public services.

CONCLUSION

This chapter has examined the original implementation of CPP/D and initial program changes and disability policy debates over the prime ministerial era of Pierre Trudeau. According to Jim Coutts, who worked in the prime minister's office of Lester Pearson from 1963 to 1966 and then as principal secretary to Pierre Trudeau from 1975 to 1981, "the Trudeau government neither set out for, nor achieved, major social reform. It mostly held the line against the reactionary social forces sweeping through other Western governments" (2003, 18). By contrast, as Chapter 4 indicated, Coutts names the Pearson era "the most creative and significant era of social policy in modern Canadian history" (2003, 9). To be fair, the Trudeau years, at least his first few Liberal governments, were charged with the task of implementing the major social policy innovations of the Pearson years: medicare, the CPP, Canada Assistance Plan, the Guaranteed Income Supplement, and other initiatives. These governments also experienced the loss of a majority government and the challenges of managing a minority government against an economic context of rising unemployment. Social policy making is not always about transformational and innovative initiatives; in fact, bold innovation is usually the exception (Rice and Prince 2013).

The 1970s and early 1980s are perhaps best characterized as a period of implementation in the history of the CPP/D. Yet it was not only that.

Social rights of individuals to disability income are shaped by the interconnection of states, federal-provincial relations, markets, parliamentary politics, families, and gender relations. As this chapter has shown, a number of reform proposals were put forward by civil society groups, parliamentary committees, and governments, while business groups and certain provinces resisted ideas of expanding the program, and some amendments were made to the disability benefits and to the CPP appeals system. There was also the "Great Pension Debate" from 1978 to 1984, which mobilized more than a few stakeholders, although disability issues were not a central focus of the deliberations. In the intergovernmental arena in the early 1970s and again in the early 1980s, reforming disability income policy, including the CPP/D, was discussed then postponed to some unspecified future.[9] Even so, some notable changes to CPP/D did

9 Consider the intergovernmental process for examining a comprehensive disability income protection program. In February 1982 a working group of federal and provincial officials began analyzing this idea, promoted by the 1981 *Obstacles* report. Five years later, federal and provincial ministers of Social Services were still considering reports of the working group. A

occur in this period and some key reform ideas were later adopted. Full and automatic indexation of CPP/D benefits (along with other CPP benefits) made the CPP/D benefits more secure as a form of financial support against inflation, and more attractive as a public source of support than social assistance for the disabled because, as a general rule, provincial welfare programs then were not (and most still are not) indexed on a regular basis. Another reform to the CPP/D introduced greater flexibility in the required number of accumulated years of contributions in order to quality for disability benefits. In loosening the labour market dimension of eligibility for the CPP/D, this change had the effect of a de-commodification of applicants. Interest in increasing the flat-rate component of the CPP/D would also de-commodify the benefit and improve the minimum standard of support for meeting the needs of eligible disabled workers.

Even not-so-exciting routines of policy and practice raise matters of status and social stratification. The women's movement and other social groups mobilized critical issues of gender and family with respect to the CPP and CPP/D. CPP credits earned by one or both spouses were allowed to be split upon dissolution of the marriage; periods of no or low earnings while caring for children under age seven were excluded from determining the value of average lifetime pensionable earnings; and in families eligible for the disabled contributor's benefit, children's benefits were equalized if there were four or more children in the family. Relations of power between CPP/D appellants and the federal government were addressed, acknowledging aspects of administrative fairness and the realities of embodied citizens. For example, more flexibility was allowed in leave time and for granting of leave to appeal; someone could appeal on behalf of an incapacitated person; and, when the minister launched an appeal against a review committee decision, the minister would now pay

---

1987 federal document noted, in a classic statement of bureaucratic cautiousness, that the minister of National Health and Welfare had requested his departmental staff "to do some exploratory work to clarify the technical issues. When this is done, he will be in a better position to consider possible courses of action" (Canada, Secretary of State 1987, 31). Further federal and intergovernmental work on the idea of a comprehensive disability income plan carried on into the early 1990s. It then disappeared from federal government documents until revived, if only briefly, by the 1996 federal task force on disability issues.

any legal expenses incurred by the applicant or beneficiary. These changes point to the challenge of delivering social rights to disability income with bureaucratic justice. Social rights entail more than distributional systems for providing material benefits; social rights necessitate making and enforcing rules and mechanisms for dispute resolution. As Kathleen Jones remarks, "the citizen of the modern state as client-beneficiary" is consequently "a regulated subject" (1990, 788). If social citizenship means making claims on the state for certain benefits or services, it also means making appeals of decisions on applications. In the case of CPP/D, these can be called second- and third-stage claims for a right to income protection. The regulated subject exercises her or his rights through human agency in a context of many levels.

CHAPTER SIX

A Time of Progressive Conservatives: Enhancing CPP Disability in the Mulroney Years, 1984–1993

The language of citizenship is not properly about compassion at all, since compassion is a private virtue which cannot be legislated or enforced. The practice of citizenship is about ensuring everyone the entitlements necessary to the exercise of their liberty.

Michael Ignatieff, "Citizenship and Moral Narcissism"

The development of citizenship is not an evolutionary unfolding of the Spirit of some universal essence but rather the consequence of a whole series of particular conflicts between social groups and the development of social movements for rights and civil liberties.

Bryan S. Turner, *Citizenship and Capitalism*

Despite the Mulroney Conservatives' preoccupation with deficit control and expenditure restraint during their nine years in power, CPP/D and other disability programs were largely shielded from this restraint agenda and, in fact, were enriched.[1] However, while CPP benefits

---

1 Over several budgets from 1986 to 1991, the Mulroney government de-indexed and then froze the formula for determining transfer payments to the provinces for post-secondary education and health care. In 1990, they also introduced a ceiling on the federal share of increased transfers under CAP, for social assistance and social services, to Alberta, Ontario, and British Columbia, the three "have-provinces" that were not in receipt of equalization payments. Also introduced in the 1990 federal budget was an expenditure control plan, broadened and extended in the 1991, 1992, and 1993 Conservative budgets. Exempt from this control plan were elderly

were enriched and eligibility rules liberalized, federal expenditure
controls included staffing reductions in the Department of National
Health and Welfare, which resulted in an increase in a backlog in
appeals. Over this period, from 1984 to 1993, retirement income
reforms and CPP disability program developments clearly linked to
the earlier pension debates and reforms proposals. Connections were
apparent in the changes the Mulroney Conservative governments
made to minimum standards in occupational pension plans, to
increases in tax assistance for retirement savings vehicles, and to
broader definitions of disability for income tax deductions and tax
credits. The influence of previous pension debates and thinking was
equally apparent in reforms to the CPP. An intergovernmental consensus on CPP reforms was reached by late 1985 and federal legislation on these changes was approved by June 1986, with the changes
taking effect in January 1987. Pension reform also exhibited choices
and processes relatively distinctive to the Mulroney government, as
will be examined in this chapter.

SHAPING THE 1987 REFORMS

When the minister of National Health and Welfare, Jake Epp, introduced Bill C-166, the legislation to amend the CPP, he rightly called it
"the culmination of several years of consultation ... on the subject of
pension reform" with the provinces, parliamentarians, and Canadians.
Shortly after the Conservatives formed the government in September
1984, discussions between National Health and Welfare and Finance
officials on one side and provincial governments on the other "were
put in high gear." Within a year an agreement was reached. According
to Epp, four concerns dominated federal-provincial discussions:
"maintaining the long-term health of the plan's fund; second, ensuring

---

benefits (OAS, GIS, and Spouse's Allowances), veterans' income programs,
the CPP, and other special programs for persons with disabilities. However,
staring in 1990–91, and phased-in over three years, the OAS was subject to
a clawback, through the income tax system, of benefits from higher income
seniors. The CPP was exempt from the Conservatives' spending control
plan because CPP benefit outlays are not part of the federal government's
expenditures and thus do not directly affect the size of the federal budget
and any resulting surplus or deficit.

the affordability of premiums paid by working Canadians and their employers; third, adapting benefits to the changing needs of Canadians; and fourth, maintaining parallelism between the CPP and the QPP." In particular, Epp placed strong emphasis on the financial sustainability of the reforms: "improvements in social programs must always be carefully considered by the Government in light of present and projected financial considerations. Indeed, because expenditures on social programs normally involve a continuing and escalating outlay there is probably no area of spending that must be subject to more careful thought" (Epp 1986, 14250).

Legislation to amend the CPP passed swiftly through the House of Commons in June 1986, in a process and climate marked by nonpartisanship and cooperation between the government and the opposition parties.[2] With good justification, Epp called the legislation "one of the most important Bills that the Government will introduce during its present mandate." The reforms would have farreaching implications and significant improvements for many individuals, although, the minister assured, with "only a moderate impact upon long-term costs of the plan" (Epp 1986, 14251).

Among the major changes to the CPP that came into effect in 1987 were

- a new twenty-five-year financing schedule with the first increase in the contributions rate since 1966;
- a review of the contribution schedule every five years by federal and provincial finance ministers;
- flexible retirement benefits payable as early as age sixty and starting as late as age seventy;
- continuation of survivor's benefits if the survivor remarries (previously survivor benefits were terminated if the surviving spouse remarried);
- sharing of retirement pensions between spouses or common-law partners; and

2 Bill C-116 received first and second reading on 11 June 1986 and was then referred to committee for study and comments. On 26 June 1986, the bill returned to the business of the House of Commons. Three motions to amend the bill were debated quickly and agreed upon, and the bill was given third reading and approval.

- the extension of CPP credit splitting to include couples who separate from a marriage or common-law union.[3]

Other 1987 changes applied specifically to CPP Disability:

- The value of the flat-rate component of the benefit was more than doubled to equal that paid by the QPP.
- The contributory eligibility rule, which specified that contributions had to be made in either two of the last three years prior to disablement or in five of the last ten years before the disablement, was relaxed.
- The ceiling of the combined disability and survivor benefits to accommodate the higher flat-rate disability benefit was increased.
- Payment of two benefits where the earnings of both parents were lost due to death or disability, regardless of the child's marital status, was enacted. (Previously, only the higher of the two benefits was payable.)
- The time limit for the determination of disability was extended retroactively from twelve months to fifteen months.

The Mulroney government estimated that over the next year (1987–88) the increase in the maximum monthly disability benefit would help approximately 155,000 CPP disability pensioners; that the liberalized eligibility requirement would mean about an additional 5,000 people would qualify for benefits; and that as many as 5,000 people would benefit from the increased ceiling of combined disability and survivor payments (Epp 1986, 14252). A small number of individuals and families would also benefit from the changes in children's benefits and the extension in retroactivity claims.

Between the early 1980s pension debate to the 1986 legislation, core ideas for reforming the CPP disability program underwent a process of adoption, restriction, and rejection. Ideas for liberalizing the program ranged from probably the boldest vision, put forward by

3 As noted earlier, a 1978 legislative reform, which took effect in 1983 after Ontario dropped its opposition to the change, enabled the division of CPP credits between ex-spouses after a divorce or legal annulment. The 1987 reforms expanded this credit splitting to situations involving a separation of partners.

Table 6.1 Evolution of thinking toward the 1987 CPP disability reforms

Feature	Canadian Labour Congress Proposal (1982)	Federal Government Proposal (1982)	Bill C-166 Legislation (1986)
Flat-rate portion of the benefit	Increase to the level of the Old Age Security Benefit (about 20% higher than the QPP level)	Increase to the same as the QPP (from $71 to $228 per month)	Increase to the same level as the QPP (from $88 to $224 per month)
Earnings-related portion of the benefit	Raise from 75% to 100% of contributors' retirement pension	Raise from 75% to 100% of contributors' retirement pension	Leave at 75%
Eligibility requirement	From contributions in 5 of the last 10 years to 1 of last 2 years	From contributions in 5 of last 10 years to 1 in last 2 years	Contributions in 5 of last 10, or 2 of last 3 years

the Canadian Labour Congress, through Minister Bégin's proposals, to the intergovernmental consensus reached in late 1985 and contained in Bill C-166. Table 6.1 shows main features of these three plans.

This successive restriction in reform elements is understandable when a comparison is made among the national labour organization, a strong social Liberal minister in Bégin, a Conservative government focused on public deficit and spending control, and the political reality of obtaining broad provincial consent to proposed reforms. Jake Epp convinced Michael Wilson to take the idea of contributions in one of the last two years as the federal government's position on disability eligibility reform. The provinces, however, were not interested.

The similarity of proposals in substantially increasing the flat-rate part of the disability benefit indicates the wish to improve what was a much needed but modest income provision and to maintain uniformity of benefits between the CPP and the QPP.[4] The reforms eventually

4 The 1987 change in the CPP disability eligibility rule to making contributions in two of the last three years put the CPP out in front of the QPP, a difference between the two plans that was not closed until 1993 when the Quebec plan liberalized eligibility requirements for disability pensions (*Pension News* 1994, 7).

enacted originated from the earlier reform in the Quebec plan, the *Obstacles* report among others, policy analysis from within the Departments of Finance and National Health and Welfare, and inter-governmental negotiations in 1984 and 1985 on these issues and the wider CPP agenda of financing and retirement pensions. Public pension reform was not a central issue in the federal election of 1984, and the issue and debate effectively moved from interest group action and mass media coverage to the arena of intergovernmental relations.

Staying on the Front Burner

During third reading of the legislation that would become the 1987 reforms, the minister of National Health and Welfare acknowledged the desire among MPS to improve disability benefits even further and to reform the definition of disability used by the CPP, which many MPS saw as far too restrictive. The minister said, "passage of Bill C-116 does not mean that we are putting pension reform on the so-called parliamentary back burner. Rather, it stays on the front burner where Canadians generally and Members of the House will want to see the full heat retained" (Epp 1986, 14880). Over the next five years, if the CPP and the disability program were not continually on the front burner of the Mulroney government's agenda, they were never off the policy stove, always seeming to have something cooking politically or administratively. Numerous changes and innovations were initiated, all in the direction of the liberalization of benefits, rules, supports, and services. Table 6.2 outlines these changes.

While the changes enacted in Bill C-116 resulted from federal-provincial negotiations and agreement, most of the other changes came from the federal government. Some were accomplished through legislative amendments but many of the changes were done through departmental guidelines and management actions or by tax reforms. Many had a direct bearing on disability benefits or eligibility, while others had more indirect impacts.[5]

5 An example of a change with an indirect impact on CPP disability was the 1991 legislative amendment for assisting people denied a credit split as a result of provisions in a spousal agreement entered into before 4 June 1986. The amendment provides that applicants who were divorced or whose marriages annulled on or after 1 January 1987 receive the same amount of credits that they would have otherwise received.

Table 6.2 Changes to the CPP and disability program, 1987–1992

1987	Bill C-116 takes effect with various changes to CPP benefits and financing arrangements
1988	Pension Appeals Board, the *Leduc* decision on employability
1988–89	Regulation changed allowing initial decisions to be made by one official rather than a board of two, aimed at helping with backlog of appeals and improving the time for processing applications
1988	Applicants for CPP disability requested to submit medical reports from their physicians
1989	Departmental policy directive establishes written guidelines for assessing eligibility
1989	Departmental memo on medical conditions of older applicants
1990	Vocational rehabilitation pilot project for CPP recipients in two provinces
1991	Pilot project integrated with the 1991–96 National Strategy for the Integration of Disabled Persons
1991	Tax liability of CPP disability pensions reduced in federal income tax
1991	Bill C-260: Extension of CPP credit splitting to ensure that division of pension credits is a non-assignable right, not to be affected by separation agreements or court orders
1991	Bill C-116: Reform of CPP appeals system with the creation of the Office of the Commissioner of Review Tribunals
1992	Bill C-39: New 25-year schedule of contribution rates, increase in children's benefit, and several other amendments, including "incapacity" provision Bill C-57: Lifted the time limit on filing late applications
1992	Definition of earned income for RRSP contributions changed to include CPP disability pensions

In 1988, the Pension Appeals Board made a decision on CPP/D (the *Leduc* case) in which they adopted a more flexible approach to the definition of the *availability of gainful employment* than had been the accepted practice. The board found for the applicant, Mr Leduc, on the following basis:

The Board is advised by medical authority that despite the handicaps under which the Appellant is suffering, there might exist the possibility that he might be able to pursue some unspecified form of substantially gainful employment. In an abstract and theoretical sense, this might well be true. However, the Appellant does not live in an abstract and theoretical world. He lives in a real world, people[d] by real employers who are required to face up to the realities of commercial enterprise. The question is whether it is realistic to postulate that, given all of the Appellant's well documented difficulties, any employer would even remotely consider engaging the Appellant. This Board cannot envision any circumstances in which such might be the case. In the Board's opinion, the Appellant, Edward Leduc, is for all intents and purposes, unemployable. (CCH 1988, 6021–2)

This had the apparent effect of widening or easing the basis for determining the eligibility of an applicant for the disability benefit. In turn, this change led to a 1989 policy directive within Health and Welfare Canada that reflected the interpretation given to the *Leduc* decision by referring to local labour market and regional economic conditions as relevant considerations for officials to take into account when determining eligibility for CPP/D benefits. Further, a 1989 departmental memo from the director of Disability Operations to departmental adjudicators said that applicants over age fifty-five with medical conditions that did not allow them to do their own job or equivalent would now be deemed to have a disability for the purposes of the CPP (Torjman 2002). A similar change had been made to the QPP, through legislation, effective 1984, so that a disability pension became payable to persons between the ages of sixty and sixty-four who were not capable of carrying out their regular employment for health or medical reasons.[6]

At the time of the *Leduc* decision, it is fair to say that officials in Health and Welfare were not especially preoccupied with cost implications of the CPP disability caseloads. In fact, the department and successive National Health and Welfare ministers had long been under pressure to recognize "real-world" factors, such as the education and age of applicants and employment conditions, in determining the

6 As well, the 1984 reform to the QPP altered the eligibility criteria for persons between ages sixty and sixty-four who, for medical reasons, could not perform their regular employment. The test of participation in the workforce changed from contributions in five of the last ten years to not less than two years over their contributory period (National Health and Welfare, *Annual Report*, 1985, 12).

eligibility for disability benefits. The department felt obliged to respond to the *Leduc* decision, and interpreted the ruling as requiring and justifying them to move in that direction, thus liberalizing the interpretation of disability under the legislation.

During this period, federal officials took some steps on CPP vocational rehabilitation programming based on regulations that had existed since the 1970s but had never been implemented. For the 1990–91 fiscal year, a small-scale project to test the feasibility of rehabilitation provisions for disability clients was piloted in British Columbia and Ontario to support the policy goal of return-to-work. The next year, the pilot was added to the Mulroney government's five-year National Strategy for the Integration of Disabled Persons, which had as one of its themes the better inclusion of persons with disabilities in the economy (Prince 1992). The CPP/D vocational rehabilitation initiative was therefore extended to all provinces and given earmarked funds for the 1991–96 period of the National Strategy.

The Progressive Conservatives also announced a new way of treating the tax liability of CPP and QPP disability benefits. As a budget paper explained, "Recipients of Canada Pension Plan/Quebec Pension Plan disability pensions are taxed on these benefits in the year they are received, even though a portion of the benefit often relates to prior years. As a result, since the tax system is progressive, tax liabilities may be significantly higher than if the benefit had been paid and taxed on an ongoing basis from the date of eligibility" (Wilson 1991, 147). The 1991 federal budget introduced a measure to allow spreading the amount of a lump-sum payment over the years in which they were paid, thereby reducing the tax liability of the recipient. Another tax reform pertaining to CPP disability was made through the 1992 federal budget. For purposes of contributing to a Registered Retired Savings Plan (RRSP) the definition of "earned income" was revised to include CPP and QPP disability pensions. "This measure," the *Budget Papers* explained, "recognizes that CPP/QPP disability pensions replace the earnings of a disabled individual. It makes the tax treatment of these benefits consistent with the existing tax treatment of taxable long-term disability benefits from private plans" (Mazankowski 1993, 142). Through budgets over this period, the Conservatives also expanded the list of eligible expenses for the Medical Expenses Tax Credit, a tax measure of obvious importance to Canadians with disabilities. These various budget measures were all aimed at providing more equitable opportunities for income security.

LEGISLATIVE PLAYERS AND PROCESSES: THE 1992 REFORMS

Cabinet parliamentary government confers most of the constitutional and actual power to initiate policy on the executive – the prime minister and the cabinet, with the senior bureaucracy as influential advisor. Of key importance in financial matters is the fact that, with few exceptions, only the government can initiate legislation involving money. By and large, parliamentary government functions through intense partisan competition among political parties governed by strict party discipline. This feature of the House of Commons was most evident in the 1960s when the CPP was first proposed, debated, altered, and enacted. Partisanship of debate makes it awfully difficult for government and opposition parties to work cooperatively in the House.

CPP/D is a policy area that breaks from this norm of antagonistic legislative politics. The role of Parliament and of individual MPs has been something more than marginal and far from always being adversarial. At numerous times, legislative players and processes have been influential and consensual. A non-partisan, constructive approach was predominant in the 1964–65 Joint Committee work of the Senate and House of Commons on the original CPP legislation; the 1981 *Obstacles* report on disability issues and the 1983 parliamentary Task Force on *Pension Reform*; and the debate around Bill C-166 in 1986, which the minister of National Health and Welfare called in more than just a rhetorical flourish "one of the brighter spots in Parliament with all sides acting together on behalf of Canadians" (Epp 1986, 14249).

CPP disability as both a social program and a set of human issues has enabled individual MPs, on the government side as well as the opposition parties, through questions to the relevant minister, motions, and private members' bills to urge new action or reforms to the administration and policy on disability benefits. In a role akin to policy entrepreneurs, these questions and motions provide MPs opportunities to

- speak about the problems that constituents are having with CPP, pointing to actual gaps, limitations, or inequities of the disability program;
- communicate ideas from parliamentary bodies and other organizations, and promote the reform process by highlighting the need for changes to the disability program;

- draw out information about the appeals system (for example, processing time for applications, or the number of appeals in a year) and elicit statements of intentions from the minister about the CPP and the disability program; and
- bring pressure on or lend support to federal ministers in defending and improving benefits in meetings with their Cabinet colleagues or their provincial counterparts.

Government responses typically are polite, complimenting the member for their concern for persons with disabilities, but they are also deflective. Government MPS may review the history of the CPP, praise the initiatives already undertaken by the government, and perhaps add that any specific reform ideas advocated by individual MPS need to be considered within the wider context of the CPP and disability income system in Canada.

A fascinating sequence of parliamentary and disability pension politics took place in 1991 and early 1992, as summarized in Table 6.3.[7]

In September 1991, the Honourable Alan Redway, a former minister of Housing in the Mulroney Cabinet introduced Bill C-280, a private member's bill to amend the Canada Pension Plan Act. At first reading, Redway explained the bill was "aimed at a long-standing, but I believe only a technical injustice in the limitation period for making application for the CPP for disabled people" (Redway 1991a, 22468). Redway had been working on this issue since 1985, after becoming aware of the issue while door-to-door campaigning for the 1984 federal election. A constituent he met had been denied a disability benefit because he had not applied in time. This was not a new or unique problem to this individual. As a social policy expert

7 The year before, in June 1990, another private member's bill to amend the CPP, Bill C-260, in fact passed. It too came from a government backbencher, Bill Kempling (Burlington). Kempling worked in close consultation with and received assistance from the minister of National Health and Welfare and his staff as well as several officials in the department in drafting the bill. The purpose of Bill C-260 was to correct an error in the drafting of Bill C-116, which took effect in 1987. The private bill was to ensure that the division of pension credits was unaffected by court orders or separation agreements from 1978 to 1986. The National Council of Welfare, among other social policy groups, and the PC and NDP in the House of Commons, supported Bill C-260.

Table 6.3 Legislative stages of three bills on amending the CPP, 1991–92

Stage/bill	Bill C-280 Private Member's Bill	Bill C-39 Government Bill	Bill C-57 Government Bill (replacing Bill C-280)
First reading	20 September 1991	18 November 1991	14 February 1992
Second reading	26 November 1991	19 November 1991	20 February 1992
Third reading	26 November 1991	19 November 1991	20 February 1992
Outcome	Ruled inadmissible by Senate legal staff Raised by minister of National Health and Welfare at a federal-provincial meeting, and agreement secured	Received assent and became effective 1992	Received assent and became effective 1992

explained at the time, "Disability benefits are the only CPP pensions with a time limit for applying. Depending on a person's work history, the deadline can be anywhere from 15 months to six years. But once it has passed, entitlement is lost. Every year, almost 900 disabled ex-workers are turned away for applying too late. Unwilling to give up on ever working again, they had kept taking treatment and hoping for a recovery, unaware that time was running out. The unfairness of their plight is so compelling that virtually every MP has gone to bat for constituents caught in the deadline trap" (Shifrin 1992).

Redway began making representations to Jake Epp, the minister of National Health and Welfare, who apparently told Redway that this issue of "the deadline trap" would be addressed in the 1986 legislation. However, it ended up not being included in that package of reforms. Redway and other Conservative MPs then took the issue to the Health and Welfare Standing Committee and pressed for legislative action.[8] Again, the government's reply was that it would be taken up in the next round of changes to the CPP. In the second Mulroney government, a new minister of Health and Welfare, Benoît Bouchard, told Redway he was not aware of this issue, perhaps

8 Another Conservative backbench MP, Geoff Wilson (Swift Current–Maple Creek–Assiniboia), frequently raised the matter of amending the CPP's test of recency provision so that workers with disabilities who otherwise had legitimate applications for the disability pension had their applications for benefits rejected.

revealing the short and selective corporate memory of the department. Feeling that time was running out for action in the second and most likely last mandate for the Conservative government, Redway decided he had to resort to a private member's bill.

Under the system for private member's bills, if a bill is selected and deemed worthwhile by the House Management Committee, an all-party body, it receives three hours of debate and might then be put to a vote, for approval in principle, and then sent to the appropriate committee for public hearings. Redway's bill was selected but, after strong intervention by the government's house whip, was limited to a one-hour debate with no vote.

Redway wanted to change the limitation period for the CPP disability pension, thus allowing people to make a later application and to be eligible to receive a pension with the understanding that "they have made contributions for at least one-third of their contribution period." At second reading two months later, Redway acknowledged the assistance of Michael Hatfield, the legislative assistant to the previous minister of National Health and Welfare, Jake Epp, in drafting the wording of Bill C-280. The House Management Committee decided the bill would not be votable, but Redway argued that there was "no need to get the provinces' approval in advance. This bill could be passed, it just would not take effect until the provinces agreed" (Redway 1991b, 5380). While not mentioned during the debate, the child rearing dropout provision passed by Parliament in 1977, which did not take effect until 1983, was an example that supported Redway's argument.

At the fifty-five-minute mark of the allotted one hour for debate, an NDP member yielded the floor to Redway, allowing him to move the motion that the House allow the bill to pass all three stages, a motion that required unanimous consent of those present. During debate, several opposition MPs thanked Redway for his initiative and spoke approvingly of expanding access to benefits for Canadians with disabilities. The parliamentary secretary to the minister of Health and Welfare, Barbara Sparrow, called for a recorded vote. This undoubtedly helped the motion, as no MP wanted to be on record as opposing this motion. Unanimous consent was given and the bill was read a third time and passed unanimously, 196 to nil. The bill went to the Senate but was turned back there because it did not have "a royal recommendation."

In spite of this setback, early in 1992, the minister of National Health and Welfare sounded out the provinces on the proposal contained in Bill C-280 and obtained their approval. Certainly, the unanimity of the House of Commons on the reform proposal aided the federal government in attaining so quickly provincial agreement. The minister then informed the House that he would correct the anomaly identified in the private members' bill and would introduce an important amendment.[9] Bill C-57 went rapidly through all three stages in the House of Commons in less than a week in February 1992, made possible by all-party support and cooperation. The effect of the legislation was to lift the time limit on late applications for disability benefits, protecting people from non-eligibility solely on the basis of having filed a late application.

The Mulroney government's own major legislative measure on reforming the CPP was Bill C-39, which was tabled and approved rapidly in November 1991. The two main amendments were a revised twenty-five-year schedule of contribution rates, and a thirty-five-dollar increase in the monthly flat-rate benefits for children of deceased CPP contributors. As was set out in the 1987 reforms, the twenty-five-year schedule of CPP contribution rates was to be reviewed every five years by the federal and provincial Finance ministers. In 1991, the first such review was done and Bill C-39 revised the schedule with contribution rates increasing moderately faster than previously scheduled. Policy development on the children's benefit increase began with a federal-provincial working group established in 1986 to explore new approaches to survivor benefits. The next year, the federal government released a consultation report called *Survivor Benefits under the Canada Pension Plan* (Canada 1987), which was tabled in the House of Commons and then referred to a parliamentary committee. After holding hearings and inviting submissions, the committee released its report in April 1988, which, in turn, informed further federal-provincial discussions over the next few years. Early in 1991, the federal and provincial governments reached agreement on CPP financing and the children's benefit, forming the core of Bill C-39. Effective January 1992, the thirty-five-dollar lift in the children's benefit represented a 30 percent increase and was

9 In the 1970s, another private member's bill dealing with the CPP, specifically legal assistance for applicants under the appeals system, appeared in government legislation, and the backbench MP therefore withdrew his bill. See Coates 1976, 10452.

estimated to assist some 170,000 children of deceased or disabled CPP contributors.

Relevant to CPP disability programming, Bill C-39 also contained the following amendments:

- A CPP disabled contributor's child benefit would now be able to be converted, without need for application, to a CPP orphan's benefit.
- CPP children's benefits will be provided to a child who comes under the care and custody of a CPP contributor after the contributor becomes disabled.[10]
- Allow the sharing of information among the CPP, Old Age Security, and Family Allowance programs as well as in limited conditions with provincial administrations.
- Allow the reimbursement of CPP disability benefits to the administration of a long-term disability plan under approved conditions.[11]
- Change the timing for a ministerial review on disability benefit claims, the first-level appeal period, from twelve months to a three-month turn-around time.
- Grant late applicants with impairment the right to apply on the basis they were incapable of applying for the disability within the normal fifteen-month time limit, thus protecting the benefit eligibility of these CPP contributors.

When tabling this legislation, the parliamentary secretary to the minister of National Health and Welfare told the House of Commons that "these minor amendments are an insignificant cost. At the same time, they would improve administration, make limited improvements to eligibility rules and clarify certain sections of the legislation" (Sparrow 1991, 4887). The impact of these amendments in Bill C-57 turned out to be something more than minor. These changes

10   Until 1992, only a natural child born after the month of a disability and a child legally adopted after that month could receive the CPP children's benefit.

11   The intention of this amendment was to ensure that long-term disability plans operated by insurance companies or other government agencies "will be willing to guarantee payment of the full amount of the disability entitlement between the onset of a private benefit and the award of the CPP disability benefit" (Sparrow 1991, 4887).

resulted in an influx of applications and reapplications, more refusals and more appeals, driven in part by the "uploading" of potential disability clients from provincial social service departments.[12] The increase to the flat-rate component of the CPP/D benefit made it a much more interesting benefit for provinces to go after, and some jurisdictions made the effort to require all new social assistance applicants to apply for CPP disability. Provinces were also coming under more budgetary pressure to restrain their own program expenditures in the midst of the deep recession of the early 1990s. At the same time, some provinces did not seem to have a systematic interest in asking people to apply for CPP/D even if they were on the provincial disability assistance caseloads. From the perspective of the client and the province, if they were only entitled to a small amount, there was not much point applying for CPP/D because it would be completely offset by social assistance. So, along with some provincial uploading of the costs for disability clients to CPP/D, there was also general disinterest and inaction by other provincial governments in shifting costs of disability income support to Ottawa.

A RESTRUCTURED APPEALS SYSTEM FOR CPP

The Mulroney era also accomplished a restructuring of the appeals system for the CPP, which had not been substantially altered since the beginning of the plan. Calls by members of Parliament for making changes to the CPP appeal procedures were apparent in House of Commons debates from the early 1970s onwards, including various private member's bills. The general thrust of these proposals was to assist claimants in their appeals and to limit or remove the minister's prerogative to appeal a decision or recommendation made by a review committee under the CPP.[13]

---

12   The parliamentary secretary most likely used the term *minor amendments* in this context to signify that these changes were not "amendments of substance" as defined under the CPP legislation and therefore did not require the approval of at least seven provinces that represented at least two-thirds of the population of Canada.

13   In the 1970s, Progressive Conservative MP Robert Coates tried on a number of occasions to refine the appeal procedures under the CPP and to remove the minister's right to appeal decisions of review committees. For example, see the *Commons Debates*, 29 January 1976, pp. 10452–8.

Amendments to the CPP appeals system were passed in 1986 as part of Bill C-116, An Act to Amend the Canada Pension Plan and the Federal Court Act, but did not take effect until 1990–91. At that time, the Office of the Commissioner of Review Tribunals (OCRT) was established along with a new system of appointing and managing review tribunals. The previous system of review committees and the new review tribunals system are compared and contrasted in Table 6.4. Basic features of the appeals system such as role, powers, and size of the review bodies continued under the restructuring. Fundamental reforms involved the creation of the OCRT, a body relatively autonomous from the minister and the Department of National Health and Welfare, responsible for overseeing and supporting a new national network of panel of members.[14] The OCRT received an expanded mandate as of January 1997 when appeals under the Old Age Security Act were entrusted to it.

Both the original appeal system and the one established at this time espoused the principles of natural justice and procedural fairness that parties have a right to appeal an initial decision; that there be a hearing for affected parties to be heard; that there be notice of such hearings; that the rules of procedure be published and known; and that reasons be given for decisions. With the restructuring of the appeal system, however, an important dimension of natural justice was added or more fully realized – namely, the right to appeal to an independent body. The chair of the Pension Appeals Board (PAB) was granted greater flexibility in determining the composition of boards in individual cases, and allowed for appeals of PAB decisions to the Federal Court of Canada. A key difference between the two systems at this second level of appeal is that, with the formation of the review tribunals and the OCRT, applicants now had the opportunity to appeal ministerial decisions to an independent and impartial body for adjudication, agencies quite separate from the government officials and organization being appealed against.

14 Bill C-116 made reference to the position of the commissioner and the review tribunals but was silent on the formation of the Office of the Commissioner of Review Tribunals. Nor was the office mentioned by the minister or departmental officials in committee hearings or statements in the House of Commons. The OCRT itself then is not a statutory body, as one might expect for an administrative tribunal or a quasi-judicial body of government.

Table 6.4 Restructuring the second level of appeals for CPP decisions

	Review committees	Review tribunals
History	1967 to 1991	1991 to 2013
Jurisdiction	Make determinations on eligibility for persons claiming benefits under the Canada Pension Plan	Make determinations on eligibility for persons claiming benefits under the Canada Pension Plan and, as of 1997, the Old Age Security Act
Role	To hear an appeal from the decision of the minister on reconsideration	To hear an appeal from the decision of the minister on reconsideration, *de novo*
Powers	Confirm or vary a decision of the minister	Confirm or vary a decision of the minister
Number of members	Three	Three
Method of appointing members	Minister appoints one, appellant appoints one, these two select a third who serves as chair	Members are selected from a national panel of up to 400 appointed by the Governor-in-Council
Membership of bodies	Composition of specific committees determined in accordance with the legislation	Composition of specific panels determined by the commissioner in accordance with the legislation
	Ad hoc: Panel members changed with each appeal	Permanent: Panel members appointed for 2 to 5 years
	Unpaid laypersons	Professional and laypersons to be paid
Administration	Department of National Health and Welfare	Office of the Commissioner of Review Tribunals

This placed the CPP in fuller compliance with procedural require-ments of administrative justice.

Beyond concerns of natural justice, three other issues were at play.[15] First, it was felt that staff at National Health and Welfare was too involved in the process and, as a result, there was insufficient independence from the initial decision and the reconsideration. Second, from the department's viewpoint, it was often the case that the appointee for the appellant acted as an advocate rather than in an adjudicative role, and could thus strongly bias the outcome because their agreement on the nomination of the chair of the review

15 This discussion draws from communications with Simone Godbout and government officials, who I wish to thank for these comments.

committee was necessary. Third, there was no requirement for legal expertise on the review committees; so many legal errors were made. As the director general of Income Security Policy in National Health and Welfare explained, with the change from review committees to review tribunals,

> a very substantial proportion of the appeals that go to the review committee are subsequently turned down. We find that although the informal type of ... [committee] that we currently have has definite advantages ... [and] are composed of well-intentioned people, they do not know very much about how the act works. What we find happen is that eventually a lot of those people [making appeals] go up the line only to find out that they are being turned down. They may have won at the review committee levels, but that is subsequently reversed. We find that perhaps there should be a body of people on which we could draw, who have some experience in the process in reviewing cases, and perhaps this would reduce the number of reversal. (Fortier 1986, 34)

Because of these concerns the National Health and Wealth minister was appealing close to half of the reconsideration decisions. Thus, the aim of federal officials was to make the appeals system more professional, expert, and efficient. When the legislation was under consideration, these aims raised unease among labour groups and opposition MPs. The Canadian Labour Congress expressed various concerns about the proposed changes to the appeals system. First, labour leaders were not aware of any major criticisms of the then existing review committee system by CPP contributors. Second, there was no prior public discussion of the changes; and adding professionals to the tribunals may gain expertise but at the expense of informality and the perceived accessibility of the second level of appeals (Martin 1986, 22).

Opposition parliamentarians raised fears that the new system might become less flexible in interpreting who is eligible for disability benefits and no longer give the benefit of the doubt in a CPP application. Liberal MP Sheila Copps said, "I would hate to see the CPP system go the route which has plagued provincial compensation plans for years. They look at only the physiological aspect of the effect of any disease or illness. They do not look at the totality. That has been a hallmark which has served the Canada Pension Plan well" (Copps 1986, 14885). Other MPs made similar points during the debate, prompting the minister to remark at third reading of Bill C-116, "This is one area of the Canada Pension Plan which has a discretionary aspect, relative to medical advice. We must be sensitive to some of the points made in terms of discerning who is eligible for the disability pension" (Epp 1986, 14879).

OUTCOMES AND IMPLICATIONS

The liberalization of disability benefits, contributory requirements, and time limits on claims introduced through the legislative reforms of 1987 and 1992 had various outcomes, some anticipated and others unintended. For instance, as expected, the protection of applicants from non-eligibility solely on the basis of having filed a late application resulted in benefits for about three thousand applications.[16]

CPP disability caseloads grew through this period and at a faster rate than in the Trudeau era. The average monthly number of disability beneficiaries went from around 200,000 in 1987 to about 325,000 by 1993. Following on the *Leduc* decision, National Health and Welfare widened their interpretation of disability, which led to a general increase in applications across the country. The declining economy of the early 1990s surely influenced how panel members at local levels interpreted the rules for disability benefits, taking into account the real options for employment. This was surely another factor contributing to the rising caseloads. After averaging about 12 percent of total CPP expenditures in the previous ten years, adult disability benefits averaged nearly 16 percent in this period, while children's benefits stayed at under two per cent of total payouts.

In 1985, the maximum monthly disability pension was $414.13, and, in 1987, with the increase by the Mulroney government, the flat-rate portion was substantially increased from $91.06 in 1986 to

16 An example outside of the disability program pertains to the ability to draw CPP retirement benefits between ages sixty and seventy, actuarially adjusted, following the 1987 reforms. This wider choice of when to retire for the purposes of the CPP was an immediate hit with many Canadians. Almost 175,000 flexible retirement benefits were taken up by the spring of 1988. Still another example was that about 31,000 formerly ineligible recipients of survivor benefits were reinstated in the first few years following the 1987 reforms (National Health and Welfare, *Annual Report*, 1989, 6–8).

$242.95 a month. By 1988, the maximum monthly benefit was $660.94, and by 1993 it had grown to $812.85 (Burbidge 1996, 104). Total expenditures on CPP disability benefits jumped from $1.1 billion to approximately $2.5 billion between 1987 and 1993. Liberalization of CPP/D benefits and eligibility rules meant that the CPP and the QPP now differed on this area more than before, with the gap closed only after the QPP instituted similar reforms in 1993. Consequently, throughout the 1987–93 period, the CPP experienced striking increases in disability expenditures and caseloads that the QPP did not (Torjman 2002).

An unintended outcome of the large increase to the disability benefit was the shifting of costs upward from provinces and private insurance to this national program. Federal officials came to believe that, "the [CPP disability benefit] increase in some cases was partly offset by the private insurance sector or by provincial or municipal social assistance programs" (National Health and Welfare, *Estimates*, 1989, 6–15). This wave of "uploading" costs to the CPP was most likely, in large part, triggered by the significant increases in the flat-rate portion of the disability benefit in 1988.

Through the economic recession and rising welfare caseloads of the early 1990s, provincial governments became more active in searching for income support alternatives to social assistance or workers' compensation, including CPP disability payments. In part, there was synergy here as a result of cost concerns among all governments. Around this time, for example, Ontario's auditor reported that the province was not taking steps to ensure that provincial disability welfare recipients were referred to CPP. This led to a flood of applicants in the early 1990s. Struggling with their own fiscal restraint challenges, some provinces routinely advised new social assistance and workers' compensation applicants to first apply to CPP Disability. Private insurers and insurance companies, likewise, came to more systematically review their beneficiaries to see who might be eligible for the CPP (Wills 1996, 74). Insurance industry firms agreed to pass along the ad hoc increases to *existing* beneficiaries in 1987, but to offset the CPP benefit in full (as always) for *future* beneficiaries.

The 1991 restructuring of the CPP appeals system sought to achieve greater detachment in the proceedings for the two main parties, the appellant and the minister, along with better continuity in the membership of the review tribunals. As a result, the parties were treated impartially and equally, and tribunal members made more informed and consistent decisions. As before, disability pension cases continued to comprise about 95 percent of the CPP appeals during this period. With the review tribunal system established, it was expected that about 1,800 appeals would be received each year. Experience through the rest of the decade proved otherwise.

Increasing the flat-rate portion of benefits involved politically redefining the acceptable minimum for income protection provided by the disability program. As a uniform level of payment, the flat-rate portion is a benefit based on assumed average need for income, available to all who qualify regardless of their previous earnings level. By weighting payments in favour of lower-paid workers, the 1987 and 1992 benefit reforms modified the relationship between contributions paid and benefits received. So did the increase to the children's benefit of disabled contributors, since Canadian workers with children do not pay higher contributions for CPP coverage than workers without family responsibilities. That the disability program was seen to have departed too much from "true insurance principles" of private sector pension plans became part of the critique of CPP, especially from politically conservative quarters, through the rest of the 1990s (Robson 1996). Neither increasing the flat-rate component, nor increasing the children's benefit is a departure per se from the insurance principle. All CPP contributors pay for disability benefits that some will collect while others will not. Some will experience a severe and prolonged disability while they have young children, while other contributors will not. Contributors are protected against this commonplace risk through a collective pooling of contributions – an essential feature of social insurance programs around the world as well as this form of social rights of citizenship.

CONCLUSION

The prime ministerial era of Brian Mulroney and his Progressive Conservative governments has been described as "a decade of Tory cuts to the postwar social welfare system" (Brodie 1995, 9). With respect to CPP/D and disability policy more generally, however, the Mulroney years saw several positive developments. Among these were benefit enhancements to CPP/D, the easing of the contributory rules for determining eligibility, departmental moves towards a more expansive interpretation of disability, the first substantial action on vocational rehabilitation services for CPP/D clients, and significant improvements to the appeals system. The Mulroney Conservatives also introduced a number of tax measures related to CPP/D and disability. This approach to expanding disability income benefits seems to be an exception to the larger pattern of restraining the welfare state, so how is it explained? According to a political insider with profound Liberal credentials, "Mulroney had come to politics at a time of social reforms and was deeply in sympathy with them. The neoconservative clothing did not fit well on an essentially progressive leader who did not want to dismantle the social programs of the past 40 years; he simply wanted to run things for a while" (Coutts 2003, 18). In his finance minister for most of this period, Michael Wilson, Mulroney had an individual who personally understood issues of disability from his own family circumstances, much like another finance minister, Jim Flaherty, during the Harper era, which will be discussed in Chapter 8.

Of course, in 1984, the Mulroney government inherited an intergovernmental dialogue on an agenda of pension reforms that had already been underway for some time against the background of the Great Pension Debate of the late 1970s and early 1980s. A widely shared view was that disability benefits were far from adequate and that people with disabilities and their children were among the most deserving. What was required was not compassion, but rather legislation for ensuring entitlements. There was, in other words, a good degree of political momentum and political expectation of some changes. But no straightforward agenda-setting process of problem recognition took place. Conceptually, there were processes of suggestions of reforms for the CPP and CPP/D, a sifting and reshaping by state actors of options, and then the selection of some by federal and provincial governments. And there was the policy dynamic between the CPP and QPP where one or the other took the lead on a certain reform that, sooner or later, provoked action in the federal plan.

Importantly, as part of the 1987 reform package, premiums were scheduled to increase to maintain the CPP on sound financial footing. In that context, an increase in disability benefits was taken as eminently affordable. Within the large PC caucus of 1984–88, there were key disability advocates, such as Walter Dinsdale, Bruce Halliday, and Alan Redway, as well as other MPs who acted as policy entrepreneurs, pushing for solutions to problems with CPP/D that constituents had brought to their attention.

Constituents brought the material, embodied consequences of the cpp/d into play. Specifically, this chapter discussed the problem of the fifteen-month time limit to apply for disability benefits and the ineligibility of late applications. The embodied social citizen also appeared in relation to vocational rehabilitation projects launched in the early 1990s to explore the possibilities of a return to work for some cpp/d clients.

With the 1987 and 1992 reforms to the cpp benefits, which carried significant and lasting cost implications, governments were especially concerned with the adequacy of benefits. As a result, "cpp disability benefits ... gained attention for two reasons that were not foreseen in the mid-1980s. First, there has been some concern that recent increases in cpp disability claims might reflect the use of cpp disability as a 'de facto' early retirement program. Second, changes in assumed rates of disability ... raised the long-term estimates of the contribution rates required by the cpp" (Baldwin 1996, 72). The 1987 reforms also reduced the cpp reserve from three years to two years of equivalent benefit payments, an issue that would surface in the next period of policy debate surrounding the cpp and the cpp/d.

CHAPTER SEVEN

The Chrétien and Martin Governments: Program Retrenchment and Reorientation, 1994–2005

One of the most important policy initiatives ever undertaken in Canada was the decision over three decades ago to establish the Canada Pension Plan. The CPP is about our values as a nation. It is about the sharing of risk and the security of benefits.

Hon. Paul Martin, Minister of Finance

Inclusion and exclusion represent the two sides of citizenship's coin.

Ruth Lister, *Citizenship: Feminist Perspectives*

From 1994 to 2005, Canadian pension reform shifted from a discourse and agenda of expanding coverage of earlier times to a politics of heading for cover. This age reflects a trend apparent in many governments and social policy areas to financial restraint and cost containment as strategic priorities.[1] Writing early on in this period, Bob Baldwin stressed the importance of seeing contemporary pension debates "in the context of the wider swing to the political right and the positive currency that is associated with liberalizing market forces. The interest that is being shown in downsizing public pensions

---

1 During the 1990s, the eligibility and benefit features of public pension plans and other social security programs tightened in most European countries (Bonoli 2000; Clasen 2001). In the United States, the Reagan administration, in the early 1980s, retrenched social security benefits for persons with disabilities, cancelling income benefits and medical care to some three hundred thousand beneficiaries (Chambers 1985).

is hardly a stand-alone event. Public pensions are merely taking their place in the line-up of social programs, and other government programs as well, that are going through the downsizing ringer" (Baldwin 1997, 193).

Among governments and the general public, unease appeared to be growing over the future viability of the CPP, financially and perhaps politically across generations. While concerns about the fiscal sustainability and affordability of the CPP in general had been a recurring issue among policy makers through the late 1970s and 1980s, similar financial worries about the disability program arose only in the 1990s. As the previous chapter noted, CPP disability expenditures had more than doubled from 1987 to 1993 and disability caseloads reached a historic peak in 1993–94. In 1996, with the federal-provincial-territorial review and consultation on reforming the CPP, the size of the disability component had become a political issue and figured in plans for controlling the costs of the CPP overall.

By this time, a whole series of administrative steps were underway or in place that had a profound effect on disability caseloads and the appeals system. The *Leduc* decision, which saw a "real-world" approach to severity in deciding whether an applicant to CPP/D is incapable of pursuing any gainful employment, was superseded by a subsequent ruling that held that factors relating to social and economic circumstances should not be considered in the determination of disability under the CPP. This started affecting decisions immediately and was codified in revised administrative guidelines formally issued in 1995. A major intake of nurse adjudicators in the early 1990s gained expertise and, coupled with the implementation of the review tribunal reform, gave stronger confidence in the accuracy of the appeals system. By 1995–96, a decline in the growth rate of the caseload was visible in program statistics, and this slowdown continued until the caseload levelled off and actually began to decrease. However, the chief actuary's report, which was published in February 1995 but only accounted for events up to December 1993, projected a massive increase in the disability caseload based on past experience. This analysis strongly influenced the federal-provincial discussions on CPP reforms from late 1995 through to early 1997. In an effort to control program costs, reforms in 1998 further tightened the administration and eligibility for disability benefits.

CRITIQUES AND CONSULTATIONS

In several respects, the pension debate of the mid-1990s differed from the "Great Canadian Pension Debate" of the early 1980s, as Table 7.1 outlines. Whereas the Great Debate stressed options for improving benefits and introducing new ones, pension reform talk in the mid-1990s, including successive federal budgets, emphasized fiscal limits of the state and financial distress anticipated for the CPP and the old age benefit programs. Suggestions for reforming the CPP ranged from radical structural changes that included abolishing the plan to modifications of the present system that commonly called for increasing contribution rates, raising the retirement age for the full pension, removing the disability and survivor benefits from the CPP, and reducing benefits.

In this era of Liberal federal governments, pension reform was not as high priority as it had been a decade previous. The federal governments didn't devote as much time to pension reform, and the radius of related issues on the policy agenda narrowed. Because of the tighter time frame for dialogue, and the political stress placed on reducing the federal deficit and public debt – a defining element of the new political climate – disputes over competing ideas for reforming the CPP were relatively muted in formal discussions and media coverage.

A pension debate of sorts did occur in the mid-1990s, but it was more like a scripted talk than a grand clash of contending visions and interests. Viewpoints of social policy groups were less prominent and even marginalized in the process, since they tended to argue for further enhancements to benefits and the liberalization of eligibility rules, which government officials regarded as out of touch with the fiscal imperatives facing Canadian governments. In 1993, National Health and Welfare became Human Resources Development Canada (HRDC), which included a new focus on labour market policy and a less prominent role in pension policy making in Ottawa. In contrast, reports on the CPP by the Office of the Auditor General of Canada and the chief actuary to the plan were influential in setting the tone and parameters of the pension reform discourse, as were studies by various business groups and institutes that stressed the restraint theme.

Seeds of the decreased involvement of social policy groups and the decline of social governmental departments started earlier in the

Table 7.1 Comparing pension debates: The Great Canadian Pension Debate of the 1980s and the pension reform talk of the 1990s

	Great Canadian Pension Debate	Pension Reform Talk
Time Period	1977 to 1985	1994 to 1997
Key participants	National Health and Welfare, Finance Canada, provincial governments, parliamentary committees, financial industry, insurance industry, business associations, organized labour, women's groups, seniors groups, disability groups	Finance Canada, Human Resources Development Canada, chief actuary, auditor general of Canada, provincial governments, business associations, think tanks
Retirement policy issues on government agendas	• Better pensions for women and homemakers • Improved private pension coverage, indexing, vesting, and portability • Increased tax assistance for retirement savings plans • Alleviating poverty among current seniors • Improved CPP disability and survivor benefits • Maintaining universality of Old Age Security	• Controlling rising costs of public pensions • Maintaining protection of low-income seniors • Better targeting of Old Age Security by income testing benefits
Political climate	• Strong public confidence in public plans • Critical attention to the deficiencies of occupational pension plans and the lack of private sector coverage • Beginning to shift away from progressive social policy making, but still a sense that pension reforms can and should be done • Wide support for a mix of personal and public responsibility for retirement income and pensions	• Apprehension that pension benefits won't be there in the future • Strong preoccupation by governments with deficits and the financial sustainability of CPP • Little critical analysis of private pension plans or of continued poverty among some seniors • Shift to individual responsibility • Rhetoric about intergenerational acrimony

Sources: Baldwin 1996; Prince 1996.

1985–86 round of CPP negotiations. Basically, the role of finance departments grew and those of social policy departments diminished at federal and provincial levels. Contributions and funding became prominent and eventually the central issues in public pension reform, reinforced by the review cycle of contribution rates by finance ministers that gave them an increasing say over the benefits structure. Nonetheless, the program design expertise and administrative knowledge of the CPP residing within HRDC was needed throughout this process, and the input of the HRDC minister as the lead social policy minister, and the influence of external social policy organizations, cannot be assumed to have been trivial given the actual benefit changes made compared to those proposed at the start of the 1996 consultations and negotiations.

Table 7.2 lists a series of federal government documents from 1994 to 1997 that addressed reforming the CPP and the CPP/D program. The leading policy goals and perspectives of the documents are also noted.

The Chrétien Liberals' first budget set out the principles for the government's plan to reform Canada's social security system. The government sought to create a system "that better rewards effort and performance and offers incentives to work," while "continuing to offer security to those in need" and a "financially sustainable" social security system (Martin 1994, 19). In an early statement previewing a comprehensive review of social policy, the government referred to a bundle of values that would guide the review. The main emphasis for pension reform, though, was signalled by Finance Minister Paul Martin in his *Budget Speech*, where he indicated that the government was examining changes required to the public pension system to ensure that it remained affordable.

Reports on the Canada Pension Plan by the auditor general of Canada understandably drew attention to financial and administrative matters. In his 1994 and 1996 annual reports, the auditor general criticized the management of disability benefits, suggesting that the disability program was too loosely controlled and potentially subject to considerable fraud because of imprecise program objectives and incomplete information systems. The auditor general expressed concern that significant changes to disability eligibility practice came via guidelines rather by legislation, which properly requires formal consultations with the provinces coupled with the production and consideration of actuarial estimates.

Table 7.2 Federal government critiques of the CPP, 1994–1997:
An overview of key documents

Document	Policy Goals and Perspective
The Budget Plan, February 1994	Financial sustainability Return to work Income protection
Auditor General Reports, 1994 and 1996	Program integrity
Social Security Review, *Persons with Disabilities, A Supplementary Paper,*1994	Return to work Program integrity and efficiency
Chief Actuary, *Fifteenth Actuarial Report on the Canada Pension Plan, at 31 December 1993*, February 1995	Financial sustainability
Budget Speech, February 1995	Financial sustainability
"An Information Paper for Consultations on the Canada Pension Plan," February 1996	Financial sustainability Income protection
Report on the CPP Consultations, June 1996	Financial sustainability Program accountability
Federal Task Force on Disability Issues, *Equal Citizenship for Canadians with Disabilities: The Will to Act*, October 1996	Return to work Program flexibility and coordination A comprehensive disability income plan
Budget Speech, March 1996	Financial sustainability
The Budget Plan, February 1997	Financial sustainability Maintain income protection

Based on these critiques, the auditor general recommended that HRDC make greater efforts at checking disability claimants for the purpose of ensuring genuine applications, detecting fraud, and recovering overpayments. The auditor general also expressed concern over the length of time taken to handle applications, reconsiderations, and appeals. In response, the HRDC established a unit to verify the continuing eligibility of pension recipients, revised its quality assurance process, and took other related actions to improve service delivery. The auditor general also added his voice to the chorus about the aging of Canada's population and the consequent need to sharply raise employer and employee contributions to maintain the CPP over the next generation.

When the Liberals released their green paper "Improving Social Security in Canada" in October 1994, the CPP and other elderly benefits were explicitly excluded from this review. The intended focus of this social security review was on post-secondary education, employment, income assistance, and social services. As a consequence, pension reform was not a part of what turned out to be perhaps the widest ever public consultation exercise on federal social programs through the autumn and early winter of 1994–95. Public pension reform was largely overseen by the minister of Finance. All the same, a supplementary paper was released late in 1994 that dealt with persons with disabilities, including the CPP program (HRDC 1994). The supplementary paper gave no attention to the income support goal of the CPP, concentrating primarily on the return-to-work goal and secondarily on program integrity and efficiency. The paper noted the problem of persons applying for CPP and QPP disability benefits having to be classified as "unemployable" or "incapable of supporting themselves." Thus, disability beneficiaries who tried to return to work stood to lose their benefits entirely. To improve the incentives for beneficiaries to return to the paid workforce, the paper reported that HRDC was at that time conducting a review of the CPP/D program (HRDC 1994, 20).

The Liberals' perspective on pension reform emerged in general terms through the February 1995 federal budget. Their focus would be on the Old Age Security (OAS) and the CPP, motivated by a purpose to control the "rising costs" of these programs. A public consultation process was mentioned, though not described in any detail, and the government stated its intention to have reforms legislated to take effect in 1997. "Concerning the CPP," the finance minister declared, "the most recent actuarial report was released last week and it leaves no doubt that we will have to take steps to ensure that plan continues to be sustainable. This we shall do when we sit down this Fall with the provinces to review the CPP" (Martin 1995, 20).

A shift in the official politics of pension reform became strongly apparent in the finance minister's May 1996 federal budget speech, which chided previous governments for not taking proper action on financing the CPP. Martin expressed concern over a potential crisis and promised to consult with other governments in taking action to slow the growth rate of CPP expenditures. Martin declared gravely, "Canadians feel our very way of life is at risk. They look at Medicare – and feel it is threatened. They look at the pension system – and wonder if it will be there in the years to come" (1996, 3). He continued, "Confidence in the pension system must be restored. The party that put pensions in place for this country must now act to preserve them. The challenge is clear – it is one of sustainability. First, the CPP must be put on a sound financial footing – and done so in a way that is sustainable, affordable and fair" (Martin 1996, 12). Martin again referenced the latest report by the chief actuary to make the argument that "changes are needed to restore the CPP to health. Clearly governments should have acted some time ago to address this problem. We believe the role of government that is responsible is to act to prevent problems, rather than letting them become crises. And so, together with the provinces and the territories, we will act" (Martin 1996, 13).[2] It could have been argued quite reasonably that the early amendments to the CPP were guided by actuarial analyses and took place before the financial aspects were seen as serious consideration, and that the amendments made in the mid-1980s did occur in the context of a rescheduling of contribution rates. Such an explanation of the issue was not the dominant political frame chosen, however.

Task Force on Disability Issues

The creation of the Task Force on Disability Issues was prompted by the Chrétien government's response to the House of Commons' Standing Committee report on the 1991–96 National Strategy for the Integration of Persons with Disabilities. That response put forward the message that there was little if any future role for the

2 In a 1996 report, the chief actuary indicated that, without modifications, the CPP fund would be depleted by 2015 and that, by 2030, the combined contribution rates would have to increase to 14.2 percent to cover the growing benefit costs. Changes to the CPP in 1987 added an automatic provision for taking changes in actuarial experience into account even in the absence of federal-provincial agreement on what to do. However, the provision could only affect contribution rates twenty years out, bringing contributions to the necessary level over the medium term. When the 1996 actuarial report projected an exhaustion of reserves by 2015, the need to negotiate a federal-provincial deal to maintain the funding integrity of the plan was not really a matter of debate. To reach a deal, the challenge for Ottawa was to find a high degree of consensus among governments of all political stripes – hence the strong rhetoric by federal politicians and officials of urgency and crisis of confidence among Canadians.

federal government in disability issues, a viewpoint expressed by the minister of Human Resources Development of the day, Doug Young. In addition, significant changes to various public programs provoked growing public anxiety that basic rights of social citizenship were threatened. This sparked considerable unrest within the disability community in Canada and among many Liberal MPs, who believed that Ottawa had an ongoing if not increasing obligation to this vulnerable group of Canadians. This led to the involvement of the Prime Minister's Office on the file and the idea of the task force. In June 1996, HRDC Minister Young, Finance Minister Martin, and National Revenue Minister Jane Stewart announced the formation of a task force of four Liberal MPs to examine issues relating to the disability community, chaired by New Brunswick MP Andy Scott. The MPs were asked to report on the future role by federal government as it related to the Canadian disability community.

The task force was given four months in which to consult with individuals and groups, conduct any research, and complete their report. Six working groups were established to study issues and options, one of which was on income support, and report back to the task force before it held community consultations. During August and September 1996, the task force held fifteen forums from coast to coast and heard from about two thousand people through briefs and presentations. Several research papers by academics and experts were also commissioned.

In their October 1996 final report, *Equal Citizenship for Canadians with Disabilities: The Will to Act* (also called the Scott Report), the task force reaffirmed the critical role that the federal government should play in disability issues in the country. The task force linked a secure income for people with disabilities directly to Canadian citizenship, arguing that "the federal government was the first Canadian government to make a disability income available [a debateable claim, actually]; it remains the only government that has the potential capacity to offer a disability income that is available to all Canadians with disability, wherever they live and wherever they may move to in this country" (Federal Task Force 1996, 6:1). With its reference to national public policy and universal coverage for all people with disabilities in the country, this is a classic formulation of social citizenship linked to the national political community.

Along with CPP/D, the task force noted that Canada's disability system was a complex and inadequate patchwork of public and private sector programs, with gaps and overlaps in objectives and outcomes. Like earlier studies on this issue, such as the 1981 *Obstacles* report, the task force expressed the need to consider as a long-term reform a comprehensive disability insurance income plan administered by the federal government. "For many reasons, including fiscal constraints," however, the task force concluded, "the implementation of a universal, comprehensive program may not be appropriate at this point in time. Nevertheless, we will, no doubt, have to consider this option seriously sooner or later" (Federal Task Force 1996, 6: 3).

In the short to medium term, the Scott Report proposed a number of actions to promote workforce participation by people with disabilities and to improve program efficiencies and coordination, including implementing measures to ensure that the assessment and application procedures of CPP/D made it possible to identify and quickly refer clients who would be better served by active employment services, and integrating the CPP/D more closely with other earnings-replacement programs, such as Employment Insurance (EI) and Workers' Compensation and private insurers, to increase information sharing and reduce administrative duplication. The previous Unemployment Insurance program was revamped and renamed EI in the mid-1990s, though the sickness benefit was left untouched by these reforms. The contribution to CPP disability policy development by the task force is suggested, in part, by some of the changes later made – in particular, measures on vocational rehabilitation, information-sharing agreements, and earnings exemption for CPP disability claimants. More broadly, the task force helped to kick-start the federal-provincial process for replacing the Vocational Rehabilitation for Disabled Persons with the Employability Assistance for People with Disabilities program and, in arguing for a better recognition of the additional costs incurred by Canadians with disabilities, encouraged a series of tax assistance reforms in subsequent federal budgets (Prince 2001a, 2001c).

The 1996–1997 Intergovernmental Review of CPP
and the Ministerial Task Force

Legislative reforms made to the CPP in 1998 were preceded by two years of federal policy analysis, public consultations, intergovernmental bargaining and agreement, and parliamentary process. Table 7.3 presents the main events and timeline for this series of processes.

Table 7.3 The 1996–1997 CPP review and reform processes

Date	Activity/Event
1995	Federal Department of Finance modelling the costs and impacts of various options for changing the contribution schedule, various benefits and eligibility requirements, and investment policy
9 February 1996	"An Information Paper for Consultations on the Canada Pension Plan" released by federal, provincial, and territorial governments
6 March 1996	Federal budget outlines federal views on CPP reform
28 March 1996	Chief federal representative to consultations, MP David Walker appointed
15 April–10 June 1996	Public consultations held in all provinces and territories
18 June 1996	*Report on the Canada Pension Plan Consultations* presented to ministers
4 October 1996	*Principles to Guide Federal-Provincial Decisions on the Canada Pension Plan* released by governments
14 February 1997	*Securing the Canada Pension Plan: Agreement on Proposed Changes to the Canada Pension Plan*
14 February 1997	Draft legislation to amend the CPP tabled in the House of Commons
18 February 1997	Federal budget
28 April–2 June 1997	General federal election: Liberals returned with another majority government
25 September 1997	Legislation to amend the CPP, Bill C-2, the Canada Pension Plan Investment Board Act, tabled in new Parliament
October–December 1997	Legislation examined by the House of Commons and the Senate as well as the House of Commons Standing Committee on Finance and the Senate Committee on Banking, Trade and Commerce
18 December 1997	Bill C-2 receives royal assent
1 January 1998	Legislation takes effect, some parts retroactive to January 1997, others in January and April 1998

In 1996, as part of the statutory review of the CPP, which the federal and provincial/territorial governments must do every five years, governments agreed to a joint process of public consultations across the country.[3] David Walker, a Liberal MP and previously parliamentary secretary to the minister of Finance, co-chaired the special panel as the chief federal representative to the consultations. Despite the title, Walker was a parliamentarian, not a member of the government. In other words, he was a backbencher with a special appointment.

The panel was in effect a ministerial task force that reported directly to the government rather than a parliamentary committee, and thus it worked more closely with the public service, especially the Department of Finance. With Walker, ten other MPs and nineteen elected representatives from provincial and territorial governments served on a rotating basis, enabling governments to co-chair the joint hearings as they toured across the country. A secretariat was established, supported by the federal government, to maintain the consultation process. Several provinces held additional hearings of their own, and Quebec engaged in a parallel process related to the QPP. The ultimate package of changes for the QPP was virtually identical in terms of the long-term funding strategy and contribution rate increases, although these were not as explicitly enshrined in the QPP legislation.

Ostensibly, the aim of the consultations was to canvass views on a range of options for ensuring the financial sustainability of the CPP for future generations. The options presented in what was called a joint information paper, titled *Securing the Canada Pension Plan* (Canada, Finance Canada 1997), all dealt with various restraints or cuts to the CPP, combined with a major shift in the funding principles of the plan via private investment, partial funding, and accelerated contribution increases to create a "steady state" contribution rate. More than information was being presented in the paper, however. The unmistakable emphasis was on reducing costs by reducing the level of benefits and by tightening the access to benefits.

On CPP/D benefits and eligibility, the paper noted payments had doubled between 1987 and 1994 and that, while administration and guidelines had been tightened and claims had slowed, concerns

---

3 One of the 1998 changes to the federal legislation was that intergovernmental reviews of CPP are now required every three years rather than every five years.

remained. Several options for reducing projected disability expenditures were identified: (a) reduce the CPP disability benefit of those receiving benefits from Workers' Compensation Boards by 25 percent; (b) tighten the eligibility period for new applicants to four of the last six years; (c) convert disability benefits to an actuarially reduced retirement pension at age sixty-five so that persons on disability benefits receive a retirement pension of the same value as persons who have been out of the workforce and are receiving early retirement benefits; (d) disallow disability claims for a disability occurring up to six months after a person has starting receiving early retirement benefits; and (e) for those persons receiving a disability pension, base their retirement pension on the maximum pensionable earnings at the time of their disablement rather than at age sixty-five. At the time, the National Council of Welfare (NCW) commented that the proposals "appear to be little more than mean-spirited ways of putting the squeeze on people with disabilities" (NCW 1996, 29). The NCW saw these proposals as tinkering rather than deep thinking, and the council urged governments to postpone changing CPP/D pensions until a review of all disability programs was done, including the option of "taking disability pensions out of the Canada Pension Plan and creating a broader national disability insurance plan" (NCW 1996, 30).[4]

The ministerial task force held 33 public hearings in 19 cities across the country. In all, the task force received 140 written submissions and heard 270 formal presentations. Close to 6,000 inquiries or comments were recorded on a 1–800 information line. In addition, a special one-day session on disability issues was held, led by HRDC officials. This special session was planned because of disability community pressure and because, officially, the task force was not picking up enough ideas or options on where governments should go next on disability programming. Firm recommendations did not come from the disability session, but the testimony contained

4 Interestingly, the premiers (except for Quebec's) had put forward a proposal for a national income benefit for persons with long-term disabilities in 1996. Yet again in the modern history of disability policy in Canada, a federal-provincial working group of officials formed to explore the idea. What resulted were the modest suggestions of better harmonization of existing income programs and the removal of work disincentives in these programs (Torjman 2001).

ideas such as the need for better working relationships between the provinces and the private sector insurers.

Most provinces appointed relatively junior people to co-chair the task force, enabling Walker, with strong advisory support from Finance, to be the consistent public communicator on the range of intricate issues dealing with the CPP. The task force held roundtables at which associational groups submitted their positions and were challenged by the task force to explore and consider shared solutions. The consultations revealed several things: the CPP's complexity as a program; its deep popularity as a national social policy by the public; its low priority among most provincial governments; a strong concern from organized labour that the normal retirement age for a pension under the CPP be left at age sixty-five, rather than raised to sixty-six or higher as was being proposed by some groups; and, that within the CPP, the disability program was important but not that well-understood by the general public.

In contrast to CPP policy reviews in the 1980s or earlier, the federal government went into this consultation with no clear vision of what it wanted to achieve, aside from restoring confidence in the plan and restraining costs. Finance department officials felt the CPP was being abused and wanted it restricted. They effectively focused the review on the level of contributions, the stability of benefits, and the overall sustainability of the plan. HRDC had been tightening administration since 1994 and believed it was working. However, their program data were eighteen months behind (due to dealing with the increased caseloads and the impact of staff cuts from government restraint measures), and they could not show that their changes were working. This enabled Finance to keep their version of the issues on the top of the agenda. Finance Minister Martin wanted to achieve a 10 percent reduction in the projected growth of CPP expenditures and to keep the combined contribution rate increases to less than 10 percent. In this context, the goals of HRDC were basically defensive in nature: to preserve the basic design and integrity of the plan by avoiding any big changes, and to avoid political flashpoints arising from client concern about the future of their benefits.

In the joint consultation task force's final report, one of the main themes was, in their words, the "escalating disability costs." The topic of disability benefits generated a great deal of "often detailed and emotional discussion" at most meetings. The final report did not say whether such emotional discussion was regarded as valid, though the comment does reveal the passionate and embodied subjectivity of citizens. "Many Canadians," the report stated, "are concerned about the recent rapid escalation of the cost of disability benefits. Many favour moving the disability benefits outside the CPP – some because they favour the creation of a separate comprehensive system of support for the disabled; others because they believe disability benefits threaten the key purpose of the CPP which is to provide retirement pensions" (Canada 1996b, 13). "To protect retirement pensions as much as possible," the task force added that, "it was frequently suggested that the other benefits provided by the CPP – disability, survivor, and death benefits – should be scrutinized first and reduced, eliminated, or moved out of the CPP" (Canada 1996b, 41).

Further into the report, more significant findings are revealed about the disability program. Contrary to the main theme on disability, as presented by governments, several groups told the consultation panel that disability benefits should remain within the CPP. Their concern was that persons with disabilities "may not be better served in a separate plan which could be subject to political and economic influences" (Canada 1996b, 18). A related theme apparent in but not highlighted by the task force report was that contributors with disabilities were being unfairly blamed for the rising costs of CPP. Indeed, many participants in the consultation disagreed with the idea of making any reductions to the disability benefits, arguing that the benefits were not overly generous and should be at least maintained, if not improved. Disability groups furthermore opposed any accelerated increase in the contribution rates and called for greater attention to re-employment strategies for CPP/D clients. On the options presented in the information paper for reforming disability benefits, the consultations found many presenters supported reducing the overlap or stacking of CPP/D and WCB benefits. Groups were divided on the issue of tighter eligibility requirements, although the notion of greater attachment to the labour force resonated with some participants (Canada 1996b, 47–51).

Following the consultations, federal and provincial/territorial finance ministers participated in a series of intergovernmental meetings to negotiate a consensus on changes. Early in October 1996, finance ministers released a statement of principles to guide their decision making on reforming the CPP. One such principle stated, "The CPP is an earnings-related program. Its fundamental role is to help replace earnings upon retirement or disability, or the death of a spouse – not to redistribute income" (Canada 1996a, 1). An implication of this benchmark would be to rule out any increases to the disability benefit, especially the flat-rate component. If workers with disabilities and their families needed additional financial assistance, that should be done through the income tax system and income-tested programs funded from general revenues, not through the CPP. Another principle said that disability benefits are an important feature of the CPP, but that "it must be designed and administered in a way that does not jeopardize the security of retirement pensions" (Canada 1996a, 1).

In February 1997, Martin announced that a federal-provincial consensus on reforming the CPP had been reached. Ottawa, eight provinces, and the Northwest Territories supported the reforms, to take effect January 1998, while the NDP governments of British Columbia and Saskatchewan dissented.[5] These two provinces were opposed, in principle, to any cuts to CPP benefits. Quebec was prepared to go along with whatever the majority of the other provinces supported. Facing similar pressures in the QPP, the Quebec government privately supported the federal reform proposals but did not wish to do so publicly for political reasons. When a reform package was agreed to, Quebec announced changes to the QPP, comparable to the changes to the CPP. Agreement on the CPP was largely based on private negotiations among governments, informed by actuarial analyses of projected costs, and partly shaped by reactions during the public consultations.

The consultations revealed something of the political limits of making direct cuts to CPP benefits and tempered the scope and depth of cuts initially targeted by Finance Minister Martin and his senior officials. Neither raising the retirement age nor cutting retirement benefits directly or through de-indexation was popular with the public or politically risk-free, so the focus on making the CPP "financially sustainable" shifted to putting together a series of smaller changes on the eligibility side that would generate savings.

---

5 Probably because two provinces opposed the changes, Ottawa mentioned the NWT as part of the consensus group in press releases and public statements, even though territories do not have a formal vote in CPP amendments.

In the 1997 federal budget, Martin trumpeted the intergovernmental consensus on reforming the CPP and outlined the principles that had guided the reforms. These principles included the following:

- Governments must tighten administration as a first step towards controlling costs.
- The CPP must be affordable and sustainable for future generations. This requires fuller funding.
- Disability and survivor benefits are important features of the CPP. However, they must be designed and administered in a way that does not jeopardize the security of retirement pensions. (Martin 1997a, 119)

The language and meaning of this final principle indicates the status of the disability program as supplementary to the retirement pension, as the benefit for "citizens of that other place." This perspective became apparent in 1997 with Bill C-2, the legislation to reform the CPP.

MAJOR CHANGES TO CPP AND CPP/D, 1998

When presenting Bill C-2 to the House of Commons Standing Committee on Finance in October 1997, Finance Minister Martin described the message from the public consultations in these words: "The clearest message we heard is that Canadians want, Canadians need, and Canadians count on the Canada Pension Plan. They told us they want the CPP fixed now and fixed right – not left to drift, not privatized, and not scrapped as some have suggested. And they told us to fix it in a way that does not pass on an unbearable cost to younger generations." He added, "Canadians told us to 'go easy' on benefits. Canadians recognize the need for adjustments, but most do not want to see any dramatic changes" (Martin 1997c, 2–3).[6] Retirement pensions were left virtually untouched, while disability benefits and the other supplementary benefits were affected by the 1998 reforms. Anyone receiving CPP retirement pensions, disability

6 The National Council of Welfare made a similar observation about the impact of the public consultations on government thinking: "Representations to the committee reportedly caused governments to think twice about cuts in a variety of CPP benefits" (NCW 1996, 31).

benefits, survivor benefits, or combined benefits as of the end of 1997 was not affected by the changes. In addition, all benefits remained fully indexed to inflation. These decisions were guided by the principle of social equity and the political acumen of containing dissent. The principal changes to the CPP overall were as follows:

- Moving from pay-as-you-go financing to fuller funding. Contribution rates were scheduled to rise from 5.85 percent to 9.9 percent of contributory earnings by 2003 (rather than the previously scheduled rise to 7.35 percent in 2003) and then remain steady, rather than the projected rise to 14 percent or more by 2030.
- Investing the CPP reserve fund in a portfolio of market securities to get higher returns, something that the QPP has been doing since the start of that plan, and with the reserve managed by an investment board at arm's length from governments. The fund will grow in value from the equivalent of two years of contributions currently, to about five years of contributions.

That expenditures on disability benefits had more than tripled and the number of beneficiaries almost doubled from 1987, when the last reforms were made to the plan, no doubt prompted governments to alter the disability program. A comparison of the pre-1998 and the post-1998 reforms to the CPP, as they directly relate to disability benefits, are given in Table 7.4.

To disability benefits and eligibility, several changes were made: retirement pensions and the earnings-related portion of disability and survivor benefits were now based on the average of maximum pensionable earnings over the last five working years rather than the last three. This reform had the immediate effect of lowering maximum benefits by $147 a year. Workers now had to show greater recent attachment to the labour force. To be eligible for disability benefits, they must have made contributions in four of the last six years prior to becoming disabled. Rules for disability and survivor benefits changed to limit the extent to which these benefits were combined. In large part, this returned the benefit level to the pre-1987 arrangements. Retirement pensions for disability beneficiaries are now based on maximum pensionable earnings at the time of the disability, rather than at age sixty-five and then fully indexed to the cost-of-living index. This change sought to ensure that when

Table 7.4 CPP Disability benefits: Pre-1998 features and post-1998 reforms

CPP program element	Pre-1998 features	Post-1998 reforms
Retirement pensions and earnings-related portion of disability/survivor benefits	Based on average of last 3 years' maximum pensionable earnings (YMPE)	Based on average of last 5 years' YMPE
Contributory requirements for disability benefits	Must work and contribute to CPP in 2 of last 3, or 5 of last 10 years	Must work and contribute to CPP in 4 of last 6 years
Combined survivor/disability benefits	Ceiling equal to maximum retirement pension plus larger of two flat-rate components	Ceiling is the maximum disability pension; limits on flat rates
Retirement pensions for disability beneficiaries	Based on maximum pensionable earnings when recipient reaches age 65, then indexed to prices	Based on maximum pensionable earnings at time of disablement, then indexed to prices until age 65
Disability benefits upon death of beneficiaries	Benefits paid to estates	No longer paid to estates
Death benefit	Six times the monthly retirement pension of the deceased contributor to a maximum of $3,580 (in 1997)	Six times the contributor's monthly retirement pension up to a maximum of $2,500 (in 1998) and is frozen at that level
Year's basic exemption (YBE)	The YBE, which determines the lower earnings level for contribution purposes, was, for all benefits under the CPP, 10 percent of YMPE	For retirement, survivor, and death benefits, the YBE is frozen at $3,500, resulting in more people paying into the plan over time. For disability benefits, the YBE remains at 10 percent of the YMPE, which continues to rise each year. As of 2002, the disability basic exemption is $3,900. The result is that fewer low-income people will make contributions and therefore not qualify for disability benefits

Sources: Adapted from Finance Canada 1997, and Human Resources Development Canada 2001a.

disability beneficiaries reach sixty-five and their disability benefits are converted to retirement pensions, while they may receive pensions higher than what other people who retire are receiving, the differential will not be as large as before. Disability benefits no longer were paid to estates upon the death of the beneficiary. People already receiving early retirement benefits under the CPP are not eligible for disability benefits (unless they are found to have had a disability before starting to receive the retirement pension and were under sixty-five).

The rising basic exemption in relation to the disability program had the effect of disqualifying some workers with especially low incomes from being entitled to disability benefits. Until 1997, the year's basic exemption (YBE) and the disability basic exemption (DBE) were the same amount. For each year after 1997, the YBE is frozen at $3,500 while the DBE continues to rise, reaching $3,900 in 2002 (HRDC 2002a, 4). Contributions are made only on pensionable earnings above that amount. Indexed to the average industrial wage, the exemption will continually grow. The result is a steady elevation of the basic exemption each year, imposing what amounts to a quiet disentitlement of some very low-income earners.

In sum, the changes to disability benefits and rules went well beyond the handful of options canvassed in the information paper and debated in the consultation process of 1996. Several other options were discussed and incorporated through the intergovernmental arena, led by the federal Department of Finance. Moreover, this array of changes shows that the staunch opposition by disability groups to such cuts was virtually overridden.

Parliamentary Perspectives on Bill C-2

Finance Minister Martin described his package of reforms as being 75 percent on the financing side of contributions and the new investment policy, and only 25 percent on the benefit side. A review of the debates in the House of Commons, the Senate, the Senate Committee of the Whole, and the House of Commons Committee on Finance suggests that 90 percent or more of the debates focused on the investment and financing side; there was little discussion of changes to the way benefits are administered and calculated. Issues most commonly discussed were the increased premiums as a major tax hike, a potential decline in the Canadian economy due to this "tax grab," the composition of the investment board to be created, and the increased CPP premiums in relation to EI premiums. Tellingly, after Bill C-2 was introduced in the House of Commons, two amendments were accepted by the government, both dealing with auditing provisions in relation to the new CPP Investment Board.

As to be expected, MPs and senators from the different federal political parties assessed Bill C-2 through different clusters of beliefs about the proper role of government and about their spending and taxing measures. Reform Party members focused on the economic side of the CPP reforms. They were concerned primarily with the 73 percent increase in the premiums and with the proposed Investment Board, specifically the potential for patronage, mismanagement, and poor returns. Increases to the contribution rate were repeatedly called an extra tax burden on business and a killer of job creation. Reform MPs proposed replacing the CPP with an RRSP–like system where individuals controlled where and how their money was invested. On the disability program, Reformers were not that upset with the trimming of benefits as they did not believe the CPP should be playing this role. As one Reform MP said, "Many Canadians have disability insurance but the CPP gratuitously and unnecessarily takes that over. Even the amount the plan pays out in disability is not necessary in many cases" (Ablonczy 1997, 540).

Progressive Conservatives, then an endangered species in the House of Commons with just two members, expressed alarm over the accelerated increase in CPP premiums. They felt that if the Chrétien government was going to take billions more out of the economy through CPP payroll tax increases, they should implement tax cuts, such as through the EI program, to compensate. Conservative MPs and senators also expressed concern over the level of consultation and debate on Bill C-2, the effect of the changes on women, and the accountability and independence of the new investment board.

NDP members were disturbed about shifting an unfair portion of the burden to support the CPP onto low-income Canadians. They regarded the refinancing changes as a highly regressive way to sustain the CPP. They were, moreover, sharply critical that there was an increase in premiums, but a reduction in benefits. MPs from the NDP spoke most frequently and passionately about the cuts to disability benefits, the backlog of appeals, and the restrictive changes proposed for the program's administration. They pointed out that the CPP/D was taking a disproportionate share of the spending cuts to the CPP.

As one member asked rhetorically, "Will people with a disability get a better deal in the future? The answer to that question as a result of this legislation is also no. This legislation makes it more difficult for people suffering from a serious disability to apply for and receive Canada pension plan benefits" (Riis 1997, 1705). The NDP therefore did not support Bill C-2, seeing it as making life even harder for low-wage workers and persons with disabilities, among others struggling to make ends meet.

Bloc Québécois members were not especially concerned about the changes since they did not affect many of their constituents. Like other parties, however, they were concerned about the EI premiums, and even proposed an amendment to Bill C-2 that would require an increase in CPP contribution rates be linked to a decrease in EI premium rates. On the disability changes, some Bloc members were displeased with the tightening of the eligibility criteria while others seemed to accept the criticisms in recent years of the auditor general claiming lax administration of the CPP/D program. The QPP was presented as a superior model in dealing with disability. "In Quebec," one Bloc member said during the House of Commons debate, "those who have contributed for two of the last three years or five out of the last ten years ... are eligible for disability benefits. This makes allowance for progressive diseases, which is very important. The Government of Quebec will therefore recognize, and quite rightly, a proportionately higher number of disabled people" (de Savoye 1997, 507).

The essential rationale of the ministers of Finance and HRDC for Bill C-2 was that changes were required to save the CPP for future generations. Martin told the Standing Committee on Finance that the federal-provincial review of the CPP "had one overriding goal: to make sure that the CPP will not buckle under the weight of the demands that will be placed on it when the baby boomers retire" (Martin 1997c, 4). When confronted with challenges about the planned changes to the CPP, the ministers argued that Bill C-2 was based on the intergovernmental review and public consultations and was the outcome of a federal-provincial agreement. Compromises had to be made by all sides on the package of changes eventually accepted. The alternative, Martin argued, was to allow the plan to die from lack of change. On the "tax grab" accusation, Martin, evoking in part the line of thinking of the 1960s, told the Senate Committee examining the legislation that "CPP contributions are not a tax. They are savings that go to pensions and other family protection benefits. They go into a separate fund, not into government coffers, and will be invested like other pension plans" (Martin 1997b, 6).

On the issue of retrenching the disability program, the clearest government response during the debates came from the minister of HRDC, Pierre Pettigrew, while appearing before the Standing Committee on Finance in October 1997. "On the disability elements," Minister Pettigrew said, "there is some tightening up around eligibility, because there have been vast increases in the last few years that have been attributed to reasons that are not always clear. So the eligibility criteria were tightened in a way that we want to make sure the pensions go to the people who are covered by the law covering disabled people ... We remain committed to work in that direction" (Pettigrew 1997).

Bill C-2 passed third reading in the House of Commons on 4 December 1997 by a vote of 167 to 73. This was one of the few times that opposition parties were so significantly against legislation concerning the CPP. The very same day, Bill C-2 was given first reading in the Senate. After some debate, which concentrated on the governance of the new Investment Board and the scale and possible economic effects of the contribution rate increases, Bill C-2 was passed by the Senate on 17 December. Royal assent followed on 18 December 1997; the cabinets of the eight provinces passed supporting orders-in-council. Upon approval, the changes to the contribution rates were retroactive to January 1997, and the benefit changes and their administration went into effect 1 January 1998. The related developments of establishing the CPP Investment Board and the new investment policy were proclaimed 1 April 1998.

OTHER CHANGES TO CPP AND CPP/D, 1995–2005

In addition to the high profile reforms of Bill C-2, other reforms to the CPP policy and disability administration and benefits took place from 1995 to 2005. These were implemented through legislative amendments and involved evolving jurisprudence and numerous departmental initiatives by HRDC. These changes and their related policy emphases are presented in Table 7.5.

In the mid-1990s, HRDC took steps to streamline the appeals process for the CPP. Bill C-54, which became law in July 1995, allowed for the appointment of part-time judges for Pension Appeals Board (PAB) hearings. Another provision of this legislation relaxed the

Table 7.5 Related changes to the CPP disability program, 1995–2005

Year	Change	Policy Perspective
1993–95	Contracts with private insurance companies signed by Government of Canada	Program integrity
1995	Bill C-54: Additional medical advisors hired and part-time members appointed as judges to deal with increased number of appeals and the backlog of unheard cases; also expanded provision for the disclosure of information to better prevent mispayments and to collect overpayments	Program integrity Client service
1995	New incentives to allow beneficiaries to volunteer or attend school without losing benefits as long as they have a continuing disability; to continue to receive benefits for 3 months after returning to work; and have their application fast-tracked if the same disability again prevents them from working	Return to work Community participation
1995	New medical adjudication guidelines and appeals procedures "stress the use of medical factors and rule out the use of socio-economic factors in assessing disability"	Program integrity Financial control
1997	Bill C-54 (enacted in 1995, effective 1997): Streamlining of the appeals system at the Pension Appeals Board level; the mandate of the Office of the Commissioner for Review Tribunals extended to include appeals from Old Age Security decisions	Program integrity Client service
1997	CPP Disability Vocational Rehabilitation Program introduced by HRDC, based on previous pilot project	Return to work
1998–99	Bill C-2: Information-sharing agreements signed between HRDC and workers compensation boards of several provinces	Program integrity Return to work
2000	Bill C-23: All CPP benefits and rights extended to same-sex common law relationships	Entitlement to income protection
2000	HRDC begins mailing to all CPP contributors annual statements of their contributions	Client service Personal responsibility
2001	Allowable Earnings exemption of up to $3,800 from work while receiving CPP disability benefit	Return to work
2001	Federal Court of Canada decision in the *Villani v. Canada* case presents a more generous interpretation of the definition of a severe disability in the Canada Pension Plan legislation	Income protection
2001	Newsletter for people receiving a CPP disability benefit produced by HRDC with future issues to be mailed out at least once a year	Program integrity Client service
2004	Bill C-30 Canada Pension Plan legislation amended effective January 2005 to allow for reinstatement of a disability benefit that ceased to be payable because a client returned to work, if the person again becomes incapable of working within a two-year period after the date when payment of the CPP/D benefit ceased. Also provides for reinstatement of a disabled contributor's child benefit to the child of a person whose disability benefit is reinstated.	Return to work Income protection
2005	Program delivery for CPP and CPP/D and other federal programs transferred to Service Canada	Client service

Source: Human Resources Development Canada, *Annual Report of the CPP*, various years.

rules on delegating authority under the CPP. It permitted all PAB judges to make decisions on requests for leave to appeal to the PAB, not only the chair and vice-chair of the PAB, as occurred previously.

The never-ending issue of how to interpret the meaning of disability under the legislation was addressed in 2001 by a Federal Court of Appeal decision in *Villani v. Canada*.[7] In that case, the Federal Court noted that the CPP is social legislation with a benevolent purpose of conferring benefits and, therefore, the legislation should be interpreted in a broad and generous manner, with any ambiguity resolved in favour of a claimant for disability benefits. The court adopted a "real-world" approach to determining severity of disability, within the meaning of the plan, as against a "strict abstract" approach. Real-world details such as a person's age, education level, employment experience, and language proficiency were all relevant, the court argued, in determining whether an applicant suffers from a severe disability under the CPP. The court here employed a social model of disability, discussed in Chapter 1, to take into account a variety of personal and contextual factors that interact to produce obstacles or opportunities for disabled citizens.

An ongoing concern over the Chrétien-Martin era had to do with helping people return to work, be it their former job as it was or reconfigured, a new job, or self-employment. Several factors motivated these Liberal governments to put greater stress on the return to work goal of the CPP. In 1997, the CPP Disability Vocational Rehabilitation Program was formally established with two objectives: to provide vocational rehabilitation measures for CPP/D beneficiaries to facilitate a return to gainful employment, and to achieve cost savings to CPP by reducing the average duration of benefits of those CPP/D beneficiaries who (re)gain the capacity to work. The CPP Disability Vocational Rehabilitation Program was a response to the changing nature of the workforce and the changing attitudes of the employability of many persons with disabilities. As the HRDC wrote, "In the past, many people receiving benefits because of a severe and prolonged disability believed that they were permanently out of

7 The Federal Court allowed the application for judicial review, setting aside an earlier decision by the Pension Appeals Board and remitting the matter to the board for a re-determination by a differently constituted panel. See *Villani v. Canada* (Attorney General), (2001) Federal Court of Appeal Division, FCJ 1217.

work. Today, new technology, medical treatments and skills training are making it possible for some people with severe disabilities to become part of and remain in the work force" (HRDC 2002b, 2).

Services in the Disability Vocational Rehabilitation Program, in which participation is voluntary, include individualized guidance on assessing needs, education, and skills, and local job market opportunities; planning a return-to-work rehabilitation plan in concert with the participant's physician, the CPP case manager, and vocational rehabilitation specialist; improving skills, upgrading education, or retaining; and developing job search skills. A subsequent evaluation of the vocational rehabilitation program, the first and only done to date, found that between 1998 and 2003, 471 CPP/D clients successfully completed the program and ceased disability benefits (Social Development Canada 2004, 4).

A reform effective in 2001 allowed recipients to earn up to $3,800 a year from work without losing their benefits, and if the recipient can only work occasionally, he or she may be allowed to earn more than this amount while still receiving CPP disability benefits.[8] Continuing on this theme of promoting employment incentives in the CPP/D, in 2003, the Chrétien government announced that it would introduce a provision allowing the automatic reinstatement of CPP disability benefits if beneficiaries are unsuccessful at return-to-work attempts. This announcement followed consultations with the provincial and territorial governments who expressed their consent for the measure. Automatic reinstatement would allow CPP/D clients who decide to leave benefits to work to be reinstated if they are unable to continue working because of their disability. This provision would be available to clients for two years from the date their CPP/D benefits were discontinued. The belief was that more CPP/D beneficiaries would be encouraged to try re-entering the labour force knowing that if their return to the workplace was not successful because their disability recurred, then they were guaranteed an income safety net. With an amendment to the CPP legislation in 2004, the automatic reinstatement policy came into effect in 2005. Between 2005 and 2008, an estimated 650 claimants made use of the automatic

8 See the *Annual Report of the Canada Pension Plan, 1998–99* for more details on these and other rehabilitation measures by HRDC. On related employment-oriented initiative for persons with disabilities, see Prince 2001a, 2001b.

reinstatement provision returning to benefits after a period of regular employment. That represented approximately o.3 percent of CPP/D adult beneficiaries, a stark reminder that the large majority of beneficiaries are unlikely to return to regular employment due to the work limitations imposed by their medical conditions.

Also new projects were launched aimed at providing information more regularly to all CPP contributors as well as current disability recipients. Such information campaigns are an important, though often taken-for-granted, instrument of public policy. They not only may assist officials in providing better services to recipients; they also help to shape the knowledge and expectations of Canadians toward the public pension system. Depending on the medium and the message, information campaigns can encourage a belief in personal responsibility to comply with the rules and reporting requirements of the CPP/D.

IMPLICATIONS FOR CLIENTS WITH DISABILITIES

Earned rights to income conferred by a social insurance program are not an immutable contract between governments and individuals; they can be changed by governments. For people receiving benefits from January 1998 onwards, Bill C-2 introduced cuts to disability benefits, death benefits, combined disability and retirement benefits, and combined disability and survivor benefits. Compared to the retrenchment of EI or federal transfer payments to the provinces, cutbacks to CPP/D were relatively mild in the aggregate perhaps, but they were nonetheless belt-tightening in administration and reductions in benefits for a group of citizens who were already struggling hard to make ends meet. Eligibility for disability requirements now required a higher test of attachment to the labour force. New CPP disability beneficiaries would receive less money than before the 1998 changes, and disability beneficiaries could also receive less money at age sixty-five when their disability benefit converted to a retirement pension. CPP disability caseloads declined, reflecting stricter eligibility rules introduced in 1995 and 1998 as well as the aging of the population with proportionately more people qualifying for retirement pensions. As a percentage of total CPP benefits, disability benefits dropped to a share last recorded in the 1980s. The real value of average monthly disability benefits payable diminished, and benefits were worth about one hundred dollars a month less in

2000 than in 1993. From 1997 to 1998, there was a 15 percent decline in overall eligibility for CPP/D pensions. Changing the qualifying requirement to four of the last six years (rather than two of the last three or five of the last ten years) "resulted in a strong and immediate decrease in the number and proportion of CPP contributors eligible for CPPD pension. Younger workers, the self-employed and workers with a shorter contribution history, which disproportionately included women, were especially affected" (HRSDC 2011, 20).

Trends in restraining disability benefits and caseloads did not go undetected by parliamentarians. In 2001, the Standing Committee on Human Resources Development and the Status of Persons with Disabilities observed in a report that was endorsed by members from all five federal parties, "we recognize that during a period of cutting costs, administrative measures need to be put in place that contain expenditures but we share the concern of independent policy analysts and disability organizations that the current disability income support programs operated by the federal government, notably the Canada Pension Plan-Disability (CPP-D), has not recognized the fundamental realities of many people who live with a disability" (Bennett 2003, 17). In 2002, the Sub-Committee on the Status of Persons with Disabilities held a roundtable on the CPP/D with discussion centred on determining eligibility and administration of the program. In 2003, the Standing Committee on Human Resources Development and the Status of Persons with Disabilities studied CPP Disability in considerable depth, informed by hearings and an extensive e-consultation with Canadians. Among its many recommendations, on various aspects of program, the committee recommended that HRDC return to the pre-1998 method for calculating CPP/D benefits and retirement benefits for CPP/D recipients.

CONCLUSION

Why did Chrétien and Martin as Liberal political leaders pursue restraint measures against the CPP/D, measures that stood in contrast with the more progressive reforms of the Mulroney era or those of the final Trudeau years? Sylvia Bashevkin (2002) asks a similar question in regards to federal policy on social assistance funding. Bashevkin offers two reasons for a parallel turn of direction in that policy field between the Mulroney and Chrétien eras. One is Chrétien's political pragmatism, which, Bashevkin argues, meant that he was "prepared to operate within [the] parameters" of conservative rhetoric that "dependence on state benefits was itself faulty." Second, business interests and others joined with fiscal pressures on the public purse to push an agenda to "reduce government spending, eliminate federal deficits" (Bashevkin 2002, 2). Certainly, Canada's public pension reform debate in the mid-1990s was influenced heavily by fiscal concerns over the sustainability of pensions in the face of the aging population.

Jim Coutts calls it "ironic that the successor who came to office clothed in the mantle of 'old liberalism,' rather than 'new conservatism,' went much further toward retrenchment than Mulroney ever dared. Jean Chrétien, enthusiastically aided by his finance minister, spent nearly a decade doing little new in social policy" (2003, 18–19). Coutts reports that Chrétien "expressed the strong view that Canadians didn't *want* policy and program initiatives in this period – they wanted the government to lie low and do little" (2003, 19–20; for a similar view see Axworthy 2002). Issues over the adequacy of disability benefits and improving private insurance coverage of the workforce, prominent in other OECD countries at the time, were absent from the Liberal government agendas of Chrétien and Martin. Financial viability of the CPP retirement pension was their idée fixe.

Discourse on a social right to disability benefits, given emphasis in the Pearson, Trudeau, and Mulroney eras, was now downplayed in the interest of controlling caseloads and program expenditures and saving the CPP. Federal government leaders and officials framed the CPP/D in strongly problematic terms – terms that were contestable, and faced community resistance, but on the whole were deployed effectively. Actuarial and audit reports, a federal information paper, a public consultation report, and an intergovernmental statement of reform principles, all portrayed the CPP/D as undergoing a vast increase in recent years with rapidly escalating costs of the disability benefit, which posed a threat to the CPP retirement pension. Bruce Little describes the reforms to the CPP in 1997–98 "as one of Canada's most significant public policy success stories" (2008, xv). This assuredly is not how disability organizations and individuals with disabilities described the framing of the issues, experienced the process of policy reforms, or lived with the consequence of reduced benefits. Fixing the CPP, as a policy story, played out along the normalcy/disability binary, retrenched the CPP/D, and resulted in a less adequate, less inclusive social citizenship.

CHAPTER EIGHT

Claiming Disability Benefits as Contested Citizenship: Client–State Relations and the Harper Years, 2006–2015

Compassion and understanding for persons with disabilities, and their families. That's our Canada.

Hon. James M. Flaherty, Minister of Finance
Budget Speech, March 2007

After all, the body is political. Its form and function have been the site of powerful control and management.

Lennard J. Davis, *Enforcing Normalcy*

In exercising social rights to income maintenance, medical determination, bureaucratic administration, and judicial adjudication of claims are crucial to people with disabilities. Academic literature on citizenship and social policy at times depicts the provision of programs and exercise of public authority in positive terms of universality, equality of status, and social cohesion. These are, no doubt, principal ideas regarding the goals, mechanisms, and intended outcomes of entitlements in welfare states. This chapter presents a more critical conception of social rights to income provision. It does so by examining ways in which power is exercised in relation to people applying for CPP/D benefits and appealing denied claims for support. Claiming an earned right to a benefit can be an intensely contested practice of social citizenship. The actual outcome for many people is the eventual receipt of a disability benefit; yet, for many others, their lived experiences are of rejection, anxiety, delays, frustration, and insecurity.

Looking at practices of CPP/D social citizenship, the chapter examines legal rules, formal rights and duties, administrative procedures, and documentation. It also examines the personal understandings, status changes, and self-identities of rights claimants. What is the relation between social security and natural justice, between a social program such as CPP/D and fair processes in the adjudication of claims? This critical issue of public policy and public administration has not received the analytical attention it warrants. "Administrative law and practice," Miriam Smith observes, is an area of the Canadian state and policy that "has been largely overlooked by political scientists" (2009, 836). More attention should be given, suggests Smith, to how administrative rules set "the terms for legal claims by individuals," structure relations of power, provide effective redress or not, and foster social norms of the impartiality and legitimacy of eligibility decisions. And so, how does the administrative law and practice of CPP/D shape the social rights of contributors with disabilities when they make a claim for a disability benefit? In other words, what is the connection between public bureaucracy and social citizenship?

Social insurance is often described in the literature as a policy technique with several advantageous features. In Chapter 3, we saw a classic rationale articulated by Leonard Marsh. Under social insurance, human need is a common community risk or contingency of life as much as a personal condition. Benefits are a matter of right due to a record of employment and direct contributions paid by the client, giving the benefit a level of societal acceptability and thus little or no public stigma. In contrast to the intrusive and arbitrary nature of poor relief and social assistance, with social insurance there is highly formalized program administration with negligible contact between applicants and officials, and straightforward decisions on eligibility based on uniform rules. This chapter argues that the positive features attributed to social insurance as an earned right are more complicated and demanding in actual practice. The eligibility process for CPP/D is, at one and the same time, a method of classifying disabled workers as entitled or disqualified and regulating them by a series of relationships and decisions, some of which are formally expressed in policy and procedures and others of which are embodied in considerations and choices by clients.

What I present here is not a different or separate model of power at work in social insurance and citizenship rights, but rather a dimension of power and set of practices often overlooked. These practices embrace presentations of self, the documentation and interpretation of bodily symptoms, the construction of medical information and formulations of truth, interactions with friends and family, and always the creation of government files on program clients. Tight and loose networks of authority are at play, as are various forms of knowledge and evidence. These practices are the tangible workings of public and private power in social rights and social policy.

Regarding the prime ministerial era of Stephen Harper, the chapter will show that Conservative policy on CPP/D entailed a modest easing of eligibility for long-time contributors, more emphasis on program integrity and on the voluntary compliance by clients, and also a dramatic change in the appeal system with troubling implications for the legal rights of clients. Furthermore, changes made to the age eligibility for the Old Age Security program, from sixty-five to sixty-seven, has potential adverse consequences for the CPP/D.[1]

SOCIAL POLICY, PENSION REFORM, AND DISABILITY POLICY IN THE HARPER ERA

This section sets out the broader public policy context at the federal level of the CPP/D by describing the social policy style of the Harper government, commenting on Conservative pension reform, and then highlighting the main disability policy developments in the Harper years.

Social Policy in the Harper Years

In the Harper prime ministerial era, the federal government became less interested in extending social rights of Canadian citizenship, far less inclined to engage in intergovernmental collaboration on major issues such as poverty reduction and disability supports, and more authoritarian in political discourse, policy priorities, and legislative initiatives (Doern, Prince, and Schultz 2014). Shortly after taking office in 2006, the Harper government cancelled a federal-provincial-territorial understanding called the Kelowna Accord, brokered by the Martin

---

1 The Liberal government of Justin Trudeau, formed in November 2015, pledged in their election platform to repeal this change to the eligibility for the Old Age Security program.

Liberal government, to fund expanded and new measures for Aboriginal peoples and communities in education, health care, and housing over a ten-year period. In 2007, the Harper government terminated another Martin government social initiative, five-year intergovernmental agreements with the provinces on supporting the development of universally accessible, quality early learning and child care services. After winning a majority government in 2011, Harper announced unilaterally, rather than through negotiations with the provinces, federal health care funding arrangements for the next decade (Doern, Maslove, and Prince 2013, 99). In varying ways, these actions represented major retreats in social policy and retrenchments of the federal spending power in social policy. The Harper Conservatives were disinclined to undertake major new social programs unilaterally in federal areas of jurisdiction or collaboratively with provincial governments.

Four other developments in Canadian social policy during the Harper years are worth noting briefly. One is that for almost a quarter-century, the Court Challenges Program offered resources to equality-seeking organizations that enabled them to participate in legal cases dealing with equality rights and constitutional questions of the relationship between citizens and the state, and between the Canadian Charter of Rights and Freedoms and governments. The Harper government's termination of the Court Challenges Program in 2006 shut down a vital judicial vehicle for disability groups seeking full citizenship and a fuller measure of equality (Prince 2009). A second trend over the Harper era was the proliferation of small social tax expenditures (so-called fiscal welfare or boutique tax credits) through the establishment of new deductions or credits in the personal income and retail sales tax systems, offering a form of income-tested benefits. A third trend was the promotion of occupational welfare (that is, employer- and enterprise-sponsored provisions) such as workplace pensions and workplace day care spaces. A fourth development in federal social policy of late was the reduction in tax revenue capacity of the federal government (what is sometimes called defunding the state) from reductions in the corporate and value-added tax rates along with personal income tax relief measures.

These trends have implications for normalcy/disability relations by virtue of the fact they tend to advantage those inside the labour force and those with good jobs and middle and upper incomes. For instance, most of the tax measures recently introduced are non-refundable tax credits, which means that people who have low earnings and with little or no taxable income, such as many Canadians with significant disabilities, do not qualify for these tax credits. Overall, these developments accord with residual principles that encourage private responsibility and encumber public rights.

Conservative Pension Reform

In the 2006, 2008, and 2011 federal elections in Canada, pension reform was not a significant political issue, even though in the 2011 campaign, the major parties and their leaders addressed issues of public and private pensions. A major driving factor behind a renewed and intensified attention to pension reform was the financial crisis and economic recession of 2008 to 2010. Concerns arose over the viability of defined benefit programs, the solvency of many occupational plans, and the continued lack of coverage by most workers in the private sector of the Canadian economy. Harper governments have introduced a number of measures that offer tax relief to current seniors. As of 2006, the amount of income eligible for the Pension Income Credit doubled to $2,000; pension income splitting began in 2007; and, the age credit amount increased in 2006 and again in 2009. Some observers dubbed the 2015 budget "the senior's budget" for its inclusion of similarly generous tax measures. Regrettably, from a social policy perspective of equity, most of these tax measures promised greater benefit to better-off seniors than to low- or modest-income seniors.

Reflecting lessons from the economic and financial crisis, the Harper Conservatives strengthened rules on federally regulated private pension plans to stabilize and modernize pension arrangements. In 2009 and again in 2011, changes to the legislative and regulatory framework for private pension plans under federal jurisdiction and subject to the Pension Benefits Standards Act, 1985, sought to enhance protection and security of the plans. Under the federal Income Tax Act, which applies to defined benefit plans both federally and provincially regulated, the pension surplus threshold increased from 10 percent to 25 percent. In March 2011, clearly designed with an election in the air, the Harper government promised an increase to the Guaranteed Income Supplement (GIS) for some seniors who live in low-income circumstances, though not all seniors in restricted financial circumstances. After the May 2011 election, and the return of a now Harper majority government, the targeted GIS increase passed.

During this latest period of pension debate and reform, the federal and provincial/territorial ministers of Finance played a central role.[2] In May 2009, corresponding with the triennial review of the CPP, the ministers established a joint research working group to examine the retirement income system in Canada, chaired by the federal minister of state (Finance). A few changes to the CPP came out of the 2009 triennial review. The changes aim to make retiring later than age sixty-five more financially beneficial, and to make retiring early, between the ages of sixty to sixty-four, less financially attractive. The changes phased in over five years from 2012 to 2016.[3]

The role of provincial governments in this phase of pension reform debate occurred in three arenas. One was intergovernmental, largely through the federal-provincial-territorial (FPT) meetings of finance ministers who were supported by researchers in considering pension coverage among private sector workers and retirement incomes adequacy. A second arena was unilateral. A few provinces, usually under their finance department, commissioned expert studies on pension issues, often concentrating on private pension plans with a recent wider public consultation in Ontario. A third arena of provincial action was a unique bilateral undertaking by the BC and Alberta governments involving a joint expert panel on pension

2 By comparison, First Ministers' meetings in the Harper years played a minor role in general, especially compared to previous Liberal Prime Ministers Jean Chrétien and Paul Martin, and specifically on pension reform. At a First Ministers' meeting in January 2009 on actions to provide stimulus to the Canadian economy, leaders agreed to more action on securing Canada pension plans, in particular changes to the framework for federally regulated private pension plans.

3 By 2016, CPP will pay an additional 0.7 percent per month to those persons who begin to take their CPP retirement pensions after their sixty-fifth birthday. Waiting the extra five years, to age seventy, will mean an additional 42 percent to a person's CPP retirement pension. For people who draw their CPP pension "early," that is, between age sixty and sixty-five, the previous reduction was 0.5 percent per month for each month that the pension begins before age sixty-five. The reduction rate rises to 0.6 percent per month by 2016, which represents a 36 percent reduction in the CPP retirement benefit for a person claiming it at age sixty that year.

standards – an instance of horizontal collaboration via interprovincial cooperation. These studies generated new information, raised several issues especially on matters of pensions within provincial jurisdiction of private plans, made specific recommendations on strengthening private plans, and stimulated media attention on pension reform generally.

Parliamentary committees at both the House of Commons and the Senate participated in pension policy as a way for opposition parties to raise issues of substance and process for reform, and, at the same time, as a way for the Conservative members to limit the range of issues and to defend the Harper government's approach to consultation. At the request of Finance Minister Jim Flaherty, the Senate Standing Committee on Banking, Trade and Commerce, in March 2010 undertook a study of registered retirement savings plans (RRSPs) and tax-free savings accounts (TFSAs) and the extent to which Canadians were using them in saving for their retirement. Likewise, at the request of Finance Minister Flaherty, the Standing Committee on Finance of the House of Commons held hearings in 2010 on the retirement income security for Canadians.

Despite these committee hearings, debate on pension policy during the Harper years was relatively quiet. Policy silence is a course of non-events and inaction. In the pension reform community, there are inner circles and outer circles with recurring divisions of interests and polarization of ideas concerning the place of public pensions in the retirement income security system. Consider, in historical context, the 2008 to 2011 pension debate at the federal level. No longer is there a statutory CPP advisory committee with a range of representatives to advise the minister, due to its elimination in the late 1990 reforms; there was no green paper or white paper on pension reform issued by the Harper government as happened in the 1960s by the Pearson government and in the early 1980s by the Trudeau government. Instead, there was a four-week online consultation. There was no joint FPT series of public consultations on pension reform as took place in the 1990s under the Chrétien government; in its stead, a preference for using expert panels that report to ministry officials. The idea of a national pension summit, as occurred in the early 1980s, was rejected by the Harper Conservatives. And in Parliament, to review pension issues, there was reliance on finance and commerce standing committees with little or no role by social development standing committees of the House or the Senate. Issues pertaining to and voices of working women, low-income seniors, caregivers, and people with disabilities have largely been excluded from recent reform structures.

One final piece to the Harper record on pension has direct consequences for the CPP and CPP/D. The 2012 federal budget announced that in order to make social programs sustainable for a secure retirement, the age of eligibility for Old Age Security and the Guaranteed Income Supplement was to be raised from sixty-five to sixty-seven – a change that would start in 2023 and be implemented gradually until 2029. Besides the dubious justification for the change and the lack of democratic engagement with the general public (Prince 2012), the change in eligibility would have consequences for those persons on CPP/D who turn sixty-five and are transferred to CPP retirement pension. It will mean that, starting in 2024, those persons who are transferred from CPP/D to the CPP retirement pension will not only experience a drop in their monthly benefit income, but they will not have that decline offset form OAS/GIS for two years, until they turn sixty-seven. If this Harper reform stands (it appears the Justin Trudeau government elected in fall 2015 will reverse it), many future disabled pensioners aged sixty-five or sixty-six would need to apply for provincial social assistance to have a modicum of economic security.

Harper's Disability Policy

Major contours of disability policy development in the Harper prime ministerial era are shown in Table 8.1, with particular attention to budgetary announcements and legislative and program measures. Of the ten federal budgets from 2006 to 2015, not all were of equal significance to disability policy making by the Harper government. The most active budgets with innovative developments were the 2006 and 2007 budgets and the 2014 and 2015 budgets, bookending this period. In between were the domestic recession and global financial crisis of 2008–10, with the Conservative's Economic Action Plan, and the subsequent tentative recovery and deficit reduction agenda.

The economic recession of 2008–10 and subsequent slow recovery hit people with disabilities "harder than the broader working-age population" in Canada (OECD 2010, 3). The cold market reality is that gains made by Canadians with disabilities in labour force outcomes in the 1990s and early 2000s were lost largely due to the

Table 8.1 Disability policy developments in the Harper era, 2006–2015

- Child Disability Benefit increased and eligibility extended to most families (2006)
- Refundable Medical Expense Supplement increased (2006)
- Enhancing Accessibility Fund established (2007), renewed (2010), and made ongoing (2013)
- Canada Pension Plan legislation amended (2007)
- Working Income Tax Benefit with Disability Supplement introduced (2007) and expanded (2009)
- Registered Disability Savings Plan introduced (2007) and adjusted (2010, 2011, 2012, 2013, 2015)
- Mental Health Commission of Canada established (2007) and mandate renewed (2015)
- Medical Expense Tax Credit expanded list of eligible costs (2008, 2011, 2014)
- Employment Insurance sickness benefits, access improved for military families (2010), for claimants who receive the Parents of Critically Ill Children and Compassionate Care benefits (2014)
- UN Convention on the Rights of Persons with Disabilities ratified by Canada (2010)
- Family Caregiver Tax Credit established (2011)
- Canadian Disability Survey launched, replacing the Participation and Activity Limitation Survey (2012)
- Part III of Canada Labour Code amended to require employers in federally regulated industries to insure Long-Term Disability plans for employees (2012) in effect 2014
- Opportunities Fund for Persons with Disabilities made ongoing (2013) and with increased funding as of 2015–16
- Canadian Business SenseAbility, an employers' disability forum, funded (2013)
- Social Security Tribunal established (2013) replacing previous appeal systems for EI, CPP, and OAS
- Labour Market Agreements for Persons with Disabilities renewed (2014)
- Ready, Willing and Able program with three years of funding to connect people with developmental disabilities with jobs (2014)
- Vocational training program with four years of funding, for individuals with autism spectrum disorder (2014)
- Disability Tax Credit Promoters' Restriction Act (2014)
- Home Accessibility Tax Credit for Seniors and Persons with Disabilities (2015)
- EI Compassionate Care Benefit extended from six weeks to six months (2015) in effect 2016

Source: Government of Canada budget documents, 2006 to 2015.

recession. A weakening of work attachment and job security among people with disabilities was manifested by a decline in the labour force participation rate, a drop in the employment rate, and an increase in the unemployment rate. Furthermore, the number of hours worked by people with a disability in employment dropped, reversing the gains made in the period before the most recent recession (Spector 2012). The post-recession recovery also reinforced Conservative inclinations to oppose expansion of the CPP to meet the retirement security need of Canadians.

Employment for people with disabilities rose gradually on the Harper government agenda as a policy issue. In 2012 the Conservatives appointed a small group of outside experts to a Panel on Labour Market Opportunities for Persons with Disabilities. Their study, *Rethinking disAbility in the Private Sector* (2013), observed that this significant talent pool of people with disabilities is being overlooked. Directed at Canadian private sector employers, this report makes a business case, the most explicit to date by the federal government, for employing people with disabilities. Benefits for business firms include an educated and talented group of workers; improved company culture and reputation among the public; greater employee loyalty and commitment; lower turnover rates, thus reducing costs of training new employees; and more effective marketing to customer segments of people with disabilities. According to the report, about 795,000 working-aged people with disabilities who were not working wanted to work, and of these people, 340,000 had some level of post-secondary education.

Federal budgets provide a practical indication of the Conservative's disability agenda. For example, the 2014 federal budget announced a few targeted and modest measures on employment for certain categories of people with disabilities; specifically, it allotted $11.4 million over four years to support job training for people with autism spectrum disorder, and $15 million over three years for initiatives to connect employers with youth and working-age adults with developmental disabilities. That budget also confirmed a "new generation" of labour market agreements for persons with disabilities with the provinces, which promised stronger accountability measures but provided little in new federal dollars. The Harper government also supported the establishment of an employer disability forum to advance employment by the private sector, called Canadian SenseAbility. The 2015 federal budget featured additional measures for people with disabilities and their families. One was a new Home Accessibility Tax Credit for Seniors and Persons with Disabilities, a non-refundable measure worth up to $1,500 per year in tax relief for people who are eligible for the Disability Tax Credit, at a cost of approximately $40 million in the initial years. A second was the extension of the EI Compassionate Care Benefit from six weeks to six months to enable people to care for terminally ill family members, at an estimated annual expenditure of $37 million. A suite of new programs and enhanced spending to disabled veterans and their families was also unveiled in the 2015 pre-election budget.[4]

Certain items on the Conservative's disability agenda originated in activities and processes underway in the Chrétien and or Martin Liberal governments, including policy ideas gleaned from the Technical Advisory Committee on Tax Measures for Persons with Disabilities, from Senate committee work on a mental health strategy, and from the policy work for the Working Income Tax Benefit and Disability Supplement. The 2015 budget, for example, announced an extension to the mandate of the Mental Health Commission of Canada beginning in 2017–18. Canada's ratification of the UN Convention on the Rights of Persons with Disabilities in 2010 also had roots in intergovernmental negotiations and contributions from the disability community beginning several years earlier. With the consent of all ten provinces, ratification by Canada commits both orders of government to undertake a progressive realization of the articles in this international treaty and to periodically report on results. In the UN Convention on the Rights of Persons with Disabilities, disability refers to physical, mental, intellectual, or sensory impairments that, in interaction with various barriers, may hinder a person's full and effective participation in society on an equal basis – a definition a far cry from that found in most public programs, which tend to focus on individual bodily restrictions and to offer modest supports.

4 For disabled Canadian veterans and their families, the 2015 federal budget, following years of discontent and criticism by many veterans, announced a new Critical Injury Benefit, a new tax-free Family Caregiver Relief Benefit, a new Retirement Income Security Benefit, and expanded Permanent Impairment Allowance. For more details see Canada, Finance Canada 2015, and Prince and Moss 2015.

On income security related to disability issues, the Harper record includes small changes to improving access to the EI sickness benefits for certain groups; requiring private sector employers to insure their long-term disability plans for employees; and a minor change to eligibility rules for the CPP/D, to be discussed in the next section. More significant income security reforms were the increase in benefits to the Child Disability Benefit and extending eligibility to about 95 percent of families caring for children with severe disabilities; introduction and subsequent enhancement of the Working Income Tax Benefit and Disability Supplement for low-income working individuals and families; and introduction of the Registered Disability Savings Plan (RDSP) to help parents and other relatives save for the long-term financial security of a child with severe disabilities.

One item on the disability policy agenda, placed there by the Conservatives themselves, never saw the light of day. In their 2006 election platform, the newly formed Conservative Party had pledged a Canadians with Disabilities Act aimed at improving accessibility and inclusion for all people living with disabilities. Work commenced on developing options of a federal bill and on how to consult with the general public and stakeholders on draft legislation, but the file was never a high priority within the Harper government, and it quietly faded away, the victim of neglect by political leadership.[5]

How, then, to characterize the overall disability policy record in the Harper era? Sherri Torjman suggests the Conservatives "introduced an impressive array of disability-related initiatives" (2014, 1). The main emphasis, she notes, was on employability and labour market participation, and, in comparison to previous federal governments, the Harper government put "less emphasis on the broader goals of citizenship and inclusion" (Torjman 2014, 1). Mario Levesque and Peter Graefe (2013) offer a more critical assessment of federal disability policy – not just the Harper era but also the Chrétien and Martin years. Levesque and Graefe contend there have been "few policy developments over the last fifteen years," and policy changes have been of an "incremental nature" (2013, 172). On the issue of employment and the Panel on Labour Market Opportunities and

---

5 During the 2015 federal election, several disability organizations actively raised the issue of a Canadians with Disabilities Act with all the major political parties, and the new Liberal government of Justin Trudeau seems committed to introducing such legislation.

employer forum, Levesque and Graefe assert that "without policy ambition to more aggressively regulate private sector hiring and management practices or to provide greater supports, it is as much a stall as a step forward" (2013, 176).

The foremost example of incrementalism in Harper's disability policy was the constant tweaking of tax credits and tax exemptions for particular medical services and social supports. Then again, the RDSP is a noteworthy innovation, a tax measure with a creative and progressive program design. In addition to tax-sheltered contributions that individuals and families can make, the federal government offers up to a $3,500 grant to match families' or individuals' contributions to an RDSP, and will pay up to $1,000 in bonds to eligible low-income adults and low-income families with eligible children. The bond is not dependent on any contributions being made by a family.

CPP/D CHANGES, 2006–2014

In light of the Harper Conservatives' modest record on social policy and public pension reform and, arguably, disability policy, it is not surprising that few major changes were made to the CPP/D program, as shown in Table 8.2. A fundamental shift did occur, however, with respect to the appeal and tribunal system, with the abolition of the Office of the Commissioner for Review Tribunals (OCRT) along with three other tribunal bodies, which were replaced by the Social Security Tribunal.

Bill C-36 marked the first time since the 1998 reforms to CPP that a change to disability eligibility criteria was proposed and enacted. The bill had four policy goals: to improve the accessibility and delivery of OAS/GIS pension benefits for seniors; to enhance eligibility for CPP disability benefits for long-term contributors to the plan; to strengthen the integrity and accountability of both programs; and to enhance equitable treatment in the provision of income-tested benefits for seniors. Our interest concerns the amendment to the Canada Pension Plan, specifically eligibility rules for the CPP/D benefits.

In relation to CPP legislation and programming, Bill C-36 established a modestly more generous eligibility requirement for the CPP/D benefit for long-term contributors, that is, individuals who have contributed to the CPP for twenty-five years or more and made valid contributions in three of the last six years. The legislation also provided greater flexibility for pension credit-splitting between former common-law partners.

Table 8.2 Main changes relevant to the cpp disability program, 2006–2014

Year	Change	Policy Perspectives
2008	Bill C-36 introduced November 2006, passed in 2007 Canada Pension Plan legislation amended in effect March 2008: contributory requirements revised for plan members with 25 or more years of contributions to qualify if they have valid contributions in 3 of the last 6 years instead of the current requirement of 4 of the last 6 years	• Entitlement to income protection based on a significant history of labour force attachment
2010	Administrative penalty provisions and disclosure policy under the Canada Pension Plan became effective October 2010: provisions providing the authority to set the terms and conditions for the charging of interest in cases of misrepresentation for cpp	• Program integrity • Financial control • Client responsibility
2013	Streamlining the appeal system: termination of the Office of the Commissioner for Review Tribunals, replaced by the Social Security Tribunal	• Program integrity and efficiency
2014	cpp regulations amended adding the definition of a substantially gainful occupation at a salary greater than or equal to the disability pension	• Entitlement to income protection • Return-to-work
2014	Act to Establish the Administrative Tribunal Support Service of Canada	• Program efficiency

In regard to transparency, Bill C-36 allowed contributors to the cpp to access their Statement of Contributions more than once a year and clarified the actuarial reporting and contribution rate-setting process to ensure that new or enhanced benefit costs are fully funded. Regulation-making powers were granted also to the department for providing direction to the chief actuary for calculating such costs. As well, penalty provisions in the cpp that had been dormant (that is, never proclaimed) were reworked and included in Bill C-36 – an indication of the emphasis given to program integrity.

If there was a single focusing event for the cpp/d amendment in Bill C-36, it was the recommendation from a 2003 parliamentary report that the federal government return to the pre-1998 method of calculating cpp/d benefits of two of the past three years or five of the past ten years. In response to this proposal, the federal government said a return to the pre-1998 eligibility requirements "would jeopardize the gains made in ensuring the sustainability of the cpp." But the government quickly added "there may be value in studying the impact of the 1998 amendments to the CPP Disability program, now that a number of years have passed. In particular, the 1998 changes to the contributory requirements may have produced some unintended consequences, especially for long-term contributors. The Government is working with the provinces to explore viable options for addressing the Committee's recommendation without affecting the financing of the CPP" (Canada, Department of Human Resources Development 2003, 9).

Acting as policy entrepreneurs, reform-minded CPP/D program officials interested in improving the program's accessibility to workers with substantial labour force histories sought to shape the legislative amendment agenda. They did so by exploring a set of options and mobilizing a feasible policy solution acceptable to both Finance and Justice officials, and also critically to the provinces, thus influencing the eventual outcomes. CPP/D program officials took that issue and the opportunity of the regular review by finance ministers of CPP and linked the policy solution of new eligibility rules, and some administrative solutions, to the problem of ineligible long-term contributors to the plan.

On the idea of moderating the contributory rules for CPP/D benefits, considerations of fairness and cost for the CPP fund were prominent. In developing a disability policy reform, departmental officials generated and examined about a dozen options with respect to long-term contributors, consulting closely on analytical matters with the Office of the Chief Actuary. Concerns over the stringency of changes to CPP/D in 1998 and subsequent parliamentary attention to this issue contributed to program officials looking at this reform idea. According to program officials, unfairness existed: "A number of individuals who had tried to apply for disability benefits, who were demonstrably disabled and had worked for many years could not meet the test of four out of the last six years" (quoted in Prince 2010, 313). On how the number twenty-five years was decided upon as the definition for long-term contributors, the director general of the CPP Disability Directorate explained, "The number was a combination of what might be fair to those people who had a long attachment to work and being fiscally responsible in terms of not putting the sustainability of the CPP for the future at risk. It was a combination of a number of possible options. This option, for the Finance Department and the provinces, seemed to be the best and most reasonable option" (Canada, Standing Committee on Banking, Trade and Commerce 2007, 31).

Cost for Finance officials is always an issue, and the 1998 rule of four out of the last six years, which itself had originated from the Department of Finance, was the framework within which CPP/D was to operate. Officials in HRSDC argued the change to the eligibility requirements, therefore, in two ways: it being a reasonable and modest adjustment, reaching out to a group while respecting the general eligibility framework of the CPP; and it rewarding longevity of attachment to the workforce, not simply a recent attachment.

Data for analyzing this amendment and related discarded options came from several sources: a file review of departmental administrative data on the disability program; questions and concerns from the public to the minister and their member of Parliament about CPP disability benefits and eligibility; and compelling testimonies of Canadians from the online consultation linked to the House of Commons committee review of CPP/D in 2003, which was the first parliamentary study of the program since the early 1980s. Stories of real people converged to identify a basic unfairness in the program for severely disabled Canadian workers with a long-term attachment to the labour force. In turn, the chief actuary played an invaluable role in the process, doing cost projections of what various options would mean for CPP contributions and financial stability over time. Analysis of this disability contributory rule showed the costs to be 0.2 percent in relation to the contribution rate, and within the full funding parameters of the CPP. Departmental analysis suggested disability eligibility coverage could expand to some 80,000 contributors, resulting in an additional 3,700 contributors and 1,000 of their children receiving CPP/D benefits (Prince 2010, 314). The result was a modest and affordable cost to the CPP program and a new, second set of eligibility rules for long-term contributors, adding some further complexity to the administration of this already complex plan.

THE SOCIAL SECURITY TRIBUNAL: STREAMLINING LEGAL AND SOCIAL RIGHTS

A single paragraph in the 2012 federal budget conveyed a fundamental change to administrative justice and the civil rights of CPP/D clients: "The Minister will introduce legislative amendments to eliminate administrative duplication in appeals and tribunal services by replacing the current administrative tribunal system for major federal social security programs with a single-window decision body.

The new Social Security Tribunal will continue to provide a fair, credible and accessible appeals process for Canadians." Little was known about the Social Security Tribunal (sst) in the disability policy community or wider public as it was slipped into an omnibus budget bill. It did not flow from a broad public consultation, parliamentary investigation, or an audit report. The ocrt commissioner and the Pension Appeals Board (pab) learned about the proposed changes in the budget from outside sources. Without any effective parliamentary scrutiny, it was virtually guaranteed that persons with disabilities would have to live the consequences of every flaw, big and little, in the new process.

Impetus for the new tribunal originated within the federal bureaucracy of hrdc, informed by advice from administrative law specialists in universities. Interest in a social security federal court created through a merger of various specialized appeal boards had been raised in various studies since the late 1970s. Through the government restraint and pension reform years of the 1990s, the idea was revived. Internal departmental analysis by hrdc reviewed the administrative arrangements between the Income Security Programs Branch and the Office of the Commissioner of Review Tribunals and the Pension Appeals Board. Under consideration in the early 2000s was the issue of whether sufficient safeguards were in place to ensure the judicial independence and impartiality of the ocrt and the pab. At the time, the operating budgets and administrative support for both of these quasi-judicial bodies was provided by the Branch and funded under the cpp. Possible options to ensure independence ranged from writing formal protocol or memoranda of understanding on matters of budget and staffing; enacting clear mandates in the Financial Administration Act and other framework legislation; establishing a common administrative structure for the tribunals under the Employment Insurance Act; and consolidating the ocrt and pab with other federal tribunals concerned with social security benefits.

A 2002 study for the department by legal scholar Patrice Garant recommended the creation of a Canadian social security tribunal from merging four existing entities: ei boards of referees, ei Office of the Umpire, cpp review tribunals, and the pab. Garant was unsure of the arm's length independence of the ocrt commissioner from "the ministerial machinery" of the hrdc (2002, 57). Thinking of administrative tribunals as a meso system, a network of institutions that perform adjudicative functions, Garant argued for rationalizing the structures through integration into a larger new tribunal. Interestingly, this systems analysis left alone the Veterans Review and Appeal Board and the Disability Tax Credit appeal function, housed in other federal portfolios. Garant envisaged an administrative court of appeal with a two-tiered appeal system. The first tier would have three specialized sections, on EI, CPP/OAS, and medical or disability determination. The second tier would be a Federal Court Appeal Division to replace the Umpire and the PAB. It would be another decade until a new social security tribunal along these contours came to realization.

The SST acquired legal status in April 2013, though it was actually in operation through most of 2012. It replaced the Board of Referees and the Office of the Umpire – both associated with the EI program – as well as the OCRT and the PAB – the two bodies associated with the CPP and OAS. These bodies represented two levels of appeal, respectively, for EI and the CPP and OAS programs. The STT also comprises two levels of appeal. The General Division, the first level, includes an EI Section for EI appeals, and an Income Security Section for CPP and OAS appeals. The Appeal Division within the STT is the second level of appeal; it decides on appeals of decisions made by the General Division. As in the previous tribunal systems, the first level is a departmental reconsideration by officials in Employment and Social Development Canada (ESDC)[6] on behalf of the minister, a second and third level within the SST, and the fourth level of the Federal Court of Appeal for the judicial review of a decision (if there is an error in law or in procedure at a tribunal hearing).

The STT replaces approximately 1,000 part-time members of the EI Board of Referees, 32 umpires, and approximately 300 part-time members of review tribunals and retired judges of the PAB with 74 full-time members and some part-time members up to the equivalent of 11 full-time members. Table 8.3 presents more details on the STT.

The EI tribunals had three-person panels representing workers, employers, and government, and the CPP panels (the vast majority of which dealt with CPP/D cases) had members with medical, legal, and layperson perspectives.

6 HRSDC was rebranded as the Department of Employment and Social Development Canada in July 2013 and, then in November 2015, under the Justin Trudeau Liberal government, restructured, with the minister of Families, Children and Social Development responsible for the Canada Pension Plan and the appeals system.

Table 8.3 Social Security Tribunal (SST)

History	• Announced in 2012 federal budget, began operations April 2013
Jurisdiction	• Employment Insurance, Canada Pension Plan, and Old Age Security
Levels	• Departmental reconsideration • Social Security Tribunal General Division • Social Security Tribunal Appeal Division • Federal Court of Appeal for judicial review
Roles	• To hear appeals in the General Division from the decision of the minister on reconsideration • To hear appeals in the Appeal Division only on issues of fairness or jurisdiction or error of law
Powers	• To confirm or vary decision of the minister • To grant leave to appeal (permission for a hearing) to proceed to the Appeal Division
General principles	• To conduct tribunal proceedings as informally and quickly as the circumstances and the considerations of fairness and natural justice allow
Number of members on a tribunal	• Tribunals comprise a single member
Hearings	• May be by written submission, by appearance of the parties in person, or via telecommunication
Membership	• Up to 74 full-time and fully paid members appointed by the governor-in-council, for five year terms • Part-time members up to the equivalent of 11 full-time members, two-year terms
Administration	• Employment and Social Development Canada (ESDC)

For people with disabilities trying to appeal negative decisions on their ineligibility for a CPP/D benefit, there are serious problems with the SST. About 60 percent of initial applications for CPP/D benefits are refused. People do not succeed on the first try because of unwieldy paperwork, murky rules, failure to identify and obtain the appropriate medical and employability information, and inability to connect with real individuals who can provide genuine service. The rate of successful appeals against initial rulings on CPP/D benefits has been declining over the last decade, to just 43 percent in 2013–14. Indeed, Canada has one of the highest rejection rates for a disability insurance program among OECD countries. If, after the first decision, individuals were given detailed written decisions and a copy of their file, together with information about the appeal system, an easy-to-complete application, and a postage-paid envelope, there might be a vastly different appeal profile.

In the first year, SST inherited a backlog of an estimated 6,000 appeals on denials of CPP disability benefits to be heard. In fact, the previous tribunals made significant efforts to hear and decide appeals by the statutory deadline because the consequences for appellants were obvious. The OCRT, as the legacy body for CPP/D appeals, might have cleared more if it had not been dealing with significant budget cuts and insufficient numbers of members, and if it had been consulted in advance about the proposed reforms. In its first year of operation, the SST held just 461 hearings on appeals from people denied CCD and OAS benefits. Administrative data showed that of those appeals, 303 were dismissed. This compared badly to the thousands of hearings held the previous year by the OCRT. As of 2014, the case backlogs had grown to over 11,000 mainly of CPP/D claims, including people who were seriously ill and others terminally ill (Goodman 2014a).

In the style of damage control, the Harper government's responses to problems with the SST aimed at expediting the processing of claims. The Department of Employment and Social Development Act, which created the tribunal, was amended in 2014 to allow an increase in the number of full-time tribunal members – thus removing the original cap of seventy-four full-time staff – and to allow the removal of the limitation placed on the number of hours of part-time members (Galloway 2014). The original cost-saving limitations on tribunal staffing were now an unwelcome rigidity. An additional twenty-two part-time members were appointed and twelve members shifted from the EI section to deal with the much heavier caseload of the CPP/OAS section. A group of departmental lawyers, unofficially called "the spike unit," formed to review appeals to identify cases where settlement offers could be made conceivably without need for a tribunal hearing (Goodman 2015a, 2015b).

In the SST system, every application is heard before a single member, whereas under the previous system every application for an appeal was heard by a three-member panel that usually contained a medical specialist, lawyer, and layperson. Most members of the Income Security division of the SST are either lawyers or health professionals. The issue is not so much their specific expertise, as it is the value-added of three independent decision makers and the inherent limitations of a single perspective on complex cases. From an impartiality and integrity viewpoint, the governor-in-council appointment process of members to the STT has raised serious concerns over the appearance of the independence of the tribunal. The editorial of a major city daily newspaper remarked that "the new tribunal ... has a strong smell of patronage. At least half of its members, who earn as much as $124,000 to (slowly) pass judgment on whether ordinary Canadian should get disability pensions that average just over $10,000 a year, have ties to the Conservative party" (*Chronicle Herald* 2014; see also Goodman 2014c, 2015a).

Most troublingly with the new SST regime is that individuals who apply for CPP/D benefits have lost certain legal rights and had other rights confined. Regulations now allow the SST to summarily dismiss an appeal if it is satisfied that the appeal has no reasonable chance of success. Moreover, clients have no right to plead their case directly to a tribunal member. An in-person hearing is no longer a guaranteed right but one option among several, including a hearing by teleconference, videoconference, or on the basis of the written documents only. This change clashes with the legal rules of procedural fairness that require an oral hearing whenever there is an issue of credibility. Given the subjective component of CPP/D, in addition to the inherent embodied nature of citizens, there is always a need for an assessment of credibility. In-person hearings are critical, as an administrative lawyer and former head of a workplace compensation tribunal states: "In these cases, credibility is inevitably an important part of the decision, especially if you have a culture that views claimants with suspicion, which is always a possibility. From the adjudicator's perspective, there's the need to actually see the person in order to help judge their credibility. From the appellant's point of view, there is the deep need to look people in the eye and know that they are listening" (Goodman 2014b). In-person hearings enable the fleshy realities of appellants to come across through human encounters. This is the bodily materiality of social citizenship. Under the previous system, new evidence could be introduced by a claimant at the second level of appeal; but under the SST no new evidence or testimony can be presented before the tribunal's Appeal Division, following a decision by the tribunal's General Division. The stated aim is to move to more electronic technologies for handling CPP/D cases. However, nothing in the legislation or the regulations for the s s t requires that teleconferences or videoconferences be accessible to people with a range of impairments or health conditions. Individuals applying for c p p disability benefits are already under extraordinary stress. In all, the problematic consequences are diminished rights of working Canadians with disabilities, compromised rules of natural justice, lost expertise in decision making, and an under-resourced tribunal. Clients and their families struggle and suffer as they confront new obstacles to access to an income security program that is vital to their well-being and financial security.

LIVED EXPERIENCES IN CLAIMING DISABILITY BENEFITS

Canadian adults with disabilities, for the most part, report having three or more impairments. Most common are pain, agility, and mobility, followed by learning, hearing, seeing, and speaking, and then psychiatric, memory, and developmental disabilities. The main causes of disabilities are an accident, collision, or injury; a disease or illness; and then work conditions (Furrie 2010). The episodic nature of many disabilities has become prominent in policy discussions in Canada. At issue is the mismatch between public policies for people with disabilities – many of which base eligibility upon a prolonged and steady condition of disability – and the experiences of Canadians who have fluctuating periods of wellness and illness with variable states of severity in effects. Arthritis, cancer, diabetes, h i v / a i d s, lupus, and multiple sclerosis are examples of episodic disabilities. In part, the episodic nature of disability relates directly to work capacity and absenteeism, and to earnings and the financial security of households.

In one of the few empirical studies in Canada, Adele Furrie (2010) looked at the employment effects of those people with disabilities in the labour force who report having a limitation at work due to their condition. Frequent effects include changing the amount and the kind of work done, changing jobs, working part-time because of the condition, and being unemployed for a period. Compared to Canadians without disabilities, Canadians with disabilities are less likely to be employed and less likely to work full-time or to work full-year. As well, Canadians with disabilities are more likely to receive lower pay, attain fewer promotions, experience discrimination at work, and live in lower income households.

In what ways do people with disabilities, as applicants for benefits, experience the CPP/D program?[7] A social right to disability benefits is a claim for financial resources by individuals based on certain criteria and duties, as well as mediated through a number of discursive and regulative systems. Eric Gorham reminds us that "society and the state do not simply give ... [rights] to citizens *gratis*; citizens must subject themselves to the procedures and institutions necessary to ensure that the state can continue to provide rights" (1995, 29). In the case of CPP/D, applicants are subjected to disciplinary procedures, knowledge systems, and rules from administrative, medical, vocational rehabilitation, actuarial/financial, income security, and judicial discourses. Discursive practices influence access and shape the experiences of individuals seeking to obtain benefits to which they believe they qualify and are entitled. Multiple diagnoses include self-assessments, medical examinations, legal deliberations, rehabilitation evaluations, and even actuarial considerations regarding the financial health of the program itself. This multiplicity of discourses and associated diagnoses are integral to the nature of contestation in claiming their benefits. Even successful applicants for disability insurance who become beneficiaries experience tensions and stresses.

For many working Canadians with disabilities, the experience of seeking this social right of income support is one of rejection and denial of benefits. The earned right of CPP/D, even though based on contributions and workforce participation, does not guarantee the automatic provision of benefits. While labour force attachment is a prerequisite for entitlement to the CPP/D, as a work-related insurance plan, it is not a sufficient condition for eligibility. Further conditions must be satisfied for a worker with a disability to actually qualify and obtain financial support from the program. The individual must be found to have a severe, prolonged mental or physical disability.

This is a crucial point: CPP/D insures against a specific category of disability – severe in condition and prolonged in duration, a disability that prevents a person, it is assumed, from being able to pursue any gainful employment. CPP/D does not provide partial benefits; a person either qualifies for the full benefit or gets nothing at all from the program. For people with episodic disabilities, this

7 This section draws on Prince 2008.

can be an unfavourable design feature of the program. To determine if the person has a severe and prolonged disability, information is compiled from the applicant, his or her physician, and employer to produce a profile of the applicant, which is then used to determine medical eligibility for the income benefit. Labour market considerations also enter into decisions, informed by the relative strength of the economy and the extent of employment opportunities in a local area that may match the skills or background of an applicant.

Matters of illness, disorders, and disability contain assorted knowledge clashes. Discursive conflicts occur between expert professions as well as among laypeople and experts regarding definitions and the framing of experiences. Other points of struggle arise around diagnostic scales and assessment tools; symptoms, prevalence, and incidence; and causal relationships and the influence of other factors. Still further knowledge clashes can emerge over different understandings of the efficacy and desirability of distinct treatments, interventions, and controls. In the case of HIV/AIDS, cancer care, and schizophrenia, for example, there are many obvious and persistent conflicting perspectives. The more forms of knowledge in play in a given policy field, the greater possibility of divergent perspectives, especially if information sources are aligned with different value systems and interests endowed with authority, whether medicine, the legal process, private life insurance companies, or a state bureaucracy. With detailed investigations, reviews, and various encounters with complex organizations, for many people this social insurance program can feel a lot like a social assistance program.

Individual–Official Interactions

From a critical perspective, the liberal welfare state is a mechanism of coercion and bureaucratic administration. At the same time, it is a mechanism of compliance and self-regulation. This latter mechanism connects to practices of governmental self-formation and practices of ethical self-formation. Recognizing that these are not absolute distinctions, Mitchell Dean defines practices of governmental self-formation as "the ways in which various authorities and agencies seek to shape the conduct and capacities of specified political and social categories, to enlist them in particular strategies and to seek definable goals." Practices of ethical self-formation involve "techniques and rationalities concerning the regulation of the self by the self, and by means of which individuals seek to question, form, know, decipher and act on themselves" (Dean 1995, 563).

Dean describes social security programs as "governmental-ethical practices," suggesting these income support programs have a hybrid nature combining practices of governmental and ethical self-formation. On the governmental side are goals of income protection, perhaps the alleviation of poverty and labour market participation. On the ethical side are practices shaping "attributes, capacities, orientations and moral conduct of individuals" and defining "their rights, obligations and statuses" (Dean 1995, 567). For the CPP/D, this perspective agreeably fits. Relations of power in this disability insurance scheme are simultaneously coercive (social control) and chosen (self-compliance) as well as accepted (service provision) and resisted (contestation). Along with medical constructions and organizational processing, contested illnesses are linked utterly with self-descriptions, presentations of personal experiences, and lived realties. To establish eligibility, these self-presentations interact with multiple discourses within and among human service organizations.

Interactions between clients and experts are not all experienced as an overt struggle. Many interactions about seeking the provision of services or benefits are mostly helpful, encouraging, and productive, and give clients a sense of satisfaction and well-being. Other interactions generate a sense of quiet unease or anxiety with "the wish to suggest other issues for attention other than those given priority by the professional." In still other situations, the "interaction will be experienced more negatively as one of monitoring, surveillance and control" of individuals by experts (Leonard 1997, 170). Depending on how serious the controls and constraints, the client may feel a sense of crisis or panic. This might provoke strong resistance by clients, individually or collectively through informal or formal associations, to challenge the "knowledge claims of experts" and to seek a more equitable relationship by advancing the legitimacy of their own accounts. Many applicants to CPP/D seek out the help and support of co-workers, their employer or union, legal advocates, and their member of Parliament.

Each year significant numbers of people do not exercise their legal right to appeal an initial negative decision on their application for public disability insurance benefits. The likely reasons shed light on the context of struggle for social rights. People decline to contest a negative decision on eligibility for disability benefits because of poor personal health. Some people are concerned they may lose other supports they currently receive if they do appeal. Conversely, a disabled claimant may well lack important supports, such as accessible transportation, that would enable them to attend an appeal hearing. Family members or friends may discourage an individual from contesting a negative decision on their initial application for CPP/D. The family physician may advise a person that they do not meet the eligibility criteria. Information about rights of redress is not easily accessible and so some people are unaware of the review and appeal mechanisms. And even if they are aware of the appeal process, previous negative experiences with bureaucrats may convince them they have little or no chance of winning against the government. These explanations are rooted in personal factors and organizational processes, plus a cultural frame of beliefs and assumptions about medical science, state authority, and individual responsibility. A mix of governmental and ethical practices of self-formation is involved here. Surveillance of specific cases and the overall caseload is justified by authorities by a quality assurance discourse of ensuring program integrity and accountability so that fraud and errors are avoided and benefits are paid to those properly eligible. In the Harper era, this discourse of program control became more explicit and insistent.

CONCLUSION

Claiming social rights to disability income protection play out through myriad organized human relationships and concrete processes in the lives of disabled working Canadians. Social citizenship emerges as a complex bundle of power and knowledge relations running through state, political, and civil society structures. With their compulsory contributions and labour force attachment requirements, social insurance programs are earned rights to income benefits – important elements of social citizenship in modern welfare states. These rights are not so automatic or free from struggle to obtain, however. In comparison to classic means-tested welfare programs, social insurance policies like the CPP are claimed to have a far less "intrusive and individualised form of disciplinary relationship between the state and the applicant for benefit" (Squires 1990, 138). But in social insurance programs that address risks of illness, injury, and disability (such as workers' compensation, sickness benefits, compassionate care benefits, and public disability insurance), the state – federally or provincially or both at times for the same program – does intervene in every case, examining and verifying the information submitted by each applicant, and accepting or rejecting that information for the purposes of individual eligibility.

Disabled workers as rights bearer are subject to multiple forms of authority and information – labour market, medical, familial, administrative, and quasi-judicial. From these sources of power and knowledge, both positive and negative experiences and interpretations of needs are generated. Workers with disabilities come to the CPP/D program to receive income support and, for a relatively few, vocational rehabilitation services. Invariably, they come out of the process different from what they were before. Individuals access income security programs through their bodies, with the capabilities and limitations of their everyday physiological being. Along with work and contribution requirements, their eligibility pivots on their embodiment; a bodily status that is medically assessed, bureaucratically managed, and socially construed to be problematic. Moreover, this problematic bodily status is the basis for claiming a social right. This policy world of rules and unruly practices is far removed from the abstract, universal individual of citizenship theory. In view of these contested experiences, obtaining a disability pension is as much a personal accomplishment as it is a formal entitlement.

Over the Harper Conservative era, the discourse and practice of Canadian social policy shifted: it was less intergovernmental, less federal, and less rights-oriented at a national level, becoming more provincial, more penal, and more private sector-oriented. On CPP/D, medical criteria for qualifying for the benefits remained unaltered. Easing the eligibility rules to disability benefits for long-term contributors meant that individuals who contributed to the CPP for twenty-five years or more will meet contributory eligibility requirements for disability benefits with valid contributions in three of the last six years, instead of the standard requirement of four of the last six years. Most significantly, with the abolition of the OCRT and PAB and creation of the SST, there is a diminishment of legal rights of clients for a fair system of redress and appeal. On the evidence thus far, this restructured system of administrative justice has not generated a positive political image or enjoyed strong public confidence as an accessible, impartial, and effective tribunal.

CHAPTER NINE

Disability Governance and Social Rights

State institutions shape civil society as well as being the product of social relations. The links across the ... state, market and community are in large part organized through struggles for new rights and for the protection of acquired rights.

Jane Jenson, "Fated to Live in Interesting Times"

Disability is not actually about those of us who are disabled; it is about those with the power to call us disabled.

A.J. Withers, *Disability Politics and Theory*

What does the history of CPP/D reveal about the nature of politics and governing, of the relation between the state and market economy, and the consequences of this set of social rights and responsibilities? Employing the idea of disability governance is an effort to recognize more explicitly that governing is more than government, more than the state, and more than public policy pronounced and implemented by the state and its bureaucracies. The governance literature tends to focus on the national state, generally regarding it as a benevolent authority that, situated increasingly in dense relations with non-state organizations, has declined considerably as a force in public policy formation. By comparison, this volume focuses on the federated nature of states in Canada and has indicated that the state is a force of control and segregation as well as of support and inclusion. Moreover, the analysis shows that numerous forms of socioeconomic power have long operated in and around public policy and administration. Subject to political considerations, medical decisions, and administrative measures, disability gets worked up as a governable field. In disability governance, federal and provincial states play roles characterized at times more by steering than rowing by employing softer instruments than command and control regulatory tools. Governance of disability is a set of interacting policies, decisions, processes, laws, and values involving state agencies, political parties, business interests, non-governmental organizations, and civil society interests, individuals and families, and medical and rehabilitation professions.

This chapter first explores families, work and capitalism, and medicine. The second section surveys activists and interest groups, political parties and elections, while the third section considers parliamentary cabinet government, the internal bureaucratic politics of state action, and federalism and intergovernmental relations in Canada. Based on the literature and analysis from earlier chapters, the fourth section discusses the interplay between social policies and social rights and their implications for societal arrangements.

CANADIAN SOCIETY

This section looks at the institution of families, capitalism and work, and the role of medical science and related health professions in relation to disability and disability income provision.

Families and Sites of Social Policy

Public policy scholars sometimes depict the family as a voluntary instrument of governing and suggest that, with the exercise of just low levels of involvement, the state can rely on families for addressing social problems and providing goods and services, thus helping to achieve certain goals of public policy. How accurate is it to describe family provision as a voluntary policy instrument either devoid of state involvement or a low level of intervention? Is it voluntary because the family is seen to be a private and separate sphere of the social world?

Traditionally, and still today, governments incorporate a notion of family responsibility in many social policies, imposing a duty on families, idealized as natural providers, to care for those in need, such as aged parent, young children, and disabled relatives. Certainly, as Julia S. O'Connor, Ann Shola Orloff, and Sheila Shaver observe, social rights "depend for their effectiveness on 'private' arrangements (for example, caregiving in the family)" (1999, 31). Helen Meekosha and Leanne Dowse add that "the family may sometimes provide a safe haven and support base for people with disabilities shunned by social institutions and locked out by discriminatory processes" (1997, 53). However, they immediately remark that with respect to disabled members, families can have "contradictory and multiple intentions" (53). Families may assign fairly positive or deeply negative connotations to a condition or impairment; they may encourage or discourage particular kinds of actions by disabled members in claiming benefits or in interacting with assorted agencies and practitioners.

In CPP/D and other income support programs, families are directly implicated in the design and delivery and regulation of benefits. CPP and CPP/D interconnect with families through policies dealing with divorce, child rearing drop-out provisions, the derived social rights of survivor and children's benefits, volunteering and earnings exemptions, and the automatic reinstatement of benefits. The CPP/D program regards families as networks of earning and caring, of capacities and dependencies, and as places where people have rights and also responsibilities back to the program. For example, a child that enters the care and custody of a CPP/D recipient through birth, adoption, marriage, or common law relationship may qualify for the CPP/D children's benefit. If a child leaves their care and custody, the CPP/D recipient must inform Service Canada to ensure the termination of the children's benefit. Likewise, if the parent stops receiving a CPP/D benefit, he or she must advise Service Canada so that the children's benefit is ended. As a rule, the CPP/D children's benefit ends when the child is no longer dependent and turns eighteen, or is between eighteen and twenty-five and no longer attending school full-time, or turns twenty-five. Far from being a private world, families are thus the object of certain benefits and rules. The family is a site of self-regulation and the source of information to program administrators as to initial eligibility and continual entitlement.

Capitalism and Work

The introduction of social-insurance-based income provision for categories of disabled people directly required participation in the economic mainstream of society, the labour force. This was a notable change for traditional practices of poor relief and segregated approaches of charity and institutionalized care. The link between capitalism and disablement crystallized as injury, illness, and impairment became recognized by industrial states as general threats to interrupting work and the earned income of workers and to destabilizing families. In the words of the Marsh Report, "if earning power stops all else is threatened" ([1943] 1975, 7). By linking income entitlement in disability to the market criteria of labour force participation and previous earnings, workers are positioned as commodities, and damaged goods at that. The capitalist market economy is also a powerful creator and carrier of "cultural understandings of 'able-bodied normalcy'" (Barnes and Mercer 2003, 142). These understandings include working to a standard schedule, meeting deadlines and doing overtime if need be, and working in a built environment that takes little if any account of various impairments of employees or customers. Industrialism and the bureaucratization of work "led to the increased displacement of 'unproductive' disabled workers" (Barnes and Mercer 2003, 24).

Through social insurance, politics and markets became intertwined; in the words of Walter Korpi, political and market systems are "partly alternative, partly overlapping strategies or arenas for the mobilization of resources, the distribution of rewards, and the steering of society" (1989, 312). CPP/D is an example of social rights that come to pass through market relations. These partly alternative and overlapping arenas are apparent also in the role of private rehabilitation services, the life and health insurance industry, and the interaction between private short-term sickness and long-term disability plans with the EI sickness benefits and CPP/D benefits, respectively. As Keith Faulk observes, "the needs of the market economy have played a huge part in the form citizenship has taken" (2000, 27). Overall, CPP/D is a market-confirming benefit. There is no credible evidence that the CPP/D weakens paid work incentives, crowds out private investments in long-term disability plans, or discourages personal savings for extended health insurance (HRSDC 2011).

CPP is a social insurance program with employees and employers making compulsory contributions to the plan to both finance it and, for workers, to establish a basis for an earned right to disability, retirement, and other stipulated benefits. There is a work test of a defined attachment to the paid labour force prior to making any claims, which indicates that economic market values and practices underpin this program. To a large degree, CPP/D benefits are earnings-related. Furthermore, CPP is a first payer of benefits. This means private insurance companies and provincial program officials responsible for workers' compensation and social assistance insist that a person first apply for CPP/D benefits before they can obtain any payments from another public or private plan to which they may be entitled. This feature can generate considerable confusion and anger for people seeking to claim disability insurance benefits.

For people in the labour force, "introduction of modern social rights implies a loosening of pure commodity status. De-commodification occurs when a service is rendered as a matter of right, and when a person can maintain a livelihood without reliance on the market" (Esping-Andersen 1990, 21–2). Concrete design elements and actual practices of the CPP/D reveal a far more complicated set of relationships between social rights and the market than is usually implied by the de-commodification thesis. First, there is a *strong commodification* of entitlement. This is because eligibility depends on a person's recent labour market status as an employee or self-employed, their history of contributions, and their inability to work in any substantial gainful occupation. At the same time, there is a process of labour force detachment that occurs for many workers with disabilities years before they become CPP/D beneficiaries. Research shows that employment earnings start to substantially decline two or three years before CPP/D begins (HRSDC 2011, 30).

A form of *moderate commodification* occurs in that CPP/D benefits are partly proportionate to the labour market earnings of the client, thus reflecting wage differences in the economy. At the same time, with a flat-rate component added to the disability benefit, market value is somewhat subordinated to social welfare principles, perhaps the clearest expression of *direct de-commodification*. This flat-rate component of CPP/D shows the influence of democratic state actors in determining the overall value of the disability pension, such that the benefit is not wholly determined by participation in the labour market. On average, the CPP/D pension represents half the total income of a beneficiary; for one in eight beneficiaries, it accounts for all of their family income, helping them to alleviate poverty and live independently (HRSDC 2011). Income benefits to survivors and children of disabled contributors, of which there are over eighty thousand annually, represent *derivative de-commodification*, income support once removed from reliance on labour market participation. For a minority of the annual CPP/D caseload, a *minimal re-commodification* occurs through promotion of participating in the labour market when clients undertake vocational rehabilitation services, return-to-work programs, and make use of the CPP/D policy on earnings exemptions. Annually, 10 percent or less of all CPP/D beneficiaries has employment earnings; many of these beneficiaries have employment earnings for just one year, and the amount is typically a few thousand dollars.

A process of *re-de-commodification* happens when a client who leaves CPP/D to enter the workforce returns to the program. If they return within two years, there is an automatic reinstatement of their benefits. A 2006 survey of 155 people who had made use of this automatic reinstatement found that about half thought the provision helped them to stay at work longer than otherwise would be the case before receiving their disability pension again to maintain a basic standard of living (HRSDC 2011, 42). Yet the economic recession in 2008–10 and subsequent uneven recovery has restricted employment opportunities for many Canadians, and especially those with disabilities. Finally, a program evaluation of the CPP/D indicated that between 50 percent and 60 percent of those denied benefits had no employment earnings three or four years later (HRSDC 2011). For many disabled workers denied eligibility, *welfarization* rather than commodification seems to be a common fate.

Medical Science

Closely linked to the problem of financial insecurity, disability income provision is organized around norms of incapacity and abnormality and thus practices of diagnoses and treatments. Medical knowledge and expertise notably holds a dominant place in this policy domain. Disability income provision involves medical intervention in the welfare state and the medical gaze on citizens' bodies and minds. Workers' compensation, veterans' benefits, EI sickness benefits, and CPP/D benefits each have some medical-rehabilitation science component. Desmond Morton describes the war veterans' allowance established in 1930, for example, as "a cautious, poverty-level pension for that vague but undeniable set of symptoms first labeled 'shell shock,'" a pension for "veterans aged sixty or more, and those who were younger but unemployable for physical or mental reasons" (2004, 236). In Canada, throughout the twentieth century, medical, nursing, psychiatric, and rehabilitation sciences became the dominant forms of knowledge around human bodies and minds, positioning these professions as authoritative, as well as rival, decision makers and gatekeepers to an array of state benefits and services (Bacchi and Beasley 2002; Moss and Prince 2014).

Medicalization of modern life is especially consequential for people with impairments and for disability policy and practice. With its techniques and terminologies deployed by professionals, the medical science paradigm can shape or reshape identities of people and their sense of community. "This medicalization of disability," as Colin Barnes, Geof Mercer, and Tom Shakespeare remark, "represented the establishment of an 'individual' model of disability that became the professional, policy and lay orthodoxy through the twentieth century" (1999, 20). In this model, explanation of a person's status is primarily on diagnosing and then classifying and, if possible, treating the person's body and mind, curing or fixing their abnormalities, pathologies, and functional limitations. Departmental guidelines adopted in 1995 for determining medical eligibility to CPP/D removed the consideration of socioeconomic factors in adjudications. Along with other measures taken in the mid-1990s, this intensified medical gaze resulted, as intended, in a decrease in new beneficiaries.

The medical gaze is more heterogeneous than often popularly portrayed. Aspects of de-medicalization take place, for example, when a physician wishing not to disadvantage a patient's claim to disability support does not challenge or question their application for benefits. Physicians also may worry about stigmatizing a patient by attaching a negative label on him or her. Another kind of de-medicalization takes place when a human rights model is applied by disability activists, health practitioners, or service providers, thus shifting the focus to structural barriers and to values of equality and fair treatment. In assessing a person's state of health and then completing and submitting a medical report, physicians are described as gatekeepers to health and social services, often with the insinuation that they screen out and discourage many people with disabilities from applying for benefit programs. That may well be true, in part. However, survey research reveals that people most commonly find out about the CPP/D from medical professionals, followed by employers and family and friends. More significantly, "those whose applications were subsequently granted were more likely to find out about the program from a doctor; while denied applicants were more likely to hear about it from family or friends, or provincial disability programs" (HRSDC 2011, 33).

THE CANADIAN POLITY

A fundamental measure of the quality of citizenship rights is the capacity to shape one's social standing by having a voice in decision-making systems. This section considers activists and interest groups and the role of political parties in the political system, specifically elections, while their role in the cabinet parliamentary government is examined in the next section.

Activists and Interest Groups

The sheer human agency of people with disabilities when claiming social rights to income is evident in their interacting and negotiating with programs and wider cultural and economic institutions. Agency arises from people learning about their changing bodies and minds, and in their managing impressions around impairments. Agency is likewise exercised through gathering and exchanging information as they acquire the status of disabled worker and then as rights claimant. These activities in political affairs and in program administration "can lead to more collective forms of action to extend and defend social rights" (Lister 1997, 31).

Then there are social movement advocates and policy entrepreneurs outside of government who promote specific policy reforms to address social risks of income insecurity. It is misleading to suggest that "expansion of the welfare state in Canada was unaccompanied by intellectual rigour or any clear understanding of the relationship between market and state to which it was taking us" (Cairns and Williams 1985, 19). As Chapter 3 showed, Harry Cassidy, Leonard Marsh, and Charlotte Whitton were leading social investigators and policy advisors in Canada in the 1940s, offering empirical research, drafting blueprints for social and economic change, and recommending pragmatic reforms for administrative and professional interventions. In addition, they drew on policy lessons from other countries and debated over the relative merit of social assistance, social insurance, and the social utilities of casework and services. Their works are an important element in the heritage of liberal philosophy and practicality in social policy development and disability in Canada. By the time of the Great Pension Debate in the 1970s and 1980s, organized labour, business groups, assorted think tanks, and policy institutes were primary generators of reform ideas in civil society. In that debate, no doubt assisted by a recession in the early 1980s and rising government deficits, business and insurance industry interests were more effective in shaping policy outcomes than in the 1960s and in opposing the passage of the CPP.

Social rights to income support for disabled Canadians are located in several separate programs, with numerous categories of clientele. On the influence of interest groups seeking new or improved programs, a federal welfare official recounts that "the disabled mounted one remarkably effective campaign which led to the enactment, considerably earlier than would have otherwise been the case, of the Disabled Persons Act in 1954" (Splane 1987, 232). Categorical programs and impairment-based groups have understandable challenges in building coalitions and sustaining solidarity. Rodney Haddow points out the impact of introducing the Canada Assistance Plan (CAP) on the political influence of particular impairment groups: "Organizations of disabled persons – the old categorical groups – continued to take some interest in poverty issues during the 1970s, but the elimination of their special assistance programs in 1966 had substantially reduced their influence" (1993, 180). In contrast, creation of the CPP/D and the introduction of EI sickness benefits and disability-related tax credits produced new program constituencies that over the years have mobilized politically both individually, at the client level, and collectively, as groups. In the 1996 review of CPP led by the Chrétien Liberal government, social policy groups and disability organizations lobbied hard to limit the extent of retrenchments to the CPP/D and then, in the early 2000s, pressured MPs to review the effects of the cutbacks on disabled workers.

Political Parties and Elections

A standard critique of Canadian political parties is that they do not function as robust public policy organizations generating ideas and options or developing clear platforms for national elections. In the field of disability income policy, however, federal political parties – within their internal workings and when facing electoral situations – have played significant parts in developing policy goals and instruments and in promising specific program reforms.

In the late 1950s and early 1960s, the idea of a contributory public pension plan, with supplementary benefits for physical and mental disabilities, was of public interest and political significance. There was both electoral appeal and electoral competition among the political parties in expounding proposals on pension reform (Bryden 1997). In fact, as Chapter 4 showed, a pension plan with related benefits was an election platform priority of all three major federal political parties in the 1958, 1962, and 1963 federal elections. In the Liberal Party of Canada, politicians and officials were centrally involved in the design of what came to be called the CPP and CPP/D. On Liberal social policy in the Pearson years from 1957 to 1958, there is no question that "political actors, both in Parliament and in the backrooms, were largely responsible not only for designing the social-security legislation but also for creating its justification" (Bryden 1997, xiii; see also Kent 1988; LaMarsh 1969). I am mindful that the CPP and CPP/D story may be an exception to the rule of limited influence by political party organizations over social policy making and that, in recent times, political parties are not as programmatic in either their capacities or predilections as they might have been.

Pearson's era also saw the Canada Assistance Plan and reform of social assistance policy. Recognizably a major poverty initiative and exercise in cooperative federalism, the CAP must also be seen as a notable development in disability policy, incorporating the assistance programs for blind persons and disabled persons and mothers' allowances. Yet social assistance reform in the 1960s was led by federal and provincial social service bureaucrats, not by their political masters. The national political parties were indifferent to social assistance reform and the public was apathetic as well. Not surprisingly, poverty was not a major electoral priority given that the policy was targeted at socially and economically marginal citizens (Haddow 1993, 185–9). In comparison, the CPP and CPP/D was of interest to middle-class voters, illustrating the political point that "social programmes serve different groups of people and therefore differ in the degree of support they receive" (Mishra 1990, 104).

Disability income policy figures in the electoral politics of a country. Sheila Shaver's analysis of Australia applies well to the Canadian situation: "the income security system is a framework, historically and politically constructed, which defines legitimate claims to social rights. Social rights, once established, have become objects of budgetary and ballot-box politics, hence their terms, conditions and values are always subject to contention among competing policy agendas and citizen constituencies" (1989, 93). In several federal and provincial elections over the hundred-year period examined in this book, both governing and opposition parties announced new programs and promised enhancements to existing benefits for people with disabilities. The first modern workers' compensation plan in Canada was introduced in Ontario in 1914 during an election in that province. Between 1916 and 1920, seven of the provinces and the federal government gave women the right to vote. "It is hardly a coincidence," notes Dennis Guest, "that provincial schemes of mothers' pensions in five of these provinces should follow in such order the granting of the franchise to women" (1998, 51). On the eve of the 1930 federal election, the King Liberal government introduced the war veterans' allowance, one of the "core political issues" at the time in response to the demands of Great War veterans (Morton 2004, 235).

In the 1950s, a conservative decade for Canadian social policy, "it was not until the federal Liberal Party was dismissed from office in 1957 that its interest in social security revived" (Guest 1998, 142). The blind allowance maximum was raised twice that year, just before the election by the St Laurent Liberal government, and after by the new Diefenbaker Conservative government. Public pension figured as a prominent social policy issue in the 1962 and 1963 federal elections as did the blind allowance, with its the maximum payable ratcheted up again in both those years. During the Great Pension Debate in the late 1970s and early 1980s, federal parties yet again presented ideas and pledges for improvements to public pensions, including to disability benefits. The 2015 federal budget, before an autumn national election, figured a major extension of the compassionate care benefit to care for gravely ill family members, from six weeks to six months; confirmed plans to improve income benefits for Canadian veterans; and introduced a new tax credit for home accessibility for seniors and people with disabilities, worth up to $1,500 a year. Electoral calculations for votes and competition for success have clearly stimulated the expansion of specific disability income provisions and thus social citizenship.

THE CANADIAN STATE

Discussion on the Canadian state focuses on parliamentary cabinet government, bureaucratic politics, and working models of federalism and intergovernmental relations in effect in the CPP/D and other disability income policy.

Parliamentary Cabinet Government

It is commonplace to regard the Canadian Parliament as ineffectual and marginal in contemporary governance – what with strong party discipline and executive dominance, especially by the prime minister and central agencies. Under this view, Parliament's role in the modern welfare state has been to enact legislation shaped by interest group politics, developed by departmental officials, and managed by cabinets. Parliament's marginal role would seem compounded for the CPP/D with jurisdiction shared with the provinces, including an elaborate federal-provincial amending formula for major changes. In this context of federalism, policy developments are brought forward by responsible ministers presented to parliamentarians as carefully negotiated packages with the provinces that parliament should not reject or even try to amend but rather give assent. This too is a commonplace critique of how federalism coexists uneasily with parliamentary democracy.

A wider perspective, one that looks at policy evaluation, administrative oversight, policy community consultations, and working on behalf of constituents in the encounters with public programs, reveals that Parliament and individual MPs have been more significant, in regards to disability policy, than is typically assumed.

Over the CPP/D's fifty-year history, on various occasions the House of Commons, committees, and individual MPs have played meaningful roles in policy and practice. Even at the approval stage of intergovernmental agreements, opportunities arise for different values to be expressed, issues are raised for future negotiations, and ministerial reputations are affected. Constituents who are CPP/D applicants and clients frequently turn to their MPs for assistance in obtaining information or explanations, which, in turn, provides MPs with anecdotal evidence on problematic instances of disabled workers claiming this social entitlement. Such activities signify an exercise in political citizenship. MPs represent important resources to Canadians with disabilities both symbolically, as democratically elected representatives, and substantively, as allies in the politics of need interpretation.

In party caucuses and in standing and special committees, parliamentarians, acting as policy entrepreneurs, have exercised influence on the CPP/D program and practice. In the Pearson era, the joint House of Commons and Senate committee directly influenced the content of the CPP/D with their recommendation to add the children's benefit. In the final government of the Trudeau era, a Special House of Commons Committee on the Disabled and Handicapped produced the unanimous *Obstacles* report and a series of follow-up reports monitoring the take-up by federal agencies in adopting committee recommendations. Then in the mid-1980s to early 1990s, members of the Mulroney Progressive Conservative government caucus, especially the "Red Tory" wing, lobbied from within the ministers of Finance and National Health and Welfare for expansion and improvements to the CPP/D. The CPP legislation introduced in 1986 represented both intergovernmental and all-party consensus at that point. These efforts at influencing decisions were reinforced by a functional and activist parliamentary committee on the status of persons with disabilities and by private member's bills dealing with the CPP and CPP/D, and with some remarkable successes (Shifrin 1991, 1992). In the Chrétien-Martin years, especially from 2000 to 2005, MPs pushed back in regard to cutbacks to the CPP/D implemented in 1998, by consulting Canadians, inviting expert witnesses, questioning and challenging officials and ministers, and making a range of program recommendations.

During the Harper era, parliamentary committees declined exceedingly in relevance including the committees responsible for persons with disabilities and social policy. Having said that, the extension of the compassionate care benefit from six weeks to six months, announced in the 2015 federal budget, acknowledged the 2011 report of a parliamentary committee on palliative and compassionate care. Unique in Canadian parliamentary history, this committee was an all-party group of MPs, formed on their initiative and funded out of their member office budgets. In the words of their report, "The committee is an example of what is possible when MPs work closely across party lines on issues of profound concern to everyone. The spirit of non-partisan collaboration exhibited by the members of the committee is a great example of what parliament is at its best" (2011, 7). That there is a need for such an innovative approach by MPs regrettably points to the hyper-partisan character of recent parliaments and the strict control exercised by the Harper government over standing committees.

Bureaucratic Politics

Administrative and professional infrastructure for the CPP/D includes departmental staff in Employment and Social Development

Canada that each year handle sixty thousand new applications as well as ten thousand requests for reconsiderations of initial decisions, the involvement of nurses, physicians, and other health practitioners in determining disability in each case, reviewing a sample of files each year, the appeals and tribunals systems, the vocational rehabilitation services and related employment incentives, and the program integrity activities to ensure compliance and prevent fraud. In addition to operational and managerial tasks at call centres and regional processing offices, staff also attend to executive-level functions of policy development and liaise with other federal departments, the provinces, and Quebec Pension Plan officials.

Within this infrastructure are different interests. Bureaucratic differences are embedded in the division of labour in public administration endowing each portfolio with a distinct mandate, resources and organizational culture, policy community, and public history. The CPP is part of what Pierre Bourdieu calls "the left hand of the state," located in Employment and Social Development, a huge spending department, with traces "of the social struggles of the past," in contrast to "the right hand of the state, the technocrats of the Ministry of Finance" and private sector interests (Bourdieu 1998, 2). Both hands of the state have influenced and continue to shape the scope and direction of disability policy. This bureaucratic arm-wrestling inside the state reflects larger ideological interests and differences, and adds weight to the argument that social insurance programs are not so straightforward or free of tension. Interestingly, much of federal disability policy making over the decades has been overseen by finance ministers, most notably Michael Wilson in the Mulroney prime ministerial era, Paul Martin in the Chrétien governments, and Jim Flaherty in the Harper age. National welfare ministers also made distinctive contributions in relation to CPP/D, in particular Judy LaMarsh in the Pearson era, Monique Bégin in the final Trudeau government, and Jake Epp in the first Mulroney government.

Both the CPP's original design and those for CPP/D and QPP/D demonstrated a strong policy capacity by officials in the federal and Quebec public services. Senior administrators displayed considerable skills in examining policy options, generating relevant data, offering advice to cabinet ministers, and framing arguments for intergovernmental negotiations, then designing legislation and eventually implementing this major new social program. On the indexation of CPP benefits, there was a great battle between the federal Finance

Department and the Prime Minister's Office. A modest form of indexation was adopted, with ministers sympathetic to the idea that a public pension should rise automatically with the wage level; otherwise governments risk political trouble in adjusting benefits on an ad hoc basis. Changes to the CPP/D in 1997–98 illustrate the relative influence and divergent perspectives of federal agencies and the central role of finance officials in shaping the reform agenda and shepherding through retrenchment. To the social department responsible for the program, proposals to tighten the administration of disability benefits represented an indictment of internal management and information records. To the Finance department, however, such proposals were an opportunity to limit entitlements and to signal their minister's general message of government restraint and making public pensions sustainable for Canadians. And to the chief actuary of the Office of the Superintendent of Financial Institutions and the Office of the Auditor General, these proposals were an acknowledgment of their professional concerns raised about the integrity and accountability of the program.

Probably the most significant achievement by Finance in the 1998 amendments to the CPP was the requirement that any increase in benefits must be accompanied by a sustainable increase in the contribution rate for employers and employees to cover the additional future costs.

In recent years, the right hand of the federal state continues to prevail, with Finance officials basically content with the status quo, seeing no obvious groundswell for major changes to the CPP/D. Moreover, technocrats of the treasury have an ingrained resistance to liberalize the CPP/D whether for clients who are long-term contributors, preferring to emphasize recent attachment to work versus longevity of employment, or for clients who are terminally ill or to set up a research program funded by the CPP. Even in the Harper era, though, with a highly politicized and highly centralized government, federal public servants did shape disability income policy. Examples include the new eligibility criteria to CPP/D for long-term contributors, the creation of the social security tribunal, and the establishment of the RDSP. Laurie Beachell, former national coordinator of the Council of Canadians with Disabilities suggests that many positive changes in CPP/D policy over the years are due to responsive senior bureaucrats in the federal public service: "CPP/D continues to create incremental improvements in its process and continues to work with representatives of the disability community to remove barriers to both the receipt of the benefit as well as provide incentives to work. These changes have come about because of two factors, the input of people with disabilities and their organizations has been sought and supported, and senior civil servants running the program have demonstrated committed leadership to removing barriers and making the program more inclusive and accessible" (Beachell 2011, 114).

Canadian Federalism and Disability Income Policy

Between the federal and provincial orders of government, reflecting separate and joint constitutional powers are Canadians with disabilities as a shared and divided client group and political constituency. What, then, has been the impact of federalism on disability income policy in Canada? Has federalism been a constraint typically frustrating changes, or more a positive force enabling policy development and reforms? These are core questions asked by social scientists in trying to understand the influence of federalism on the modern welfare state.

To help address such questions, Keith Banting offers the practical observation that "different models of federalism can co-exist within an individual federal state" (2005, 90). For Canada, he identifies three models or working arrangements in federal-provincial relations in social policy and the welfare state: classical federalism, shared-cost federalism, and joint decision federalism. Classical federalism refers to the federal government or provincial government acting within its own fields of jurisdiction. Banting explains, "This model involves unilateral decisions by both levels of government, with minimal efforts at co-ordination even when decisions at one level have implications for the other" (2005, 95). With shared-cost federalism, "the federal government offers financial support to provincial governments on specific terms. In practice, the substance of such programmes tends to be hammered out in bargaining between the two levels. In formal terms, however, the model involves each government making separate decisions" (Banting 2005, 95). In the model of joint decision federalism, "the formal agreement of both levels of government is required before any action is possible. Unilateralism is not an option here." Indeed, "nothing happens unless formal approval is given by both levels of government" (ibid.).

Disability income policy in Canada illustrates each of these three models in action. The earliest developments in income provision for people with disabilities were expressions of classical federalism, whether exclusive action by one or other province on workers' compensation or mothers' allowances, or action by the federal government on war veterans' benefits. Later examples would be the establishment of youth allowances in 1964, the inclusion of sickness benefits in the unemployment insurance program in 1971, and, since the 1990s, introduction and expansion of an array of disability-related tax measures, largely by the federal government, though some provinces have adopted similar independent measures.

With regard to shared-cost federalism, also called cooperative federalism, notable disability income policy initiatives entailed the blind persons' allowance beginning in 1937, followed by the disabled persons' allowance, old age assistance, and vocational rehabilitation, mostly brought under the umbrella agreement of the Canada Assistance Plan, which was in effect from 1966 to 1996. As discussed in Chapter 3, much of this collaborative federalism in disability income provision is a record of federal initiative on policy design, provincial responsibility for administration, shared responsibility on financing and, in certain programs, a federal role in auditing provincial accounts and documentation.

In social policy, the foremost case of joint decision federalism is CPP. Another example of joint decision federalism field is Canada's ratification in 2010 of the UN Convention on the Rights of Persons with Disabilities. As argued in earlier chapters, we would not have a national public disability insurance program without the CPP as a national contributory retirement income program. Joint decision federalism, therefore, is integral to the CPP/D.

In the 1980s, political assessments of the CPP concluded that while major change was possible, it was not easy, given the need to secure the support of Ottawa, Quebec, Ontario, and five other provinces. With shared and divided authority over the CPP, a broad intergovernmental consensus was required under the decision rules, consequently making it a conservative force in Canadian pension policy (Banting 1984, 1987). This became the conventional view of the CPP in the social policy and Canadian federalism literatures. This pessimistic view of possibilities for changing CPP also reflected the very modest results from the Great Canadian Pension Debate and National Pensions Conference in that period. In subsequent writing, Banting has noted three effects of the joint decision model on the CPP. First, in practice, this model of federalism diversified the ideological perspective influencing the policy; second, it slowed change due to the complex formula of multiple veto points for provincial consent and because of the aim of keeping the Canada and Quebec pension plans broadly parallel; third, on the issue of retirement income policy, it deflected electoral pressures away from the CPP and towards other policies within the exclusive control of the federal government such as the Guaranteed Income Supplement (Banting 2005, 108).

In relation to the CPP/D program, this analysis has limited application. The goal of maintaining close comparability between the Canada and Quebec pension plans, including on disability benefits, has yielded an occasional dynamic of innovation between the two plans, with one plan taking the lead on a given reform followed then by the other plan to ensure reasonable similarity between them. Since the writings of the mid-1980s, the CPP/D has undergone significant reforms, both expansions and contractions. Intergovernmental agreements have been reached on different occasions dealing with several issues. A major expansion of CPP/D eligibility and benefit amounts took place in the Mulroney years, followed by a modest degree of retrenchment in the Chrétien years, and then a minor liberalization in eligibility in 2006 at the start of the Harper years. Attention to disability income reform has not been so much deflected away from the CPP as directed simultaneously at other programs at federal and provincial levels, be it social assistance reforms in the provinces or, at the federal level, improvements to employment standards, sickness benefits, tax credits, and veterans' benefits. Federalism certainly plays a role in the politics of disability income reform advocacy.

In the modern history of Canadian federalism, the CPP/D is an important policy development. And the history of the CPP/D indicates that several distinct models of federal-provincial relations can operate in and around an individual social program. According to David Cameron and Fraser Valentine, federalism is central to the disability policy formulation process and "bargaining between powerful federal and political executives comprises the heart of the policy nexus" (2001, 2). The analysis presented in Chapter 4 showed the CPP/D originated essentially in bilateral negotiations between Ottawa and Quebec in a form of executive federalism between a small group of cabinet ministers and senior officials. The regular schedule of federal-provincial meetings of ministers every five years, instituted in 1987, and every three years since the 1998 reforms, facilitates this dialogue among governments, especially among Finance and Treasury officials.

The actual ability of the federal government to propose disability and survivor benefits as part of the CPP required an exercise in constitutional federalism whereby the provinces agreed to an amendment to the BNA Act of 1867, enabling the federal government to enact a contributory pension plan with supplementary benefits such as for disability. (In retrospect, the 1940 constitutional amendment giving authority to Ottawa to enact an unemployment insurance plan eventually enabled the federal government to introduce a sickness benefit and later a compassionate care benefit as special benefits associated with that plan.) The CPP's amending formula requires the consent of the Canadian Parliament as well as at least two-thirds of the provinces that represent no less than two-thirds of the Canadian population. The amending formula applies to amendments of substance in the national legislation pertaining to the CPP, including the CPP/D. Areas of major amendments include the general level of benefits provided, the classes of benefits offered, the rates of contributions, the formula for calculating the contributions and benefits payable, the management of the CPP Account and CPP Investment Fund, and, until it was abolished in 1997, the constitution and duties of the CPP advisory committee. These changes require a two-year notice before coming into effect unless all provinces agree to waive the notice requirement.

A distinctive feature of the CPP and CPP/D is that this is a field of collaborative federalism anchored legally in concurrent jurisdiction by the two orders of government. As Alan Puttee writes, "by including a disability component in the Canada Pension Plan (CPP) in the mid-1960s, the federal government (together with the Quebec government with respect to the Quebec Pension Plan) initiated Canada's first nationwide disability insurance plan, an example of federal-provincial collaboration in the disability area" (2002, 6). With the CPP operative in every province and territory, except Quebec, which operates its own plan, this area of social policy exhibits a strong de jure form of asymmetric federalism.

Increasingly in the 1990s, after the CPP/D had been enhanced and the Mulroney and Chrétien governments retrenched various federal programs and transfer payments to the provinces, a version of competitive federalism became increasingly obvious. Under this model, government at one or other or both levels endeavour to shift program costs within their responsibility onto the other level. CPP/D policy became a target of this ploy with regular referrals by provincial officials of clients for social assistance or workers' compensation to CPP/D. As Bruce Little explains, "Provincial governments had a special incentive in that all were struggling with large deficits; any costs they could shuffle off to CPP would help them with their own finances" (2008, 75). Lastly, there is a fascinating element of classical federalism that concerns the appeal procedures and structures for the CPP and CPP/D. When the original legislation for CPP was introduced, the appeal system was purposefully not included as an area in which changes would be regarded as a substantive amendment necessitating provincial consent; the rationale was that appeals were an "administrative feature" of the CPP that did not go to the basis of what a beneficiary is entitled to receive or what a contributor is obliged to pay (Thorson 1964, 449). This has allowed the federal government leeway in making decisions and implementing changes about how the appeals and tribunal system is structured, staffed, and funded as well as the nature and scope of legal rights associated with it. Although this may not be blunt unilateralism, it affords the federal government a degree of relative autonomy of action within an area of shared jurisdiction. Not all aspects, then, of the CPP are subject to the multiparty rules of joint decision federalism.

CONSEQUENCES OF SOCIAL RIGHTS

On the connection among social policies, social rights, and societal arrangements, four interpretations emerge from the earlier chapters. Among these readings is the orthodox view that social policies have important integrative effects that contribute to social cohesion and community solidarity. In a more critical assessment, social policies reflect and produce divisions and status hierarchies within the economy and society. A third interpretation maintains that identities associated with social programs and rights are multiple and often fluid, thus complicating notions of solidarity while also celebrating differences. In contrast, a fourth viewpoint suggests that social policies of the welfare state amount to the construction and regulation of normalcy/disability relationships.

Social Cohesion and Solidarity

Initially, the dominant perspective on social policy as social rights equated them with a sense of belonging, community membership, and societal cohesion. The Marsh report on social security for Canada ([1943] 1975, 241) spoke of those persons in need as being in the company of all other citizens through the collective pooling of resources and communal provision of benefits against shared risks. The seminal work on social citizenship by T.H. Marshall (1964) emphasized notions of equality of status, economic security, sharing in the social heritage, universal rights, collective duties, and a common national community. The result, in short, became a discourse of social solidarity in regards to social rights. This discourse often conveys a totalizing perspective that is transcendental – inspiring yet also otherworldly. Banting expresses this perspective this way: "National social programmes create spheres of shared experience in a country otherwise marked by territorial diversities, and strengthen the links between the central government and individuals across the country" (2005, 130; see also Banting 1999). Federal social policy and federal spending power help to define a shared public community by nurturing political identities and by creating broad constituencies and mass solidarities. In short, they act like social glue and hold the country together. The end result, according to Banting, is "the underlying sense that, at some level, all citizens are part of a common political community with shared commitments to each other" (2005, 137).

The CPP and CPP/D were proud achievements of the Pearson Liberals. These programs symbolized a period of innovative social policy making and cooperative federalism in Canadian history (Coutts 2003; LaMarsh 1969). However, unlike Medicare, the CPP and CPP/D are not viewed as such fundamental symbols that define Canada and distinguish it from the United States. In fact, as Chapter 3 showed, the CPP and CPP/D followed social security reform in the United States and were influenced by program experience there, particularly the administrative challenges of implementing a disability benefit program. More concretely, a sociological assessment of CPP/D points to the role of several structures and institutions that mediate relations between the social citizens and the larger political community. Substantive practices operating through the CPP/D include those of the medicalization of bodies, the contested interpretation and categorization of needs, and the official acceptance or rejection of claims. There is much more at work here than the discourse and dream of social solidarity.

Social Stratification

An alternative perspective on the relation between social policies, social rights, and societal arrangements focuses on the categorization and ranking of people with resulting divisions and inequalities. Building on the work of Marshall, Gösta Esping-Andersen argues that a "welfare state may provide services and income security but it is also, and always has been, a system of social stratification. Welfare states are key institutions in the structuring of class and the social order. The organizational features of the welfare state help determine the articulation of social solidarity, divisions of class, and status differentiation" (1990, 55).

CPP/D is an important expression of cultural relations and identities as they pertain to impairments, illnesses, and capacities. This program is not a universal or comprehensive national program for all Canadians with disabilities whatever the cause or type of disability. The program addresses a defined group of people considered as a category of risks: employed workers between the ages of eighteen and sixty-five that, in social insurance terms, are insured against the contingency of certain mental and physical disabilities. There are no partial benefits. To qualify, a person must be determined, through a process of medical assessment, to have a severe and prolonged disability that does not allow them to pursue gainful employment. In these terms and demarcations is a particular construction of disability, ability, and eligibility – a construction particularly shaped by biomedical knowledge and experts. The eligibility determination process for CPP/D also generates a series of social dualisms. One is between those covered and those who are not. Like any other program, this one marks off some people as entitled, in principle, because of the severity and prolonged nature of their disability, from the many others who, because their disability is deemed to be mild or moderate and is more episodic in nature perhaps, are excluded in practice. Another dualism is between those workers with intermittent workforce attachments, who would not meet the work test, and those workers with more traditional employment records who do meet this test. There are further distinctions between direct and derived social rights to income benefits reflecting historical gender relationships. Such dualisms might pose political challenges in efforts to build solidarity among workers with disabilities as well as in forming coalitions with other disability groups to mobilize and advocate for policy reforms. In this manner, CPP/D, like other social insurance programs and social assistance programs, offers an uneven base for social citizenship and incomplete structure of income security for Canadians with disabilities. For those not covered, for those ineligible, and for those denied benefits after an appeal, income programs generate prevalent experiences of social distance and exclusion from public entitlements (Prince and Moss 2015).

Multiplicity of Differences

A third view of social policy and social rights looks at the multiplicity of differences. Here the basic focus is on the specificity of contexts, the variety of roles and identities people inhabit and their often shifting quality. While the solidarity perspective notes the institutionalization of rights over many decades, especially the age of the Keynesian welfare state, this perspective highlights the fluid and changing nature of entitlements and clients (Cowen 2008; Redden 2002). In modern and postmodern welfare states, there is no single, universal image of citizen. As Sheila Shaver states, "constituencies formed in welfare politics reflect the multidimensional character of social rights, engaged in interests rooted in various and often crosscutting social interests" (1989, 3–4).

Whether understood as interest-group pluralism, identity politics, or status politics, in the construction of income benefits for disabled Canadians, the figure of the social citizen is unquestionably partial and multiple; we get the injured industrial worker, the damaged war veteran, the mother in need, the visually impaired person, the totally incapacitated adult, the wage earner who develops a severe and prolonged physical or mental disability, the dependent spouse and child of a disabled contributor to a public program. The federalized nature of the Canadian state amplifies these differences of citizenship – the simultaneous roles and orientations as federal and provincial citizens linked to programs aligned with one or the other level of government.

Dealings with institutions beside federalism are of real significance in producing diverse affiliations and identities. These include interacting with medical practitioners and other health care workers, participating in peer support groups, consultations with lawyers, dealing with life insurance companies, and transactions with employers or trade union officials. Social citizenship is a multi-level and multi-institutional phenomenon. The citizen occupies numerous roles, adopts various identities, and acquires labels assigned by others in an assortment of authority relationships. All of this, along with state entitlements, forges attachments as well as provokes resistance, shaping the character of memberships and participation opportunities in communities. While the literature can give the impression that state-based cohesion is the principal outcome of social policy, the actual network of multiple social, political, and state interactions may not foster broadly shared experiences of being in a caring and sharing national community (Glenn 2011).

Normalcy/Disability Relations

From critical disability studies comes a fourth perspective on the relation between social policies, social rights, and societal arrangements. On social solidarity, this disability outlook asks, belonging and cohesion on whose terms and by what standards prevailing in society? How does stigma associated with the flawed body and mind fit with the benign abstractions of solidarity discourse? In the words of one scholar, "disabled people are still excluded from the public role and from societal structures of power. Disability is still in collusion with the underside of appearance and with the established" (Michalko 2002, 165). On stratification, critical disability draws attention to the systemic inequalities between the disabled and non-disabled – evident in part by differences in access to different types of income programs and tax measures – as well as differences between people with different impairments, a so-called hierarchy of disablements between, for example, people with visible and hidden disabilities. Looking at Canadian society, Richard Devlin and Dianne Pothier observe that "not all share equally in the good life, or feel adequately included. Among those who face recurring coercion, marginalization, and social exclusion are persons with disabilities" (2006, 1). Federal social policy and federal spending power help to constitute systematically a fractured political community by creating specific constituencies and particularistic groups based on embodied identities.

On multiple identities and the politics of difference, this perspective points to the marginal status of people with disabilities and how social and political systems are always operating in relation to human bodies. Definitions of disability in public programs in Canada tend to incorporate medicalized dichotomies that a person is either able-bodied or disabled. The general effect, because of a shared medical orientation, is to individualize and pathologize a person's condition, to emphasize the inability to work rather than focus on work capacity, to ignore fluctuating or episodic conditions, and consequently to exclude some people from qualifying for specific programs. When most buildings, public spaces, and transit systems are unreachable, when common forms of information and communication are inaccessible, when general attitudes are uninformed and popular assumptions toward people with impairments are negative, regarding them as tragic figures and abnormal, when practices in everyday spheres of living are restrictive, when work is a domain where people with disabilities are sidelined and materially disadvantaged, when public policies create or replicate obstacles, then Canadian society is routinely experienced as disabling.

CONCLUSION

This chapter has considered the governance of Canadian disability income policy and social rights. The aim has not been to determine the most influential actors or institutions, or to imply that all are equally significant. The analysis suggests that in reality institutions and groups do not push in the same direction or with the same purpose. Different actors have distinct and competing effects on disability policy and social rights, the nature of which are historically constructed and can vary over prime ministerial eras. Social rights and citizenship more generally operate within a complex matrix of embodied power and knowledge relationships.

Family life is not a private domain detached entirely from public policy or political structures. CPP/D links the private and the public spheres, recognizing specific dependent relationships within families and imposing obligations on beneficiaries to report changes – in this case, those families with an eligible disabled contributor. Depending on the character of interpersonal roles and relations, the family can be an important site in influencing a disabled worker's decision to claim a benefit or to appeal a negative decision regarding CPP disability eligibility. In addition to what goes on in the "private world" of families, the exercise of social rights is shaped as well by interactions and practices in the "public world" of paid employment and organized medical care.

Canada's liberal approach to social policy and liberal discourse on social citizenship privilege labour market participation, earned benefits, private insurance, and categorical diagnoses of bodily impairments. CPP/D supports the market economy in several ways, including by basing eligibility on labour force attachment, relating benefits largely to wage levels, and serving as first payer ahead of private insurance plans. CPP/D also supports the market by offering a modicum of income support to contributors who are deemed unable to work, providing vocational rehabilitation services, and, in more recent times, introducing return-to-work incentives. In relation to capitalism, CPP/D has a modest de-commodification role, most apparent in the flat-rate portion of benefits, joined with commodification and re-commodification elements built into the program design itself. In our market-based society, where paid employment is a major prerequisite for social rights, many Canadians with disabilities experience an incomplete citizenship.

Political parties and general elections are important to disability income policy developments. Moreover, individuals MPS and Parliament are more effective than they are portrayed in standard generalizations, although this may be due at least partly to the character of the disability policy field as a public issue. Parliament has mattered in the origins and in the development of the CPP/D through the work of caucuses, debates, and private member's bills, as well as through the work of committees in monitoring the program's administration, enabling the voices of disabled Canadians to be heard, and making policy recommendations. The lesson here is to not automatically assume that Parliament is totally irrelevant in the policy and program delivery, or in the lives of ordinary citizens.

Policy developments in income supports for disabled person do not result from a collective conscience of compassion or social justice; nor are they the steady implementation of some ideal of equality of status or universality. Certainly, they reflect aspirations and demands for a better, more secure life in the face of industrialization, warfare, and other risks. Social rights represent personal struggles and conflicts between organized interests of workers and employers, industry and the state, federal and provincial governments; and always the interplay of problematic values of normalcy and disability is at stake here. Entitlements to income programs have complicated relationships and contradictory consequences for citizens, policy communities, and larger social structures.

Social Citizenship, the Disabled, and Income Security

Citizenship in post-industrial society is still a work in progress. We are in the midst of a debate about the rules, the responsibilities, and the rights of citizens and about what we expect from the state.

Janice Gross Stein, *The Cult of Efficiency*

Experiences with disabilities are a source of social innovations.

Deborah Stienstra, *Disability Rights*

Struggling for Social Citizenship has explored how Canadian governments contemplated, introduced, expanded, constrained, and restructured disability income programs, specifically the Canada Pension Plan Disability program. The genesis of CPP/D was shaped by electoral strategies, policy work by Liberal Party members and by federal and Quebec bureaucratic officials, constitutional considerations, and intergovernmental bargaining. The book has analyzed the CPP/D in relation to a number of key political factors, including families, labour markets, medical science, and administrative justice processes. This Conclusion offers comparative assessments of the prime ministerial eras of the past five decades in Canadian politics and disability policy making. I present conclusions related to the changes and continuities in policy and practice of the CPP/D, and the quality of social rights for working-age Canadians with disabilities as offered by the CPP/D. Lastly, I make several suggestions for addressing the ongoing struggle for social citizenship that is the everyday reality of so many Canadians living with disabilities.

MEANINGS OF SOCIAL CITIZENSHIP AND POWER

Social rights are not political universals. This volume, therefore, has abstained from adopting a wholly normative and abstract conception of social citizenship, to instead consider actually constructed policies and practices. Most social citizenship theory holds a conception of public power that is juridical and liberal in character. From this perspective, benefits are held as rights that can be possessed by citizens. Such rights are established by sovereign authorities, enacted through legislation, and implemented via state organizations. Social rights are then granted directly or, as derived rights, indirectly to an individual or family member. These qualities are most apparent in social-insurance-based programs like the CPP in which the right is acquired or earned through a record of employment and financial contributions to the plan. Entitlement is thus based on an exchange or contractual arrangement. Running through this reality is a notion of public power that is essentially positive and empowering.

I have examined the workings of social rights and power from more of a critical realist perspective. Every social citizenship regime is a historically specific creation with particular institutional arrangements intertwined with numerous relations of power. Actors and organizations in political and civil society institutions contribute in various configurations to shaping disability policies and social rights. Federal and provincial states do exercise degrees of autonomy; politics do matter; and civil society institutions are more than an undemanding environment for public policy. The citizenship literature distinctly has a state-centred orientation and this book focuses on social rights and social policies. So what image of the Canadian state emerges from this study of people with disability and income security? Plainly, the state in Canada is not culturally unbiased, nor is it an institution altogether responsive to the needs of vulnerable individuals and marginal groups in society. Disability gets constructed in explicitly normative ways and in politically specific contexts. Furthermore, the interpretation of needs, even within established public policies, is frequently contested and closely regulated. Viewed as a liberal form of welfare regime, the Canadian state is certainly interventionist. It is interactional, too, upholding labour market interests and creating strategic spaces for medical and legal practices. One result is the circulation of competing discourses of citizen–state relations and the distribution of rights and responsibilities.

The state's power base anchors in the constitution, legislation and program mandates, and the expertise of officials. The politics of federalism and public bureaucracies point out that the Canadian state is also highly differentiated in terms of jurisdiction and organization. Far from neutral, the state is conditioned by economic and market relations of power in our capitalist society. In addition to the structurally privileged position of business interests in liberal democracies, biomedical interests have a privileged role in relation to several aspects of disability policy. Generally speaking, across most domains of life, people with disabilities do not have the same educational advantages, employment opportunities, material resources, or social status as people without disabilities. In this sense, the state is an expression of and site for the production of ability/disability relations. These relations and attendant inequalities and tensions are a defining feature of modern society.

Rights to public benefits have multiple and contradictory effects for individuals and societal arrangements. Social citizenship concerns not only the nation-state intervening in society or regulating the market economy; it is about federal and provincial states interacting with societal institutions and relying on market structures. If a national policy embraces Canadians within general public services, it also creates dualisms and divisions in coverage. For most social programs, purposes of meeting human needs are modest in nature, designs are categorical in focus, and outcomes involve anticipated and unwelcome consequences. For countless Canadians with disabilities, their encounters with the state, as citizens with rights to a benefit, are convoluted and uncertain experiences. From the kingdom of the well to the land of the unwell, social right claimants must regularly pass through more than a few social organizations in addition to state institutions to secure a disability income benefit. In this context, that social cohesion is what rights claimants actually experience is not so obvious (Prince and Moss 2015).

Struggles in seeking rights and claiming access to income benefits have been a major theme of this book. Macro-level struggle is imagined in terms of power imbalances among institutions and contestation against domination. At a meso- or middle-range level, struggles over social citizenship entail mêlée over program design and content: the basis of entitlement and eligibility rules; financing methods, the scope of coverage, and quality of benefits. And with whatever form social rights take, at the micro level are issues of physician–patient relations and legal matters regarding the procedural rights and duties of claimants as well as those for program administrators. At all these levels, the Canadian state is a site of citizenship struggles.

Struggles reveal the problematic nature of traditional understandings of citizenship for people with disabilities, and struggles emphasize the importance of the classification of citizen bodies. Through the twentieth century, the emergence of six citizen figures constituted the expanding field of public income protection for disability. These figures are the injured factory worker, the shell-shocked or burnt-out veteran, the family with a disabled male breadwinner, the blind person, the permanently disabled person, and the insured disabled employee with a severe physical limitation or mental condition. These identities of the disabled person are programmatically constructed with separate benefit structures, distinct bodies of knowledge, and peculiar systems of rules. Their political significance also varies in terms of public profile, governmental budgets, and mobilization by organized interests. Other figures of people with disabilities – for example, individuals with episodic conditions, those with hidden impairments, or with illnesses still contested by established medicine – vie for recognition of their embodied needs and thus entry to one or more of these income programs. In other terms, there is no meta-domain of disability, no general policy that integrates these numerous categories of disabled citizens in Canadian life.

T.H. Marshall partly defined social citizenship as the right to live the life of a civilized being according to societal standards. From a critical disability perspective, the standards prevailing in society usually mean standards of normal bodies. As Michael Orsini puts it, "The idea that disability itself is a form of diversity that need not always be overcome is a difficult one to grasp; especially through the lens of liberalism" (2012, 810). Social standards that bear on disability and disability policy involve ableist norms of prejudice about bodies and appearance, legal norms around competence, and medical norms of functioning and activity limitations. The citizen's material body is governed through rules on labour force attachment, records of financial contributions to insurance plans, and medical assessments of health conditions.

The Significance of Social Citizenship for Canadians with Disabilities

To incorporate disability more fully into accounts of citizenship and social rights is a basic aim of this study. Informed by critical social science, critical policy studies, and critical disability theory, the focal point has been on what social security policy means for persons with various kinds of disabilities. Disablement poses a challenge to conventional notions of citizenship as robust participation in mainstream society, the capitalist economy, and liberal polity. Through the twentieth century, disability became viewed as something more than a personal pathology – as the product of social forces, such as industrial accidents, general unemployment, wartime wounds, poverty, and family need. Accordingly, this book has understood disability policy as the use of state and social powers to construct identities of disablement and to organize relations of ability/disability in the population.

As a public policy issue, disability is bound up with the growth of health professions and rehabilitation sciences and therapies. In critically important ways, modern social rights to income support are medicalized rights. Disability programs have been shown to be collectivist social policies of public and private interventions, yet this collectivism operates in conjunction with individualist notions of bodily limitations and potential workforce capacities. The social significance of disability income support is evident in how human differences and needs are authoritatively interpreted, in how groups and identities become recognized in public policies and private plans, and in how roles are distributed among professions and other societal institutions. For example, an applicant claiming the CPP/D is required under the program's regulations to supply a report of any physical or mental disability including (i) the nature, extent, and prognosis of the disability, (ii) the findings upon which the diagnosis and prognosis were made, (iii) any limitation resulting from the disability, and (iv) any other pertinent information, such as recommendations for further diagnostic work or treatment. An applicant must also provide a statement of his or her occupation and earnings, education, employment experience, and activities of daily life.

Our modern politics of disability income provision involve the regulation of impairments along with the recognition and non-recognition of disablement. As a cultural formation, the state assumes particular beliefs about disablement, persons with impairments and ability/disability relations. During the Keynesian welfare state era, disabled people were frequently segregated and marginalized. This was not a golden age with a benevolent consensus for many Canadian living with significant impairments. Deemed to be controlled by their body, individuals with significant disabilities tend to be under government surveillance more than full citizens; certainly, they are frequent objects of medical scrutiny. Yet disabled bodies are politicized working bodies. Like other social identities, people living with a mental or physical disability elicit reactions and enact performances. People with disabilities actively participate in both constituting and claiming social rights of citizenship as workers, as contributors to social insurance programs, as applicants and recipients, and as appellants of negative decisions on their entitlement claims.

The social right foundations for CPP/D incorporate aspects of economic substance and personal status. The program confers an entitlement by requiring certain market achievements in the labour force and by recognizing certain personal incapacities verified by medical personnel. With these eligibility criteria, disability benefits are an individual entitlement based on market and medical references, along with other considerations. As a national disability insurance program, the benefit is a social right to partial compensation for the loss of work capacity and earned income. Despite the elaborate apparatus of the CPP/D, the situation of many disabled workers is initial ineligibility, strenuous experiences through appeal processes, and eventual rejection for benefits, all the while experiencing changes in their material being and social status. The result undoubtedly limits many disabled people in living in accordance with prevailing societal standards. Such gaps between provision and promise contribute to ongoing political debates and personal struggles for social rights to income security.

HISTORICAL ORIGINS AND PRIME MINISTERIAL ERAS

Successive Liberal and Conservative governments, both minority and majority administrations, built disability income policy and the CPP/D regime collaboratively – sometimes incrementally, sometimes substantively, and sometimes with restraint.

International influences, particularly American influences, on Canadian disability policy making are evident. When the first Canadian province, Ontario, established a government-administered workers' compensation scheme in 1914, more than half of American states had such legislation in place. Introduction of income support for mothers with young children whose husband had died or was incapacitated was influenced by domestic interest group and electoral politics, which were bolstered by the mothers' pension movement in the United States. Some years before Canada, the US

Congress established public assistance for the blind and those totally and permanently disabled as well as national legislation on vocational rehabilitation. For both countries, these were statuses deserving of public income support.[1]

Canadian thinking on social security, including provision for disablement, was actively expressed in books by reformers, reports by advisory committees and think tanks, and policy papers by governments. The addition of disability insurance to the United States' Social Security, a national contributory pension scheme, in 1957 contributed to public interest in Canada. The next year, the Diefenbaker Conservative government commissioned a comparative study of the Canadian and American systems in retirement pensions and disability and survivor benefits. Later, when designing the CPP in detail, federal government welfare officials found that Canadian statistics related to long-term disability under the Disabled Persons Act "disclosed little information that seemed directly pertinent to possible future experience under the CPP. Thus, for purposes of the current estimates, disability rates were based almost wholly on disability experience that has developed under the Old Age Security Disability Insurance system of the United States" (National Health and Welfare 1965, 78). The appeal system included in the original Canada Pension Plan legislation, discussed in Chapter 4, was modelled somewhat along the lines of the American old age security legislation, along with experience of comparable Canadian social programs.

A major difference, though, between CPP/D and the US Social Security Disability Insurance program concerns the locus of administration. In the United States, state governments have a direct role in the administration of disability insurance, including the determination of eligibility by state employees; whereas, in Canada, the management and rule making for the CPP/D is more centralized under federal government departments and agencies.

In the politics of marketing the CPP proposal, the American example was convenient and familiar to many Canadians, perhaps helping to allay the concerns of fiscal conservatives within the

1 From the other direction, Canada legislated on old age assistance before the United States (1927 v. 1935) and consolidated welfare assistance before the United States did (1966 v. 1972–74). At the same time, both countries enacted veterans' benefits during or after the Great War and the Second World War.

federal bureaucracy, Parliament, and the private insurance and pension industry. These American influences on Canadian social policy are illustrative of exogenous policy and administrative learning at the middle-range level of governing, external effects on a specific policy system in Canada. Formation of the Social Security Tribunal in 2013 was influenced by similar appeals structures in Australia and Britain as well as thinking and developments in administrative justice in Canadian provinces (Garant 2002). These influences are also suggestive of specific sources of liberal qualities in the Canadian welfare state regime. Once implemented, the CPP developed a trajectory of its own – with its financing and lending policy, growing caseloads and appeals, program changes, and policy debates – that was subject to the influences of Canada's political economy, practices of the QPP, federalism, and cabinet parliamentary government. In the other direction, CPP has affected the policy context too, and Chapter 9 discussed political implications of the CPP/D program.

Across prime ministerial eras since the 1960s, the history of CPP/D policy development shows both consistencies and differences across the partisan divide, differences that reflect contrasting views on the Canadian state and on persons with disabilities. Chapter 4 examined the policy formation phase under the Lester Pearson Liberals from 1963 to the introduction of CPP/D in 1970. "Disability was not originally included in the proposed Canada Pension Plan," Havi Echenberg recalls, but it was included through intergovernmental and parliamentary processes. "As a mandatory contributory plan, the CPP disability benefit removed the restrictive notions of 'charity' and/ or 'compensation' from income support for persons with disabilities. Pearson could be painted as an inadvertent or unintentional hero" (Echenberg 2003, 47). Jim Coutts's assessment of this and other Pearson era social policy reforms is more positively definitive: "I believe that Prime Minister Pearson came through with reform in the end because the combination of his diplomatic skill and basic social outlook were exactly right for this particular window of opportunity" (2003, 17).

In examining the Pierre Trudeau Liberal era, Chapter 5 examined the policy implementation, adaptation, and pension debate phase spanning 1970 to 1984. In the historical arc of the Keynesian welfare state, CPP/D began operation just as the postwar consensus on social welfare went into crisis. In this period, crisis politics in social policy took various forms, including retrenchment and defending and maintaining the welfare state. CPP/D was, of course, part of this larger context, yet it had its own temporal and intergovernmental dynamic and the intergenerational and funding dynamics of the CPP retirement benefit. In the Trudeau years, CPP/D politics largely concerned realizing legislative and intergovernmental commitments that were forged in the mid-1960s. From 1980 to 1984, the Trudeau government's pursuit of public pension reform was impacted by economic recession and austerity politics, against a "deteriorating fiscal position" (Axworthy 2002, 1). Overall, the Trudeau Liberals "mostly held the line against the reactionary social forces sweeping through other Western governments" (Coutts 2003, 18).

Chapter 6 appraised the Brian Mulroney Progressive Conservatives from 1984 to 1993. In coming to power with a massive majority, the Mulroney Conservatives not only accepted the CPP, they instituted positive reforms, some of which had been under discussion with the provinces during the last Trudeau Liberal government. Mulroney-era reforms included major changes to the CPP program and the liberalization of disability benefits. Within the Mulroney government, cabinet ministers and caucus members actively supported enhancement to disability benefits. Such changes fit with segments of the Progressive Conservative party who were Red Tories and others who held a sense of compassion and *noblesse oblige* toward this vulnerable and deserving group of Canadians.

The Liberal years of Jean Chrétien and Paul Martin from 1994 to 2005, assessed in Chapter 7, differed from the three previous prime ministerial eras in CPP and disability pension policy. The Chrétien and Martin period was characterized by intensive critiques of the Canada Pension Plan, the reorientation of CPP/D policy goals, and the retrenchment of CPP disability benefits. Termination of the Canada Assistance Plan (CAP) in 1996–97 ended a seventy-year involvement by the federal government in cost-sharing with the provinces income assistance for people with disabilities. In retrospect, the time-limited cap on CAP increases in federal transfers by the Mulroney Conservatives in 1991 looked quite modest by comparison to "Martin's Draconian 1995 budget" (Axworthy 2002, 1). Ending CAP eroded the social citizenship regime for the large number of Canadians with disabilities living in low-income circumstances. Neither the unconditional Canada Social Transfer nor non-refundable tax credits for the disabled are adequate substitutes for the loss of the CAP. Chrétien-Martin cuts to CPP Disability in

1997 were immediate and significant. In addition, more emphasis was given to fostering work incentives in the CPP/D with new measures such as the allowable earnings provision, three-month trial paid work periods, fast-track reapplications, and automatic reinstatement. These measures involve a redefinition of some CPP/D clients as having the potential to be active citizens in the labour market. It remains the case, however, that relatively few CPP/D beneficiaries have income from employment and that those that do have low levels of annual earnings.

Chapter 8 surveyed the Stephen Harper Conservatives from 2006 to 2015, a period of policy maintenance for CPP and minimal initiatives on CPP/D benefits. The Harper years were characterized by general caution and incremental moves on many social policy issues facing the country, including CPP and CPP/D. The Harper Conservatives, for example, refused to expand the CPP to improve the retirement income security of Canadians. The promise of a specific piece of federal legislation for Canadian with disabilities, first made by the Conservative Party in 2005, fell quietly by the wayside once they won office. At a fundamental level, such reforms fit uneasily with Harper's conception of the federal state and what it should do and not do in the contemporary world. Like many other prime ministers in relation to social reform, Harper relied on disability policy initiatives from others, notably his Finance Minister Jim Flaherty. On an initiative generated from within the federal bureaucracy, however, the Harper Conservatives made major changes to the appeal and tribunal system for important federal income programs in 2013 with the creation of the mega-tribunal on social security.

CPP/D has multiple policy objectives, the core one having to do with a providing a modicum of income protection against disability for working Canadians and their families. From the start, CPP/D featured other policy goals – return to work, program integrity, and financial sustainability – all of which received greater emphasis through the 1980s and 1990s, while the income security goal has been the object of some restraint in more recent periods. Each of these policy goals also has its own meaning, which over time have shifted somewhat. Income support has had a social insurance purpose to replace earnings lost, rather than an anti-poverty purpose of providing a guaranteed basic income to all. Program integrity, for example, has expanded beyond initial ideas about rights to an appeals process, to include control measures, client services, and communication efforts.

Each of the five prime ministerial eras reveals partisan stances, ideological differences and similarities, as well as some surprising policy decisions set in particular political and economic climates of each regime.

Continuities Spanning the Prime Ministerial Eras

A substantial element of continuity in policy, practice, and politics surrounds CPP/D's program history. CPP remains a national social insurance program operating in nine provinces and the territories alongside the Quebec Plan. The statutory definition of eligibility to CPP/D benefits has always included reference to a prolonged and severe mental or physical disability. The right to appeal decisions affecting CPP benefits may be launched by the applicant or beneficiary, an advocate, trustee, an estate, or the minister responsible. The original goal of a modest level of income replacement, with a defined benefit that is indexed, taxable, and portable, continues. CPP and QPP retirement pensions are still limited to 25 percent of average earnings, to leave considerable room for occupational pensions and personal retirement savings plans. However, the distribution of income protection for disability available through private industry plans and savings arrangements remains very uneven for Canadians. While CPP/D is a first-payer program, provincial income assistance programs remain a foundational safety net for masses of Canadian with disabilities. Indeed, reliance on social assistance by Canadians with disabilities is proportionally higher today than when the CPP was first introduced in the 1960s (Prince 2015).

There are many reasons for these continuities. Likewise, there are multiple reasons why changes are often slow or difficult, including faith in the private sector and the belief that providing retirement income security is an individual responsibility. Concerns, held by many, about the financial costs and sustainability of public pension reforms are also factors.

Then there is the reality that the disability program is one part of a larger program, the CPP retirement pension, which, in turn, is one component of a complex system of public and private sector pension plans. As an intergovernmental program, the CPP is both a valuable source of stability and an impediment to quick and easy change. As a federalized social contract, the CPP is a response to key public needs and the product of hard governmental bargaining and hot parliamentary debate.

The CPP constitutes a complex web of obligations, entitlements, and expectations. In part, continuities in the CPP represent an honouring of these past commitments. At the same time, however, another continuity is that ideas about and demands for reforming the CPP have never been far from the public policy agenda.

Innovations and Changes in Disability Income Policy

Before CPP/D became the country's national public disability insurance program, several innovations took place in disability income policy making in Canada. From the early 1900s to the 1960s, new roles emerged for the provinces and the federal government in the provision of income maintenance to people with disabilities. Provincial and federal governments recognized new program categories of disabled citizens, including injured factory workers and shattered war veterans. Eventually, through cost-sharing arrangements, intergovernmental relations were forged. Beginning in 1937, the federal government cost-shared allowances for blind persons, a practice codified in specific legislation in 1951. In 1954, the Disabled Persons Act marked yet another new form of federal involvement in income support for a group of Canadians with disabilities. This federal initiative followed provincial disability allowance programs in place in Alberta, Newfoundland, and Ontario. Once federal legislation was in place, the other provinces all quickly adopted Ottawa's cost-shared program. Gradually through the 1950s, and then established in legislation in 1961, the federal government began cost-sharing for vocational rehabilitation services for working-age adults with disabilities, a practice that continues today through the Labour Market Agreements for Persons with Disabilities.

While continuities are apparent in CPP policy, change in many respects has been a normal state of affairs for disability policy and practice. The nature and content of main policy changes, legislative amendments, and administrative developments were set out in Chapters 5, 6, 7, and 8. I draw concluding attention to them to make the basic point that the CPP and CPP/D have changed many times in many ways. In all, there have been approximately fifty substantial changes in policy and practice since the program began.

Among innovations to the CPP, the automatic indexation of benefits stands out as significant for determining the quality of a social right to income maintenance. As Dennis Guest explains, "For the first time in

Canada's history of social security, the decision was taken, while drafting the provisions of the Canada and the Quebec Pension Plans, to provide for an automatic increase in benefits in line with increases in the cost of living" (1998, 154). The original formula of indexation against inflation, which took effect in 1968, was for an annual increase of not less than 1 percent and not more than 2 percent. Other noteworthy changes to the CPP include an enhanced method of indexation (1974), elimination of the retirement or earnings test for retirement pensions (1974), and the enactment of international Social Security Agreements (starting in 1979). Later changes to CPP included revisions to the contribution rates schedule (1987, 1992, 1998), instituting a review of program performance by finance ministers on a five-year cycle (1987), which was later changed to a three-year interval (1998), and the move from pay-as-you-go financing to partial funding of the plan (1998). Organizational modifications involved the lead department's portfolio structure and delivery systems for services (various times), the abolition of the CPP Advisory Committee (1998), and the creation of the CPP Investment Board (1998).

Significant changes to the CPP/D program, and their dates, are as follows: increases to the amount of benefits payable to disabled contributors and to children (1978, 1987, 1992), contributory requirements for disability (1969, 1975, 1980, 1987, 1998), the shift from review committees to review tribunals at the second level of appeals (1992), revised interpretations of what constitutes a severe and prolonged disability (1988, 1992, 1995, 2001), introduction of the CPP Disability Vocational Rehabilitation Program (1997), adoption of an earnings exemption for disability beneficiaries (2001), adjustment of eligibility requirements for long-term contributors (2006), and the abolition of the review tribunals system replaced by the Social Security Tribunal (2013).

Changes in policy and organizational practices were accomplished through a mix of regulatory and procedural governing instruments. The mix of instruments encompassed legislative amendments via government and private member's bills, new legislation, administrative guidelines, and policy directives within the department, and through Federal Court decisions and accords between the federal government and other governments. Other changes reflect shifts in the economy and society, such as the decline in the age of CPP disability beneficiaries over time and the shift in the gender mix of beneficiaries, with a growing presence of women on the caseloads

(HRSDC 2011). Pressure for changes has come from claimants and their families, in their struggles with the department and the appeals system, from MPs advocating on behalf of constituents and their own political beliefs, and from the federal Department of Finance, which wants to control costs.[2]

The push for progressive change came also from social policy groups representing women, persons with disabilities, and older workers. With an increase in divorces, shifts in family sizes and forms, the growing labour participation of women, people retiring earlier than age sixty-five, and other trends in social attitudes, the assumptions embedded in the program from the 1960s and earlier became less conventional and reflective of the human tapestries of Canadian experience. Official discourse on disability issues – the language used by decision makers in talking about public policy actions – has also shifted somewhat in recent decades. Language commonly employed in documents in the 1980s spoke of "helping the disabled," while more recent documents speak of "helping Canadians with disabilities in achieving equal citizenship." However, as all too many social groups learn, a positive change in words does not necessarily mean a progressive change in well-being.

Overlaps across Prime Ministerial Eras

Prime ministerial eras have been an analytically useful and historically applicable method of examining the political and policy developments of the CPP/D program. Looking across specific eras helps to reveal both innovations and continuities. Also there are overlaps

2 The abolition of the CPP Advisory Committee in 1998, for example, was not publicly discussed in the 1996 consultations and was not particularly an issue for the provinces. The Advisory Council was not liked by Finance officials, who commonly viewed the council as a source of expansionary pressures on CPP program spending. The official rationale within the federal bureaucracy for killing off the Advisory Council was that it was no longer needed given the three-year cycle of review of the CPP by governments and that similar boards had been eliminated by recent federal governments as part of the restraint drive. With the change in financing the CPP and the creation of the investment board in 1998, it seems clear that the federal government, along with the provinces, wanted to do business differently with respect to the governance of the CPP.

or connections in policy developments that relate to prime ministerial eras.

The CPP was enacted in the Pearson years, but CPP/D did not come into effect until 1970, in the early part of the Trudeau era. Federal-provincial negotiations on CPP reform, underway in the final years of the Trudeau era, continued through late 1984 and 1985 under the new Mulroney government and shaped policy decisions that the Progressive Conservatives introduced. Overlaps in disability policy between the Mulroney and Chrétien eras included the National Strategy for the Integration of Persons with Disabilities (1991–96) and in the CPP/D the vocational rehabilitation program (1991–97). In the Chrétien years, especially his first government of 1993–97, changes to the CPP/D were a negative reaction to decisions made during the Mulroney era, and the overall package of reforms in 1997 placed the CPP on a different pathway somewhat. In 2003, the Martin government established a Technical Advisory Committee on Tax Measures for Persons with Disabilities, which influenced not only Liberal federal budgets in 2004 and 2005 but also Harper Conservative budgets in 2006 and beyond. On the CPP/D, work on changing eligibility requirements for long-term contributors, which the Harper government enacted, had begun during the Martin years. These overlaps are examples of policy legacies, of how decisions made or processes underway in one prime ministerial era can influence CPP/D policy making in the succeeding era.

SOCIAL INSURANCE AND SOCIAL RIGHTS
FOR DISABLED CANADIANS: WHAT IS THE FUTURE?

In just over fifty years, the CPP/D program has gone through several phases of development. While a particular reform process represented by a major piece of legislation may start and stop, disability policy is never finished and the pension system never totally completed. As Kenneth Bryden explains, "Policies rarely take the precise form of the demands which gave rise to them. The demand is often that 'something' be done; the policy is only one of several possible some things. For many it may satisfy the original want only in part, and for both them and theirs it may give rise to new wants by raising expectations" (1974, 16). With disagreements over definitions of severe and prolonged disability, shifting priorities on policy goals, time constraints, and other resource limitations, policy and practice reforms are never precisely on target. And, let us remember, disability pension policy reform is inherently a political process. The continued, serious inadequacies of pension coverage in the private sector of Canada's workforce served, at times, as a stimulus for calls of further action in public pension, though such calls were ignored or resisted by private sector interests and the Harper Conservatives.

What is the future for social security for disabled citizens? From an international perspective, Marjorie O'Loughlin argues that "because of the realities of globalising capitalism at the present time, and in light of the decline in popularity of notions of state welfare, such economic advantages as unemployment benefits, disability allowances and the like are no longer seen as rights" (2006, 157). In the case of the CPP/D, few people would call the benefit an economic advantage but most, including political parties and leaders, still see it as an earned right. As noted earlier, the entitlement is established before any claim on the basis of work and financial contribution. In Canadian public policy, social rights and social citizenship remain meaningful ideas. In examining the content of social citizenship, Lois Harder contends that "the tenuous legitimacy of social rights in Canada results from their challenge to the established constitutional and economic order" (2003, 175). However, with respect to the CPP and CPP/D, their legitimacy and limitations derive from *compliance* with the constitutional order and economic market system. Any increase in benefits, for example, must go together with an intergovernmental consensus on a permanent increase in the contribution rate to cover future incremental costs.

Mark Weber (2009) explores the compatibility between social insurance programs that provide income support to people with disabilities and the ideas of the disability rights movement. Because contributory-based statutory disability insurance is based on medical assessments and notions of risks or tragedies, Weber suggests that social insurance does not reflect "the civil rights approach to disability," an approach that rejects disability being a risky defect and that rather asserts disability is "a maladaptation of society to human variation" (2009, 576). Still, Weber argues that social insurance has a role to play in disability policy, noting that this policy instrument "protects people against the hazards of modern life ... while encouraging ... long-term participation in the work force." Specifically on disability-related social insurance, it "protects against the harms of discrimination that stem from the social barriers that block persons with disabilities from reaching their full potential in the workplace." In this regard, Weber concludes that social insurance "is consistent with a civil rights approach to disability" (604).

The social insurance approach, as envisaged in the 1940s and again in the 1960s, was based on a series of normative assumptions: breadwinners and homemakers were distinct and stable roles; breadwinners had full-time careers; significant disabilities rendered people permanently unemployable; means-tested social assistance would fade in importance as a source of income for those in need; and private sector life insurance and workplace disability schemes would become available to most working families. That these assumptions no longer reflect reality or, in fact, never became reality does not make social insurance obsolete. It suggests, rather, that policy approaches must be rethought and reformed.

A major role remains in Canadian public policy for provision of payments to people in financial need due to injuries, chronic and episodic illnesses, physical impairments, and mental health conditions. Given Canada's aging population, among other factors, the occurrence of disablement as a known risk to economic security is more prevalent today. Inclusion of physical and mental disability in CPP/D coverage has allowed the program to address conditions not foreseen when it was designed in the 1960s. Moreover, the contributory basis for social rights remains a core value of the liberal welfare state and wider socio-political culture of the country. If there is an overall structure of beliefs that legitimate Canadian social policy, a strong argument can be made that these beliefs include paid work, insuring against risk, and exercising mutual and self-responsibility. This is not a notion of social citizenship informed by moral generosity or institutionalized compassion; the practice is of making contributions and earning rights. This is the essence of social liberalism. Not all is well in social policy, however.

Social rights for people with disabilities are disabled rights. They are disabled rights as state-organized provision of income support for certain categories of people who are medically assessed to have disabilities. This financial benefit is then made available to those claimants who have been determined as eligible according to the relevant legislation and by administrative consideration. This is the promise of the formal status of social citizenship. As J.M. Barbalet reminds us, "Social legislation does bring changes and reforms, certainly; and ordinary people benefit from these. But such legislation can serve to preserve an existing pattern of power and privilege and may leave it essentially intact" (1988, 63).

Social rights are disabled rights as well in their actual practice as experienced by individuals and families. Through their administrative effects, social programs are inaccessible and restrictive for many people with disabilities. Far from accidental, these circumstances are integral to the design and interaction among programs: clawbacks or offsets between different income support programs; narrow eligibility criteria to many tax credits; the absence of accommodation and retraining for a worker with the onset of a health condition. The income support system and employment services for Canadians with disabilities, as for all Canadians, are complex, fragmented, and piecemeal. Large numbers of people with serious illnesses or disabilities are ineligible for EI and even more so for CPP/D since the 1997 reforms. The consequences for individuals and their families involve declining household incomes, depleting savings and possibly retirement funds, and taking on debt to cover the cost of medical treatments. Disabled people rely heavily on the social assistance programs in provincial welfare systems to an extent today that would astound social reformers of the 1940s.

Widespread struggles of people with disabilities represent a sharp and meaningful challenge to public beliefs about the adequacy of Canada's social security programs. An international study on the Canadian sickness and disability policy system recommends making the federation work better for persons with disabilities by clarifying the roles of the different levels of government and promoting good practice learning. The study calls for moving towards a client-oriented framework by implementing systematic case management, improving the program coverage and take-up by persons with disabilities of income benefits as well as employment programs, promoting early intervention and access to supports at the onset of health problems, and strengthening the role of private disability benefit plans (OECD 2010). The great goal sought after in this policy field may be a universal, comprehensive disability income program. Interestingly, federal-provincial officials gave this considerable consideration in the early 1980s, and the 1996 Scott task force report expressed the belief that sooner or later this option will have to be considered seriously.

Outlines of a reform agenda for disability policy, income provision and the CPP/D are available in academic writings, community reports, and documents from Parliament and the federal government. One

fiscally prudent and socially progressive reform would be the introduction of partial benefits for contributors who work less than full
time because of health restrictions. A partial CPP/D benefit could
complement the income earned from part-time employment for people
with lifelong episodic disabilities and partial capacities to work. This
reform would shift eligibility away from unemployability toward the
willingness to work by individuals experiencing episodic conditions
such as chronic pain, chronic fatigue syndrome, and fibromyalgia.
Another proposal, following on the child care dropout provision in
the CPP, is to include comparable dropout provisions in CPP/D for
workers attending school or training or for caregiving a family member. Raising the level of CPP/D benefit levels is not heard as much as
some might expect, although a parliamentary committee did recom-
mend a return to the pre-1998 method for calculating CPP/D benefits
in order to improve the adequacy of payments. In a similar way, community advocates call for making CPP/D benefits non-taxable. Beyond
CPP/D, other income security reform options include extending the
duration of EI sickness benefits from the current fifteen weeks, and
making the Disability Tax Credit refundable and therefore available
to those low-income Canadian with disabilities who do not pay taxes.

The CPP legislation is old and creaky. Disability program elements
are scattered throughout the act and need to be reviewed, consolidated, and revised to enhance the responsiveness of the program.
Legislative authority should be established to permit the program
to engage in social innovations. Families, Children and Social
Development Canada (formerly Employment and Social Development
Canada), in partnership with the provinces as stewards of CPP/D,
should have the ability to implement demonstration projects on new
ways of offering early intervention, perhaps in collaboration with the
EI sickness benefit program, or of linking vocational rehabilitation,
training, and work incentives for beneficiaries to return to employment. Also worth considering is statutory authority to spend money
on non-beneficiaries to assist them in reintegration to the workforce.
As one policy analyst writes, "social rights of citizenship should
include a right to satisfying work and human self-development," a
conception that encompasses adult education and active labour market programming (Stephens 2010, 514). Doing case management
with people requires ongoing and meaningful interaction between
program staff and clients. Genuine case management is tailored to
the specific needs and circumstances of the individual; it considers the

intangibles of abilities to cope with stress, risk-taking behaviours, opportunities and barriers in the community and labour market, and the presence of family and other supports.

In the immediate future, the social rights for disabled Canadians will be shaped at the national level by Justin Trudeau's Liberal government. Formed in November 2015, the Trudeau federal government has articulated a series of policy and program initiatives that bear on several aspects of employment and disability policy, income security, and social citizenship (Liberal Party of Canada 2015).

On Employment Insurance, for example, the Trudeau Liberals promise to reduce the waiting period for benefits from two weeks to one and to introduce more flexibility in parental benefits and in accessing the compassionate care benefit. For those individuals not employed and those who do not qualify for EI, the plan is to expand federal investments by $200 million per year in training programs led by the provinces and territories for a range of groups disadvantaged in the labour market. The Canada Labour Code is to be amended to grant federally regulated workers the legal right to formally request more flexible working conditions from their employers, an important feature of job accommodations for many people with and without disabilities.

Injured and disabled veterans and their families figure prominently in the Liberal's platform, with commitments to re-establish lifelong pensions for injured Canadian veterans; increase the earnings loss benefit and the value of the disability award; expand access to the permanent impairment allowance as well as index that allowance; and introduce a new $80-million per-year education benefit to support post-secondary and technical education for veterans. In addition, vocational rehabilitation and other services for veterans' families plan to be enhanced through $100 million in new support. A related pledge is to introduce a public safety officer compensation benefit of $300,000 to families of firefighters, police officers, and paramedics killed or permanently disabled in the line of duty. The Trudeau Liberals intend to review federal tax expenditure spending with the aim of targeting tax loopholes that benefit the wealthiest one percent. At the same time, disability organizations would welcome that policy review to improve tax measures for the benefit of Canadians in low- to modest-income households.

In terms of bolstering rights of social citizenship for disabled Canadians, the Liberals commit to consult with provinces and other stakeholders on the idea of introducing a National Disabilities Act, an initiative that would complement their 2015 election promises of progressively implementing the UN Convention on the Rights of Persons with Disabilities and on reinstating the Court Challenges Program of Canada, a program that the Harper government terminated several years ago. With respect to the CPP disability program and the Social Security Tribunal, the Liberal Party's platform for the 2015 election was silent, though the Liberals did commit to an expansion of the CPP retirement benefit. Now in power, the Trudeau Liberals should take steps to improve the application processing time for CPP/D benefits and address the backlog of appeals on denials of CPP/D. Moreover, the Trudeau government should take steps to ensure the impartiality and subject-matter expertise of tribunal members and take steps to restore legal rights and procedural fairness for CPP/D clients, including the fundamental right to an in-person hearing. Social citizenship, after all, must always begin with the embodied self in connection with legislative measures and larger structural realities.

Bibliography

Ablonczy, Diane. 1997. *Commons Debates.* 6 October, p. 540.

Alford, Robert F., and Roger Friedland. 1985. *Powers of Theory: Capitalism, the State, and Democracy.* Cambridge: Cambridge University Press.

Arts, Wil, and John Gelissen. 2002. "Three Worlds of Welfare Capitalism or More? A State-of-the-Art Report." *Journal of European Social Policy* 12:137–58.

Auditor General of Canada. 1994. *Report of the Auditor General of Canada to the House of Commons.* Ottawa: Minister of Supply and Services.

– 1996. *Report of the Auditor General of Canada to the House of Commons.* Ottawa: Minister of Supply and Services.

Axworthy, Thomas S. 2002. "Social Cohesion and the New Liberalism: How to Move Social Policy from Neutral to Go." Searching for the New Liberalism, Toronto, 27–29 September.

Bacchi, Carol Lee, and Chris Beasley. 2002. "Citizen Bodies: Is Embodied Citizenship A Contradiction in Terms?" *Critical Social Policy* 22 (2): 324–52.

Bach, Michael, and Marcia Rioux. 1996. "Social Policy, Devolution and Disability: Back to Notions of the Worthy Poor?" In *Remaking Canadian Social Policy: Social Security in the Late 1990s,* edited by Jane Pulkingham and Gordon Ternowetsky, 317–26. Halifax, NS: Fernwood Publishing.

Baldwin, Bob. 1996. "Income Security Prospects for Older Canadians." In *Aging Workforce, Income Security, and Retirement: Policy and Practical Implications,* edited by Anju Joshi and Ellie Berger, 69–74. McMaster University Summer Institute on Gerontology Proceedings, Hamilton, ON.

– 1997. "Comments." In *Reform of Retirement Income Policy: International and Canadian Perspectives,* edited by Keith G. Banting and Robin Boadway, 191–8. Kingston: School of Policy Studies, Queen's University.

Banting, Keith G. 1984. "The Decision Rules: Federalism and Pension Reform." In *Pensions Today and Tomorrow: Background Studies*, edited by D.W. Conklin, J.H. Bennett and T.J. Courchene, 189–209. Toronto: Ontario Economic Council.

– 1987. *The Welfare State and Canadian Federalism*. 2nd ed. Montreal and Kingston: McGill-Queen's University Press.

– 1999. "Social Citizenship and the Multicultural Welfare State." In *Citizenship, Diversity, and Pluralism: Canadian and Comparative Perspectives*, edited by A.C. Cairns, J.C. Courtney, P. MacKinnon, H.J. Michelmann, and D.E. Smith, 108–36. Montreal and Kingston: McGill-Queen's University Press.

– 2005. "Canada: Nation-Building in a Federal State." In *Federalism and the Welfare State: New World and European Experiences*, edited by Herbert Obinger, Stephen Leibfried, and Francis G. Castles, 89–137. Cambridge: Cambridge University Press.

Banting, Keith G., and Robin Boadway. 1997. "Reforming Retirement Income Policy: The Issues." In *Reform of Retirement Income Policy: International and Canadian Perspectives*, edited by Keith G. Banting and Robin Boadway, 1–26. Montreal and Kingston: McGill-Queen's University Press.

Barbalet, J.M. 1988. *Citizenship: Rights, Struggle and Class Equality*. Milton Keynes, UK: Open University Press.

Barnes, Colin, and Geof Mercer. 2003. *Disability*. Cambridge: Polity Press.

Barnes, Colin, Geof Mercer, and Tom Shakespeare. 1999. *Exploring Disability: A Sociological Introduction*. Cambridge: Polity Press.

Barry, Norman. 1999. *Welfare*. 2nd ed. Minneapolis: University of Minnesota Press.

Barton, Len. 1993. "The Struggle for Citizenship: The Case of Disabled People." *Disability & Society* 8 (3): 235–48.

Bashevkin, Sylvia. 2002. *Welfare Hot Buttons: Women, Work, and Social Policy Reform*. Toronto: University of Toronto Press.

Beachell, Laurie. 2011. "CPPD Reforms: An Example of Leadership within the Civil Service." In *Celebrating Our Accomplishments*, Council of Canadians with Disabilities, 113–14. Winnipeg: CCD.

Beasley, Chris, and Carol Bacchi. 2000. "Citizen Bodies: Embodying Citizens – A Feminist Analysis." *International Feminist Journal of Politics* 2 (3): 337–58.

Beckett, Angharad E. 2005. "Reconsidering Citizenship in the Light of the Concerns of the UK Disability Movement." *Citizenship Studies* 9 (4): 405–21.

Béland, Daniel. 2013. "The Politics of the Canada Pension Plan: Private Pensions and Federal-Provincial Parallelism." In *How Ottawa Spends, 2013–2014 – The Harper Government: Mid-Term Blues and Long-Term Plans*, edited by G. Bruce Doern and Christopher Stoney, 76–87. Montreal and Kingston: McGill-Queen's University Press.

Bennett, Carolyn. 2003. *Listening to Canadians: A First View of the Future of the Canadian Disability Plan Disability Program.* Report of the Standing Committee on Human Resources Development and the Status of Persons with Disabilities. Ottawa: House of Commons.

Berkowitz, Edward D. 1987. *Disabled Policy: America's Programs for the Handicapped.* Cambridge: Cambridge University Press.

Bliss, Michael. 1975. Preface to *Report on Social Security for Canada*, 2nd ed., by Leonard Marsh, ix–xxxi. Toronto: University of Toronto Press.

Bonnett, Laura. 2003. "Citizenship and People with Disabilities: The Invisible Frontier." In *Reinventing Canada: Politics of the 21st Century*, edited by Janine Brodie and Linda Trimble, 151–63. Toronto: Pearson Education.

Bourdieu, Pierre. 1998. *Acts of Resistance: Against the Tyranny of the Market.* Translated by Richard Nice. New York: The New Press.

Boyce, William, Mary Tremblay, Mary Anne McColl, Jerome Bickenbach, Anne Crichton, Steven Andrews, Nancy Gerein, and April D'Aubin. 2001. *A Seat at the Table: Persons with Disabilities and Policy Making.* Montreal and Kingston: McGill-Queen's University Press.

Boychuk, Gerald W. 1998. *Patchworks of Purpose: The Development of Provincial Social Assistance Regimes in Canada.* Montreal and Kingston: McGill-Queen's University Press.

Braidotti, Rosi. 1994. *Nomadic Subjects: Embodiment and Sexual Differences in Contemporary Feminist Theory.* New York: Columbia University Press.

Brodie, Janine. 1995. *Politics on the Margins: Restructuring and the Canadian Women's Movement.* Halifax, NS: Fernwood Publishing.

– 1997. "Meso-Discourses, State Forms and the Gendering of Liberal-Democratic Citizenship." *Citizenship Studies* 1 (2): 223–42.

– 1999. "The Politics of Social Policy in the Twenty-First Century." In *Citizens or Consumers? Social Policy in a Market Society*, edited by D. Broad and W. Antony, 37–45. Halifax, NS: Fernwood Publishing.

– 2009. "The Social in Social Citizenship." In *Recasting the Social in Citizenship*, edited by E.F. Isin, 20–43. Toronto: University of Toronto Press.

Brown, Joan C. 1977. *A Hit-and-Miss Affair: Policies for Disabled People in Canada.* Ottawa: Canadian Council on Social Development.

Bryden, Kenneth. 1974. *Old Age Pensions and Policy-Making in Canada*. Montreal: McGill-Queen's University Press.

Bryden, P.E. 1997. *Planners and Politicians: Liberal Politics and Social Policy, 1957–1968*. Montreal and Kingston: McGill-Queen's University Press.

Burbidge, John B. 1987. "Social Security in Canada: An Economic Appraisal." Tax paper no. 79. Canadian Tax Foundation, Toronto.

– 1996. "Public Pensions in Canada." In *When We're 65: Reforming Canada's Retirement Income System*, by John B. Burbidge et al., 93–128. Toronto: C.D. Howe Institute.

Burns, Eveline M. 1956. *Social Security and Public Policy*. Toronto: McGraw-Hill.

Cairns, Alan. 1986. "The Embedded State: State-Society Relations in Canada." In *State and Society: Canada in Comparative Perspective*, edited by Keith Banting, 53–86. Toronto: University of Toronto Press.

Cairns, Alan, and Cynthia Williams. 1985. "Constitutionalism, Citizenship, and Society in Canada: An Overview." In *Constitutionalism, Citizenship, and Society in Canada*, edited by Alan Cairns and Cynthia Williams, 1–50. Toronto: University of Toronto Press.

Cameron, David, and Fraser Valentine. 2001. "Comparing Policy-Making in Federal Systems: The Case of Disability Policy and Programs – An Introduction." In *Disability and Federalism: Comparing Different Approaches to Full Participation*, edited by D. Cameron and F. Valentine, 1–44. Montreal and Kingston: McGill-Queen's University Press.

Canada. 1982. *Better Pensions for Canadians*. Ottawa: Minister of Supply and Services.

– 1985a. *The Canada Pension Plan: Keeping It Financially Healthy*. Ottawa: Minister of Supply and Services.

– 1985b. *Changes Proposed to Canada Pension Plan*. Ottawa: Department of Finance.

– 1987. *Survivor Benefits under the Canada Pension Plan*. Ottawa: Minister of Supply and Services.

– 1996a. *Principles to Guide Federal-Provincial Decisions on the Canada Pension Plan*. Ottawa: Department of Finance, October.

– 1996b. *Report on the Canada Pension Plan Consultations*. Ottawa: Department of Finance, June.

– Department of Human Resources Development. 2003. *Government of Canada Response to "Listening to Canadians: A First View of the Future of the Canada Pension Plan Disability Program."* The Fifth Report of the Standing Committee on Human Resources Development and the Status of Persons with Disabilities. Report (November). Ottawa: Public Works and Government Services Canada.

– Finance Canada. 1997. *Securing the Canada Pension Plan: Agreement on Proposed Changes to the CPP*. Ottawa: Department of Finance.
– Finance Canada. 2015. *Strong Leadership: A Balanced-Budget, Low-Tax Plan for Jobs, Growth and Security*. Tabled in the House of Commons by the Honourable Joe Oliver, Minister of Finance, 21 April. Ottawa: Her Majesty the Queen in Right of Canada.
– Secretary of State. 1985. *Obstacles: Progress Report*. Ottawa: Minister of Supply and Services, Status of Disabled Persons Secretariat.
– Secretary of State. 1987. *Obstacles: 1987 Report Update*. Ottawa: Minister of Supply and Services.
– Senate. Standing Committee on Banking, Trade and Commerce. 2007. Proceedings. Evidence, Issue 20. 39th Parliament, 1st Session, 18 and 19 April. Ottawa: Public Works and Government Services Canada.
Canadian Welfare Council. 1946. *Dominion-Provincial Relations and Social Security*. Ottawa: The Council.
Cassidy, Harry M. 1943. *Social Security and Reconstruction in Canada*. Toronto: Ryerson Press.
Chambers, D.E. 1985. "The Reagan Administration Welfare Retrenchment Policy: Terminating Social Security Benefits for the Disabled." *Policy Studies Review* 2:207–15.
Chouinard, Vera, and Valorie A. Crooks. 2005. "'Because *They* Have All the Power and I Have None': State Restructuring of Income and Employment Supports and Disabled Women." *Disability and Society* 20 (1): 19–32.
Chronicle Herald (Halifax). 2014. "Disgraceful Treatment of Would-Be Disability Pensioners." Editorial, 2 December.
Clasen, J., ed. 2001. *What Future for Social Security? Debates and Reforms in National and Cross-National Perspective*. The Hague: Kluwer Law International.
Coates, Robert C. 1976. *Commons Debates*, 29 January, p. 10452.
Coffey, Amanda. 2004. *Reconceptualizing Social Policy: Sociological Perspectives on Contemporary Social Policy*. Maidenhead, UK: Open University Press.
Coleman, William, and Grace Skogstad. 1990. *Policy Communities and Public Policy in Canada: A Structural Approach*. Toronto: Copp Clark Pitman.
Commerce Clearing House (CCH). 1968. *Canada Pension Plan and Old Age Security Legislation, with Regulations, Revised Edition, 1968*. Don Mills, ON: CCH Canadian Limited.
– 1988. "Edward Leduc v. Minister of National Health and Welfare." In *CCH Canadian Employment Benefits and Pension Guide Reports*,

Transfer Binder, 1986–1992, 6021–2. Don Mills, ON: Commerce Clearing House Canadian Ltd.

Copps, Sheila. 1986. *Commons Debates,* 26 June, p. 14885.

Coutts, Jim. 1990. "Expansion, Retrenchment and Protecting the Future: Social Policy in the Trudeau Years." In *Towards a Just Society: The Trudeau Years,* edited by Thomas S. Axworthy and Pierre Elliott Trudeau, 177–201. Markham, ON: Viking.

– 2003. "Windows of Opportunity: Social Reform under Lester B. Pearson." *Policy Options,* November, 9–20.

Cowen, Deborah. 2008. *Military Workfare: The Soldier and Social Citizenship in Canada.* Toronto: University of Toronto Press.

Cruikshank, Barbara. 1999. *The Will to Empower: Democratic Citizens and Other Subjects.* Ithaca, NY: Cornell University Press.

Curran, R. 1964. Testimony before the Joint Committee of the Senate and House of Commons to Examine and Report on Bill C-136. *Minutes of Proceedings and Evidence.* No. 6, 8 December, p. 338.

Dahrendorf, Ralf. 1988. *The Modern Social Conflict.* Berkeley: University of California Press.

Daly, Mary. 2002. *Access to Social Rights in Europe.* Strasbourg: Council of Europe.

Davis, Lennard J. 1995. *Enforcing Normalcy: Disability, Deafness, and the Body.* New York: Verso.

Dean, Hartley. 1999. "Introduction: Towards an Embodied Account of Welfare." In *Social Policy and the Body: Transitions in Corporeal Discourse,* edited by K. Ellis and H. Dean, ix–xxv. New York: Palgrave Macmillan.

Dean, Mitchell. 1994. *Critical and Effective Histories: Foucault's Methods and Historical Sociology.* London: Routledge.

– 1995. "Governing the Unemployed Self in an Active Society." *Economy and Society* 24 (4): 559–83.

Deaton, Richard Lee. 1989. *The Political Economy of Pensions: Power, Politics and Social Change in Canada, Britain and the United States.* Vancouver: University of British Columbia Press.

Devlin, Richard, and Dianne Pothier. 2006. "Introduction: Towards a Critical Theory of Dis-Citizenship." In *Critical Disability Theory: Essays in Philosophy, Politics, Policy, and Law,* edited by Dianne Pothier and Richard Devlin, 1–22. Vancouver: University of British Columbia Press.

De Savoye, Pierre. 1997. *Commons Debates.* 6 October, p. 507.

Dietz, Mary G. 1987. "Context Is All: Feminism and Theories of Citizenship." *Daedalus* 116 (4): 1–24.

Dixon, John, and Mark Hyde. 2000. "A Global Perspective on Social
Security Programmes for Disabled People." *Disability & Society* 15 (5):
709–30.

Dixon, Robert G. 1973. *Social Security Disability and Mass Justice: A
Problem in Welfare Adjudication*. New York: Praeger.

Doern, G. Bruce, Allan M. Maslove, and Michael J. Prince. 2013.
*Canadian Public Budgeting in the Age of Crises: Shifting Budget
Domains and Temporal Budgeting*. Montreal and Kingston: McGill-
Queen's University Press.

Doern, G. Bruce, Michael J. Prince, and Richard J. Schultz. 2014. *Rules and
Unruliness: Canadian Regulatory Democracy, Governance, Capitalism,
and Welfarism*. Montreal and Kingston: McGill-Queen's University Press.

Dwyer, Peter. 2000. *Welfare Rights and Responsibilities: Contesting Social
Citizenship*. Bristol: Policy Press.

– 2004. *Understanding Social Citizenship: Themes and Perspectives for
Policy and Practice*. Bristol: Policy Press.

Echenberg, Havi. 2003. "Fifty Years of Social Issues: Playing "Hide and
Seek" with Villains and Heroes." *Policy Options*, 1 June. http://
policyoptions.irpp.org/issues/the-best-pms-in-the-past-50-years/
fifty-years-of-social-issues-playing-hide-and-seek-with-villains-and-heroes/.

Eckert, Julia. 2011. "Introduction: Subjects of Citizenship." *Citizenship
Studies* 15 (3–4): 309–17.

Ellis, Kathryn. 2005. "Disability Rights in Practice: The Relationship
between Human Rights and Social Rights in Contemporary Social
Care." *Disability and Society* 20 (7): 693–706.

Enns, Henry, and Aldred H. Neufeldt, eds. 2003. *In Pursuit of
Participation: Canada and Disability at Home and Abroad*. Concord,
ON: Captus Press.

Epp, Hon. Jake. 1986. *Commons Debates*. 26 June, pp. 14249–52, 14879–80.

Erkulwater, Jennifer L. 2006. *Disability Rights and the American Safety
Net*. Ithaca, NY: Cornell University Press.

Erlanger, Howard S., and William Roth. 1985. "Disability Policy: The
Parts and the Whole." *American Behavioral Scientist* 28 (3): 319–45.

Esping-Andersen, Gösta. 1990. *The Three Worlds of Capitalism*.
Cambridge: Polity Press.

Faulks, Keith. 2000. *Citizenship: A Critical Introduction*. London:
Routledge.

Federal/Provincial/Territorial Ministers Responsible for Social Services.
1998. *In Unison: A Canadian Approach to Disability Issues: A Vision
Paper*. Hull, QC: Human Resources Development Canada.

Federal Task Force on Disability Issues (Chaired by Andy Scott). 1996. *Equal Citizenship for Canadians with Disabilities: The Will to Act.* Ottawa: Government of Canada.

Fortier, Pierre. 1986. *Minutes of Proceedings and Evidence.* Standing Committee on National Health and Welfare, issue no. 5.

Foucault, Michel. 1990. *The History of Sexuality, Volume I: An Introduction.* New York: Vintage Books.

– 2003. *"Society Must Be Defended": Lectures at the Collège de France, 1975–1976.* London: Picador.

– 2004. *Abnormal: Lectures at the Collège de France, 1974–1975.* London: Picador.

– 2006. *Psychiatric Power: Lectures at the Collège de France 1973–1974.* London: Picador.

Fraser, Nancy. 1987. "Women, Welfare and the Politics of Need Interpretation." *Hypatia: A Journal of Feminist Philosophy* 2 (1): 103–21.

– 1989. *Unruly Practices: Power, Discourse and Gender in Contemporary Social Theory.* Minneapolis: University of Minnesota Press.

Furrie, Adele. 2010. *Towards a Better Understanding of the Dynamics of Disability and Its Impact on Employment: Final Report.* Ottawa: Adele Furrie Consulting Inc.

Gabrielson, Teena, and Katelyn Parady. 2010. "Corporeal Citizenship: Rethinking Green Citizenship through the Body." *Environmental Politics* 19 (3): 374–91.

Galloway, Gloria. 2014. "More Tribunal Members Hired for Backlog of 11,000 Social Security Appeals." *Globe and Mail,* 27 November.

Garant, Patrice. 2002. *A Canadian Social Security Tribunal: Final Report.* Prepared for Human Resources and Development Canada. 30 November.

Glenn, Evelyn Nakano. 2011. "Constructing Citizenship: Exclusion, Subordination, and Resistance." *American Sociological Review* 76 (1): 1–24.

Goffman, Erving. 1968. *Stigma: Notes on the Management of Spoiled Identity.* Harmondsworth: Penguin.

Goodman, Lee-Anne. 2014a. "Critics Wonder Why Seriously Ill Seekers of Disability Benefits Being Denied." *The Canadian Press,* 2 December.

– 2014b. "Fewer In-Person Hearings Being Heard by Social Security Tribunal." *Winnipeg Free Press,* 18 December.

– 2014c. "Harper, PCO Approved the Long Hiring Process for Social Security Tribunal." *The Canadian Press,* 17 December.

– 2015a. "Government on Hot Seat about Dying Albertan Denied CPP Disability Benefits." *Globe and Mail,* 26 February.

– 2015b. "Kenney Pledges to Wipe Out Social Security Tribunal Backlog by This Summer." *Globe and Mail*, 6 February.

Gorham, Eric. 1995. "Social Citizenship and Its Fetters." *Polity* 28: 25–47.

Guest, Dennis. 1998. *The Emergence of Social Security in Canada*. 3rd ed. Vancouver: University of British Columbia Press.

Haddow, Rodney S. 1993. *Poverty Reform in Canada 1958–1978: State and Class Influences on Policy Making*. Montreal and Kingston: McGill-Queen's University Press.

Harder, Lois. 2003. *State of Struggle: Feminism and Politics in Alberta*. Edmonton: University of Alberta Press.

Harris, David. 1987. *Justifying State Welfare: The New Right Versus the Old Left*. Oxford: Blackwell.

Heclo, Hugh. (1974) 2011. *Modern Social Politics in Britain and Sweden*. 2nd ed. New Haven, CT: Yale University Press/European Consortium for Political Research Press.

– 1995. "The Social Question." In *Poverty, Inequality and the Future of Social Policy*, edited by Katherine McFate, Richard Lawson, and William Julius Wilson, 665–92. New York: Russell Sage.

Held, David. 1987. *Models of Democracy*. Cambridge: Polity Press.

Human Resources Development Canada. Various years. *Annual Report of the Canada Pension Plan, 1994–2000*. Ottawa: Minister of Supply and Services.

– Various years. *Estimates, Part III, Expenditure Plans*. Ottawa: Minister of Supply and Services.

– 1994. "Improving Social Security in Canada, Persons with Disabilities: A Discussion Paper." Minister of Supply and Services, Ottawa.

– 2001a. "1998 Changes to the Canada Pension Plan." *Annual CPPD Newsletter*.

– 2001b. *Staying in Touch: A Newsletter for People Receiving a Canada Disability Benefit*. November.

– 2002a. *Canada Pension Plan Benefit Rates 2002*. Ottawa: Income Security Programs Branch.

– 2002b. "The Canada Pension Plan Disability Vocational Rehabilitation Program." Ottawa: Income Security Programs Branch.

Human Resources and Skills Development Canada (HRSDC). 2011. *Summative Evaluation: Canada Pension Plan Disability Program, Final Report*. Gatineau, QC: Evaluation Directorate, Strategic Policy and Research Branch.

Ignatieff, Michael. 1984. *The Needs of Strangers: An Essay on Privacy, Solidarity and the Politics of Being Human*. Toronto: Penguin Books.

– 1989. "Citizenship and Moral Narcissism." *Political Quarterly* 60 (1): 63–74.

Jenkins, Richard. 2004. *Social Identity*. 2nd ed. New York: Routledge.

Jennissen, Therese, Michael J. Prince, and Saul Schwartz. 2000. "Workers' Compensation in Canada: A Case for Greater Public Accountability." *Canadian Public Administration* 43 (1): 23–45.

Jenson, Jane. 1997. "Fated to Live in Interesting Times: Canada's Changing Citizenship Regimes." *Canadian Journal of Political Science* 30 (4): 627–44.

– 2003. "Social Citizenship, Governance and Social Policy." Paper prepared for the Canada-Korea Social Policy Research Co-operation Symposium, Seoul, Korea, 21 November. http://www.cccg.umontreal.ca/pdf/SocialCitizenshipGovernance.pdf.

Joint Committee of the Senate and House of Commons to Examine and Report on Bill C-136. 1964. *Minutes of Proceedings and Evidence*. No. 2, 1 December, Appendix B, pp. 133–45.

Jones, Kathleen B. 1990. "Citizenship in a Women-Friendly Polity." *Signs* 15 (4): 781–812.

Jongbloed, Lyn. 2003. "Disability Policy in Canada: An Overview." *Journal of Disability Policy Studies* 13 (4): 203–9.

Kent, Tom. 1988. *A Public Purpose: An Experience of Liberal Opposition and Canadian Government*. Montreal and Kingston: McGill-Queen's University Press.

King, Desmond S., and Jeremy Waldron. 1988. "Citizenship, Social Citizenship and the Defence of Welfare Provision." *British Journal of Political Science* 18 (4): 415–43.

Korpi, Walter. 1989. "Power, Politics, and State Autonomy in the Development of Social Citizenship: Social Rights during Sickness in Eighteen OECD Countries since 1930." *American Sociological Review* 54:309–28.

Lalonde, Hon. Marc. 1973. "Working Paper on Social Security in Canada." Department of National Health and Welfare, Ottawa.

– 1984. *Action Plan for Pension Reform: Building Better Pensions for Canadians*. Ottawa: Department of Finance.

LaMarsh, Judy. 1964. "Testimony before the Joint Committee of the Senate and House of Commons to Examine and Report on Bill C-136." *Minutes of Proceedings and Evidence*. No. 1, 25 November.

– 1965. *Commons Debates*. Vol. 2, Session 1964–65, 1 March, pp. 11837–46.

– 1969. *Memoirs of a Bird in a Gilded Cage*. Toronto: McClelland and Stewart.

Lawand, Nancy, and Rita Kloosterman. 2006. "The Canada Pension Plan Disability Program: Building a Solid Foundation." In *Disability and Social Policy in Canada*, 2nd ed., edited by Mary Ann McColl and Lyn Jongbloed, 267–83. Concord, ON: Captus University Publications.

Leonard, Peter. 1997. *Postmodern Welfare: Reconstructing an Emancipatory Project*. London: Sage.

Levesque, Mario, and Peter Graefe. 2013. "'Not Good Enough': Canada's Stalled Disability Policy." In *How Ottawa Spends, 2013–2014*, edited by G. Bruce Doern and Chris Stoney, 172–83. Montreal and Kingston: McGill-Queen's University Press.

Liberal Party of Canada. 2015. *Real Change: A New Plan for a Strong Middle Class*. Ottawa: Liberal Party of Canada.

Lister, Ruth. 1997. *Citizenship: Feminist Perspectives*. London: Macmillan.

– 2007. "Inclusive Citizenship: Realizing the Potential." *Citizenship Studies* 11 (1): 49–61.

Little, Bruce. 2008. *Fixing the Future: How Canada's Usually Fractious Governments Worked Together to Rescue the Canada Pension Plan*. Toronto: University of Toronto Press.

Marsh, Leonard. (1943) 1975. *Report on Social Security for Canada*. 2nd ed. Toronto: University of Toronto Press.

Marshall, T.H. 1964. *Class, Citizenship, and Social Development*. Westport, CT: Greenwood Press.

Martin, Dick. 1986. *Minutes of Proceedings and Evidence*. Standing Committee of National Health and Welfare, issue no. 5.

Martin, Hon. Paul. 1994. *Budget Speech*. Ottawa: Department of Finance, 22 February.

– 1995. *Budget Speech*. Ottawa: Department of Finance, 27 February.

– 1996. *Budget Speech*. Ottawa: Department of Finance, 6 March.

– 1997a. *The Budget Plan*. Ottawa: Department of Finance, 18 February.

– 1997b. "Notes for Remarks by the Hon. Paul Martin before the Senate Standing Committee on Banking, Trade and Commerce on Bill C-2." Ottawa: Department of Finance, 17 December.

– 1997c. "Notes for Remarks by the Hon. Paul Martin to the House of Commons Standing Committee on Finance on Bill C-2." Ottawa: Department of Finance, 28 October.

– 1998. *The Budget Speech: Building Canada for the 21st Century*. Ottawa: Department of Finance, 24 February.

– 2000. *The Budget Plan 2000: Better Finances, Better Lives*. Ottawa: Department of Finance, 28 February.

Mazankowski, Hon. Don. 1993. *The Budget 1993*. Ottawa: Department of Finance, 26 April.

McColl, Mary Ann, and Lyn Jongbloed, eds. 2006. *Disability and Social Policy in Canada*. 2nd ed. Concord, ON: Captus Press.

McCreath, Graeme. 2011. *The Politics of Blindness: From Charity to Parity*. Vancouver: Granville Island Publishing.

McLaren, Margaret A. 2002. *Feminism, Foucault, and Embodied Subjectivity*. Albany: State University of New York Press.

Meekosha, Helen, and Leanne Dowse. 1997. "Enabling Citizenship: Gender, Disability and Citizenship in Australia." *Feminist Review* 57:49–72.

Michalko, Rod. 2002. *The Difference that Disability Makes*. Philadelphia: Temple University Press.

Mishra, Ramesh. 1981. *Society and Social Policy: Theories and Practice of Welfare*. 2nd ed. London: Macmillan.

– 1990. *The Welfare State in Capitalist Society: Policies of Retrenchment and Maintenance in Europe, North America and Australia*. Toronto: University of Toronto Press.

Morris, Jenny. 1993. "Feminism and Disability." *Feminist Review* 43:57–70.

Morton, Desmond. 2004. *Fight or Pay: Soldiers' Families in the Great War*. Vancouver: University of British Columbia Press.

Moss, Pamela, and Michael J. Prince. 2014. *Weary Warriors: Power, Knowledge, and the Invisible Wounds of Soldiers*. New York and Oxford: Berghahn.

Moss, Pamela, and Katherine Teghtsoonian. 2008. "Power and Illness: Authority, Bodies, and Context." In *Contesting Illness: Processes and Practices*, edited by Pamela Moss and Katherine Teghtsoonian, 3–27. Toronto: University of Toronto Press.

Munro, Hon. John. 1970. "Income Security for Canadians." White paper. Department of National Health and Welfare, Ottawa.

National Council of Welfare. 1996. *Improving the Canada Pension Plan: A Report by the National Council of Welfare*. Ottawa: Ministry of Supply and Services Canada.

National Health and Welfare. Various years. *Annual Report of the Canada Pension Plan, 1966–1993*. Ottawa: Queen's Printer and Minister of Supply and Services.

– Various years. *Report on the Administration of Allowances for Blind Persons in Canada*. Ottawa: Queen's Printer.

– Various years. *Report on the Administration of Allowances for Disabled Persons in Canada*. Ottawa: Queen's Printer.

– 1965. *The Canada Pension Plan, Actuarial Report, as of November 6, 1964*. Ottawa: Queen's Printer.

- 1983. *CPP Disability Applicants Study*. Ottawa: Income Security Programs Branch.
- 1986. *Estimates, 1986–87, Part III, Expenditure Plans*. Ottawa: Minister of Supply and Services.
- 1989. *Estimates, 1989–90, Part III, Expenditure Plans*. Ottawa: Minister of Supply and Services.
- 1990. *Estimates, 1990–91, Part III, Expenditure Plans*. Ottawa: Minister of Supply and Services.
- 1996. *Improving the Canada Pension Plan*. Ottawa: Minister of Supply and Services.
- 1999. *A Pension Primer*. Ottawa: Minister of Supply and Services.

Neary, Peter. 2009. "'Without the Stigma of Pauperism': Canadian Veterans in the 1930s." *British Journal of Canadian Studies* 22 (1): 31–62.

Neumann, W. Lawrence. 2006. *Social Research Methods: Qualitative and Quantitative Approaches*. 6th ed. Boston: Allyn and Bacon.

O'Connor, Julia S., Ann Shola Orloff, and Sheila Shaver. 1999. *States, Markets, Families: Gender. Liberalism and Social Policy in Australia, Canada, Great Britain and the United States*. Cambridge: Cambridge University Press.

OECD. 2003. *Transforming Disability into Ability: Policies to Promote Work and Income Security for Disabled People*. Paris: Organisation for Economic Co-operation and Development.

- 2010. *Sickness, Disability and Work: Breaking the Barriers, Canada: Time for Structural Reform*. Paris: Directorate for Employment, Labour and Social Affairs, Organisation for Economic Co-operation and Development.

Office of the Commissioner of Review Tribunals. 2001. *Annual Report 1999–2000*. Ottawa.

O'Loughlin, Marjorie. 2006. *Embodiment and Education*. Dordrecht: Springer Netherlands.

Orsini, Michael. 2012. "Autism, Neurodiversity and the Welfare State: The Challenge of Accommodating Neurological Difference." *Canadian Journal of Political Science* 45 (4): 805–27.

Orsini, Michael, and Miriam Smith. 2007. "Critical Policy Studies." In *Critical Policy Studies*, edited by Michael Orsini and Miriam Smith, 1–16. Vancouver: University of British Columbia Press.

Panel on Labour Market Opportunities for Persons with Disabilities. 2013. *Rethinking disAbility in the Private Sector*. Ottawa: Employment and Social Development Canada.

Parliamentary Committee on Palliative and Compassionate Care. 2011. *Not to Be Forgotten: Care of Vulnerable Canadians.* Ottawa, November.

Pension News. 1994. 8 (3): 7.

Pettigrew, Hon. Pierre. 1997. Remarks before the Standing Committee on Finance on Bill C-2. Ottawa, 28 October.

Pinker, Robert. 1971. *Social Theory and Social Policy.* London: Heinemann Educational Books.

Porter, Bruce. 2007. "Claiming Adjudicative Space: Social Rights, Equality, and Citizenship." In *Poverty: Rights, Social Citizenship, and Legal Activism,* edited by M. Young, S.B. Boyd, G. Brodsky, and S. Day, 77–95. Vancouver: University of British Columbia Press.

Porter, John. 1965. *The Vertical Mosaic: An Analysis of Social Class and Power in Canada.* Toronto: University of Toronto Press.

Prince, Michael J. 1985. "Startling Facts, Sobering Truths and Sacred Trust: Pension Policy and the Tories." In *How Ottawa Spends 1985: Sharing the Pie,* edited by Allan M. Maslove, 114–61. Toronto: Methuen.

– 1992. "Touching Us All: International Context, National Policies, and the Integration of Canadians with Disabilities." In *How Ottawa Spends, 1992–93: The Politics of Competitiveness,* edited by Frances Abele, 191–239. Ottawa: Carleton University Press.

– 1996. "From Expanding Coverage to Heading for Cover: Shifts in the Politics and Policies of Canadian Pension Reform." In *Aging Workforce, Income Security and Retirement: Policy and Practical Implications,* edited by A. Joshi and E. Berger, 57–67. Hamilton, ON: McMaster University Summer Institute on Gerontology Proceedings.

– 2001a. "Canadian Federalism and Disability Policy Making." *Canadian Journal of Political Science* 34 (4): 791–817.

– 2001b. "Citizenship by Instalments: Federal Policies for Canadians with Disabilities." In *How Ottawa Spends 2001–2002: Power in Transition,* edited by Leslie A. Pal, 177–200. Toronto: Oxford University Press.

– 2001c. "Tax Policy as Social Policy: Tax Assistance for Canadians with Disabilities." *Canadian Public Policy* 27 (4): 487–501.

– 2002. *Wrestling with the Poor Cousin: Canada Pension Plan Disability Policy and Practice, 1964–2001.* Research report for the Office of the Commissioner of Review Tribunals Canada Pension Plan/Old Age Security, Government of Canada.

– 2008. "Claiming a Disability Benefit as Contesting Social Citizenship." In *Contesting Illness: Processes and Practices,* edited by P. Moss and K. Teghtsoonian, 28–46. Toronto: University of Toronto Press.

- 2009. *Absent Citizens: Disability Politics and Policy in Canada.* Toronto: University of Toronto Press.
- 2010. "Avoiding Blame, Doing Good, and Claiming Credit: Reforming Canadian Income Security." *Canadian Public Administration* 53 (3): 1–30.
- 2012. "Blue Rinse: Harper's Treatment of Old Age Security and Other Elderly Benefits." In *How Ottawa Spends, 2012–2013,* edited by G.B. Doern and C. Stoney, 64–75. Montreal and Kingston: McGill-Queen's University Press.
- 2014. *Disabling Poverty, Enabling Citizenship: Recommendations for Positive Change.* Winnipeg: Council of Canadians with Disabilities.
- 2015. "Entrenched Residualism: Social Assistance and People with Disabilities." In *Welfare Reform in Canada: Provincial Social Assistance in Comparative Perspective,* edited by Daniel Béland and Pierre-Marc Daigneault, 273–87. Toronto: University of Toronto Press.
Prince, Michael J., and Pamela Moss. 2015. "Under Siege: Canadian Veterans, Veterans Affairs and the Harper Legacy." In *How Ottawa Spends: 2015–2016: The Liberal Rise and the Tory Demise,* edited by Christopher Stoney and G. Bruce Doern, 144–70. Ottawa: School of Public Policy and Administration, Carleton University.
Procacci, Giovanna. 2001. "Poor Citizens: Social Citizenship versus Individualization of Welfare." In *Citizenship, Markets, and the State,* edited by C. Crouch, K. Eder, and D. Tambini, 49–68. Oxford: Oxford University Press.
Puttee, Alan, ed. 2002. *Federalism, Democracy and Disability Policy in Canada.* Montreal and Kingston: McGill-Queen's University Press.
Quebec. 1978. *Financial Security of Aged Persons in Quebec.* Quebec: Confirentes' Report.
Redden, Candace Johnson. 2002. *Health Care, Entitlement, and Citizenship.* Toronto: University of Toronto Press.
Redway, Hon. Alan. 1991a. *Commons Debates.* Vol. 2, 3rd Session, 34th Parliament, p. 2468.
- 1991b. *Commons Debates* Vol. 4, 3rd Session, 34th Parliament, pp. 5380–3.
Rice, James J., and Michael J. Prince. 2013. *Changing Politics of Canadian Social Policy.* 2nd ed. Toronto: University of Toronto Press.
Riis, N. 1997. *Commons Debates.* Vol. 1, 1st Session, 36th Parliament, p. 1705.
Rioux, Marcia H., and Michael J. Prince. 2002. "The Canadian Political Landscape of Disability: Policy Perspectives, Social Status, Interest Groups and the Rights Movement." In *Federalism, Democracy and*

Disability Policy in Canada, edited by Alan Puttee, 11–28. Montreal and Kingston: McGill-Queen's University Press.

Robson, William B.P. 1996. "Putting Some Gold in the Golden Years: Fixing the Canada Pension Plan." *Commentary*, no. 76. Toronto: C.D. Howe Institute.

Rooke, Patricia, and R.L. Schnell. 1987. *No Bleeding Heart, Charlotte Whitton: Feminist on the Right*. Vancouver: University of British Columbia Press.

Rose, Nikolas, and Peter Miller. 1992. "Political Power beyond the State: Problematics of Government." *British Journal of Sociology* 43 (2): 1–31.

Sarvasy, Wendy. 1997. "Social Citizenship from a Feminist Perspective." *Hypatia* 12 (4): 54–73.

Scully, Jackie Leach. 2012. "Disability and the Thinking Body." In *Embodied Selves*, edited by Stella Gonzalez-Amal, Gill Jagger, and Kathleen Lennon, 139–59. New York: Palgrave Macmillan.

Shaver, Sheila. 1989. "Gender, Class and the Welfare State: The Case of Income Security in Australia." *Feminist Review* 32 (1): 90–110.

Shields, John, and Mitchell B. Evans. 1998. *Shrinking the State: Globalization and Public Administration*. Halifax, NS: Fernwood Publishing.

Shifrin, Leonard. 1991. "CPP Bill Sneaks Through." *Toronto Star*, 9 December.

– 1992. "A Reform No One Expected." *Toronto Star*, 3 February.

Simeon, Richard. 1972. *Federal-Provincial Diplomacy: The Making of Recent Policy in Canada*. Toronto: University of Toronto Press.

Sjöberg, Ola. 1999. "Paying for Social Rights." *Journal of Social Policy* 28 (2): 275–97.

Skocpol, Theda. 1985. "Bringing the State Back In: Strategies of Analysis in Current Research." In *Bringing the State Back In*, edited by Peter B. Evans, Dietrich Rueschemeyer, and Theda Skocpol, 3–41. Cambridge: Cambridge University Press.

Smith, Miriam. 2005. *A Civil Society*. Peterborough, ON: Broadview Press.

– 2009. "Diversity and Canadian Political Development." *Canadian Journal of Political Science* 42 (4): 831–54.

Social Development Canada. 2004. *Evaluation of the CPP Disability Vocational Rehabilitation Program, Final Report*. Gatineau, QC: Audit and Evaluation Directorate.

Sontag, Susan. 1978. *Illness as a Metaphor*. Toronto: McGraw-Hill Ryerson.

Sparrow, Barbara. 1991. *Commons Debates*. 18 November, pp. 4887–90.

Spector, Aaron. 2012. "Ageing in an Age of Increasing Inclusion: Changes in Labour Market Participation Rates for Older Workers with Disabilities." PowerPoint Presentation, Canadian Research Data Centre Network National Conference, Fredericton, NB, 23–24 October.

Spicker, Paul. 1984. *Stigma and Social Welfare*. Beckenham, UK: Croom Helm.

Splane, Richard B. 1987. "Social Policy Making in the Government of Canada." In *Canadian Social Policy*, rev. ed., edited by Shankar Yelaja, 224–65. Waterloo, ON: Wilfrid Laurier University Press.

Squires, Peter. 1990. *Anti-Social Policy: Welfare, Ideology and the Disciplinary State*. London: Harvester Wheatsheaf.

Stein, Janice Gross. 2002. *The Cult of Efficiency*. Rev. ed. Toronto: Anansi Press.

Stephens, J.D. 2010. "Social Rights of Citizenship." In *The Oxford Handbook of the Welfare State*, edited by F. Castles, S. Leibfried, J. Lewis, H. Obinger, and C. Pierson, 511–25. Oxford: Oxford University Press.

Stienstra, Deborah. 2012. *Disability Rights*. Halifax, NS: Fernwood Publishing.

Stone, Deborah A. 1984. *The Disabled State*. Philadelphia: Temple University Press.

Struthers, James. 1994. *The Limits of Affluence: Welfare in Ontario, 1920–1970*. Toronto: University of Toronto Press.

Thomas, Helen. 2013. *The Body and Everyday Life*. New York: Routledge.

Thorson, D. 1964. "Testimony before the Joint Committee of the Senate and House of Commons to Examine and Report on Bill C-136." *Minutes of Proceedings and Evidence*. No. 9, 11 December, p. 449.

Titchkosky, Tanya. 2003. *Disability, Self, and Society*. Toronto: University of Toronto Press.

Torjman, Sherri. 2001. "Canada's Federal Regime and Persons with Disabilities." In *Disability and Federalism: Comparing Different Approaches to Full Participation*, edited by David Cameron and Fraser Valentine, 151–96. Montreal and Kingston: McGill-Queen's University Press.

– 2002. *The Canada Pension Plan Disability Benefit*. Ottawa: Caledon Institute of Social Policy.

– 2014. *Disability Policy Highlights*. Ottawa: Caledon Institute of Social Policy.

Tremblay, Marcel R. 1991. *Commons Debates*. 26 November, p. 5389.

Tremblay, Mary. 1998. "Going Back to Main Street: The Development and Impact of Casualty Rehabilitation for Veterans with Disabilities,

1945–1948." In *The Veterans Charter and Post-World War II Canada*, edited by Peter Neary and J.L. Granatstein, 160–78. Montreal and Kingston: McGill-Queen's University Press.

Turner, Bryan S. 1986. *Citizenship and Capitalism: The Debate over Reformism*. London: Allen and Unwin.

– 1988. *Status*. Minneapolis: University of Minnesota Press.

– 1993. "Contemporary Problems in the Theory of Citizenship." In *Citizenship and Social Theory*, edited by Bryan S. Turner, 1–18. London: Sage.

– 1996. *The Body and Society*. 2nd ed. London: Sage.

Twigg, Julia. 2000. "Social Policy and the Body." In *Rethinking Social Policy*, edited by Gail Lewis, Sharon Gewirtz, and John Clarke, 127–40. London: Sage.

– 2004. "The Body in Social Policy: Mapping a Territory." *Journal of Social Policy* 31:421–40.

Vick, Andrea. 2012. "Theorizing Episodic Disabilities: The Case for an Embodied Politics." *Canadian Social Work Review* 29 (1): 41–60.

Vickers, Jill. 1997. *Reinventing Political Science: A Feminist Approach*. Halifax, NS: Fernwood Publishing.

Weber, Mark C. 2009. "Disability Rights, Disability Discrimination, and Social Insurance." *Georgia State University Law Review* 25 (3): 575–606.

Wendell, Susan. 1996. *The Rejected Body: Feminist Philosophical Reflections on Disability*. New York: Routledge.

Whitton, Charlotte. 1943a. *The Dawn of Ampler Life*. Toronto: Macmillan.

– 1943b. "Social Security for Canadians." *Behind the Headlines* 3 (6). Toronto: Canadian Association for Adult Education.

Willard, Dr Joseph. 1964a. "Testimony before the Joint Committee of the Senate and House of Commons to Examine and Report on Bill C-136." *Minutes of Proceedings and Evidence*. No. 1, 26 November, p. 60.

– 1964b. "Testimony before the Joint Committee of the Senate and House of Commons to Examine and Report on Bill C-136." *Minutes of Proceedings and Evidence*. No. 2, 1 December, pp. 247 and 250.

Wills, E. 1996. "Canada Pension Plan: Disability Benefits." In *Roundtable on Canada's Aging Society and Retirement Income System, June 5, 1995*, by Caledon Institute of Social Policy, 73–5. Ottawa: Caledon Institute of Social Policy.

Wilson, Hon. Michael H. 1991. *Budget Papers*. Ottawa: Department of Finance.

Withers, A.J. 2012. *Disability Politics and Theory*. Halifax, NS: Fernwood Publishing.

Young, Iris Marion. 1990. *Justice and the Politics of Difference*. Princeton: Princeton University Press.

Yuval-Davis, Nira. 1997. "Women, Citizenship and Difference." *Feminist Review* 57:4–27.

Index